ON WINGS OF ANGELS

ALEX SYTNYK

JOSEPH SHOCKEY

Published in the United States by selfpublishing.com.

All scripture taken from the New King James Version®. Copyright © 1982 by Thomas
Nelson. Used by permission. All rights reserved.

Names: Alex Sytnyk, Author.

Contributors and Publisher, J. G. Shockey & Associates, LLC (Joseph G. Shockey and
David B. H. Wiliams)

ISBN: 979-8-89694-878-0 - eBook

ISBN: 979-8-89694-879-7 - Paperback

ISBN: 979-8-89694-937-4 - Hardcover

"This book describes my father's miraculous escape and survival from certain death during WW II. His mother (my grandma) didn't make it. As a three-year old orphan, young Alex had everything he needed to venture into the unknown: his mother's assurance that God would care for him and guide him to safety and happiness. Her profound faith instilled a lasting sense of fearlessness, trust and gratitude into my dad's life which has also carried through to me.

I was blessed to have the nurturing and comfort of one loving mother and father in my life. My dad, however, had several kindhearted people providing food and shelter for him and was finally adopted when he was ten.

My dad has always shown kindness, helpfulness, encouragement and inspiration to others because total strangers throughout the world have been there for him when he was in need. I know that anyone reading this book will have a deeper appreciation of God's gift of freedom and opportunities, the power of faith and above all, God's endless, bountiful love for each one of us."

— *Alexander Great Wilding (Jason A. Sytnyk)*

"The epitome of inspiration! From my earliest memories to the present, Uncle Alex represents a shining light rarely available in today's world.

He has always been encouragingly positive regardless of the situation, and has an amazing ability to see good in everything and everyone. I feel extremely fortunate to have him in my life."

— *Glen J Sytnyk*

"I first learned of Alex's background when we were neighbors and attended bible study classes together. Reading his book, "On Wings of Angels," 1 found it very inspirational, heartwarming and spiritual as he ever so vividly described the power of faith which never ceased to guide him.

His story of survival and escape in the midst of WWII and his ever changing life in the free world thereafter, makes it hard to put the book down. Alex has become my lifelong friend."

— *James E. Stanley, MD.*

DEDICATION

To my biological Mother, your last words of strength and profound faith
"RUN, ALEX; RUN AS FAST AS YOU CAN—AWAY FROM HERE.
DON'T BE AFRAID OF ANYTHING. GOD AND HIS ANGELS WILL
WATCH OVER YOU AND CARE FOR YOU. NOW, RUN QUICKLY
AND DON'T EVEN LOOK BACK" made my escape possible and sent me
on a lifetime journey that saved my life;

To Lady Elizabeth, the bravest angel imaginable;

To Mary Sytnyk, my adopted Canadian mother;

And to my beautiful wife, Patricia, the love of my life.

CONTENTS

INTRODUCTION

Hypermnesia is an unusual power or ability of vivid memory recall in one's lifetime, typically enhanced under abnormal conditions, such as trauma. In my autobiography, I have, to the best of my memory, from a very early childhood age of about three, detailed my most unforgettable and heart-wrenching experiences. Yet, throughout my journey, there were many happy events—carrying me on wings of angels away from genocidal killings that were occurring through the Eastern European war zone of World War II, between the orphanages and foster homes in Western Europe, and across the Atlantic Ocean. All the events are almost as vivid in my mind and heart today as when they first occurred. I changed some of the names in my story due to privacy concerns.

My story is just one of the many millions of victims who endured the effects of World War II brought about by two of the most ruthless and murderous dictators of the 20th century. By the grace of God, I was spared, thanks to the deep faith of my dear biological Ukrainian mother, who, as a last resort, tearfully tore my tight grip from her and sternly commanded me to quickly run into God's awaiting embrace and loving care as she continued the forced march to her final genocidal destiny along with countless innocent women, children and older men. From that unforgettable and painful moment and for the rest of my life, her parting words would continue to dwell within my heart and soul.

"RUN, ALEX; RUN AS FAST AS YOU CAN—AWAY FROM HERE. DON'T BE AFRAID OF ANYTHING. GOD AND HIS ANGELS WILL WATCH OVER YOU AND CARE FOR YOU. NOW, RUN QUICKLY AND DON'T EVEN LOOK BACK."

Throughout history, there have always been bold and brave individuals such as my mother who refused to become prisoners of fear, even at the ultimate sacrifice of their own lives—as revealed more recently with flight 93 over Shanksville, Pennsylvania on 9/11, when Todd Beamer and several fellow bold and brave air passengers, with a shout of "let's roll," overpowered the armed terrorists. Although the plane crashed into an open field, killing all aboard, the action of those patriotic passengers saved countless lives and major destruction had they allowed the terrorists to carry out their intended plan.

Having lived in five countries, in several orphanages, and at times under the cover of bomb shelters, I was blessed by a number of kind-hearted people who provided warmth and comfort in their homes for me. I never feared anything or anyone, learned several languages, obeyed most rules, and with a smile, put forth my best effort—always with a complete trust that the faith and assurance with which my mother sent me off into God's care, would carry me to safety, freedom, and lasting joy one step at a time.

Only through divine intervention was my escape and survival possible. As I wandered aimlessly, near starvation through the deadly war zone, I received comfort in a trench amid Ukrainian soldiers with guns ablaze, was whisked up by an armed German soldier with his speeding motorcycle, crossed several Eastern European countries by horse and buggy to avoid capture by the Soviets, and was aided by a German officer and his wife to safety via an America-bound ship.

With the ever-changing adventurous, and, at times, dangerous life unfolding around me at a somewhat rapid pace, I felt that I had already lived a full life by the time I turned eight. But, when I stepped off the ship in Canada, a rainbow of bright colors and a new exciting future greeted me beyond anything I could ever have dreamed or imagined. It felt like the gates of Heaven—filled with love, joy, laughter, beauty, peace, and freedom were all opened to welcome me. I'm certain that my faithful mom, watching me from Heaven at that moment, was smiling and praising God for answering her desperate plea in such a miraculous way.

In many ways, I can relate my survival to the uplifting words in the very popular song, "You'll Never Walk Alone" composed in 1945 for a Broadway musical production by Rodgers and Hammerstein.

CHAPTER 1
ZHYTOMYR, UKRAINE -
(1939 - 1942)

I was in somewhat of a similar predicament as a disoriented and helpless little earthworm wiggling and squirming on an asphalt road or walkway, trying desperately to escape the rapidly increasing summer afternoon heat. Like the struggling earthworm, I would certainly have perished were it not for my mom's profound faith and for God's love and mercy.

FROM A PIT OF EVIL

My very first awareness and remembrance of life began when I was about three years old, shivering cold and clinging very tightly to my mother's right leg with both my arms for a sense of safety, warmth, and security. Like cattle in a stockyard awaiting slaughter, we were crammed tightly among many other people inside a large, very old, dirty, cold, and foul-smelling building. The atmosphere was extremely frightening as most everyone around us was wailing, crying, even screaming and very audibly praying.

Being only knee-high, all I could see were countless bare bony knees and legs surrounding us—like tree trunks in a dense forest. I was totally confused and wanted to ask Mom why we were here, where we were going, and why everyone was so afraid. The warmth and security of just holding onto my mother's knee dispelled any great personal fear I would otherwise have had. Every youngster around us, also reacting to their mother's emotions and tears, was either glued to their mother like I was, or crying and holding on as tightly as possible to their necks.

It truly was the pit of anguish, fear, and evil from which there was no escape—like a most frightful nightmare. Every adult in the building was surely well aware what imminent fate awaited them—they were all about to be massacred.

Realizing that time was about to run out, that the doors were now locked, that there was no escape, and that the armed guards had the place surrounded, my fearful mom, with tears gushing down her face, visibly trembling and sobbing uncontrollably, stooped down, enveloped me with both her arms, and squeezed me ever-so-tightly against her teary wet cheeks.

She then followed through with her bravest and most sacrificial act of faith imaginable—something that no one else in that place dared to attempt. She sternly commanded me to quickly make my way to the edge of the building, find even the smallest crawlspace near the ground, squeeze through it, and then run as fast as possible away from this horrible place, not to even glance back. She assured me that God and His angels would always be at my side to protect me.

In Exodus 23:20, we read, "Behold, I send an Angel before you to keep you in the way and to bring you into the place which I have prepared."

My mother's profound faith assured her that God would lead me to safety. As she pried my tightening and resisting grip from her arms and legs, she promised me that God would surely lead me to a safe and happy place, that He would always guide me and care for me, and that I wasn't to be afraid of anything. I took that to heart—every word she said—and relied on it from that moment forward. I also didn't cry or reflect any signs of fear as I wanted to assure her that I would be obedient, brave, and fearless.

She then held my body ever-so-tightly against her bosom—tighter than ever, so that I could barely breathe. Grasping my cheeks with both her hands, she pulled me up to her sobbing and quivering face—her eyes only two to three inches from mine like a laser piercing my heart, she kissed me one final time and sent me off into God's waiting hands.

"RUN, ALEX; RUN AS FAST AS YOU CAN—AWAY FROM HERE. DON'T BE AFRAID OF ANYTHING. GOD AND HIS ANGELS WILL WATCH OVER YOU AND CARE FOR YOU. NOW, RUN QUICKLY AND DON'T EVEN LOOK BACK."

Those were her final words, and our most painful and precious moments together. I would repeat these words throughout the rest of my life, especially when there was nowhere else to turn. I was instantly transformed from a confused, scared baby clinging to his mama, into a responsible young man, filled with hope, trust, and assurance that God's angels would be waiting for me outside the building. My mom completely relied upon her deep, unshakeable faith and I simply acted on a child's trust and obedience.

I would never see her or hear of her again the rest of my life. I didn't even know her name, except that she was my mommy. In fact, I don't recall ever spending any tender moments at home with her. I have no recollection of having a father or any siblings.

More than likely, as would have been the case throughout Ukraine, Russia, Germany, and most of Europe, all able-bodied men would have been forced to serve in the brutal onslaught of World War II.

Many young boys were being taken away for military training to take up arms against the enemy as quickly as possible, usually to the front line, the most dangerous position, in which most of them would not survive. Since I was her last and youngest, she would certainly have done everything within her power to protect me at all costs.

No doubt, my mother, like everyone else around her, knew that the German army had already set up their military control center in Ukraine as it continued its hot pursuit toward Moscow. There would be no way for me to avoid running directly into the line of fire of the widespread deadly war zone of which she was well aware. However, in desperation, it was her only alternative.

Once the German forces had broken through the fortified Russian line of defense in 1941 and occupied Ukraine, Heinrich Himmler established his headquarters near Zhytomyr, a city west of Ukraine's Capital city—Kiev. He was one of the chief engineers in Hitler's vision of Europe, a vision without Jews. He was appointed by Hitler as the head of the European special police division (more commonly known as the most feared "Gestapo" or "S.S."). Heinrich Himmler carried out his resettlement activities by the elimination of Jews and the reduction of Ukraine's civil population to further his plans of establishing a German colony by using the reduced Ukrainian population as slaves.

By relying on my simple childlike trust that God would watch over me, my life henceforth would be void of fear or doubt. I permanently etched my mom's parting words into my mind, heart, and soul, fully believing that I was embarking on a thrilling, adventurous journey to a most wonderful place somewhere—somewhere of God's choosing.

However, just the thought of the dagger in my mom's heart when she forced herself to separate herself from my tight grasp and then, be herded like cattle, along with all the others inside that satanic warehouse to their fate, would never cease to stir my emotions.

Most assuredly, she completely trusted and believed that God had a special place reserved for little children and widows, and that my life would be saved and protected. She knew God's angels would take me from that most evil place on earth to a special happy spot somewhere far, far away.

In my mind and heart, I have replayed those unforgettable final moments so many, many times and wondered how anyone, especially a mother with a toddler, could possibly be so strong and have such a profound faith.

"FAITH POSSESSES THE MIGHTIEST POWER IN THE UNIVERSE. IT IS THE CONFIDENT ASSURANCE THAT WHAT WE HOPE FOR IS GOING TO HAPPEN." (commonly attributed to W. Clement Stone)

I'm amazed by the similarity of instruction in the book of Joshua of the Old Testament after the death of Moses, the Lord spoke to Joshua to lead His people across the Jordan River:

"Have I not commanded you? Be strong and of a good courage; do not be afraid, nor be dismayed, for the LORD your God is with you wherever you go"
(Joshua 1:9).

Within the approximate same period of time (1941–1942), and in somewhat similar circumstances as my mom's and mine, another genocidal event was being carried out—also near Kiev, Ukraine—in Babyn Yar:

(Kiev is the traditional English name. It became disfavored in many Western media outlets during the outbreak of Russia's invasion of Crimea and Donbas in 2014. Kyiv, commonly used today, is the Romanized official name replacing Kiev.)

BABYN YAR

On the northern edge of Kiev is a historic place called "Babyn Yar," known for its natural beauty, where in peaceful times, young people used to enjoy playing, swimming, and strolling leisurely. Today, it is a stark reminder of a systemic genocidal slaughter by the German Nazis as they brutally overran the city of Kiev during Hitler's campaign against the Soviet Union.

In September 1941, two years after Hitler invaded Poland to begin World War II, estimates between 100,000 to 200,000 Jewish women, young children, and elderly men were rounded up by the Nazis and brought to a place called Babyn Yar, Ukraine, where they were stripped naked and forced to stand by a deep ravine into which they would fall following a mass machine gun killing. The able-bodied men had previously been taken by force to join the Russian or German army and those that resisted had already been executed beforehand.

The reason all the helpless people were forced to strip before they were killed was so that the guards could later search for any valuables like money, gold, rings, and watches. But most cruelly and inhumanely—it was to strip the people of their identity and dignity.

Yevgeniva Podovskaya, a twenty-four-year-old Jewish mother, stood at the edge of that ravine, awaiting her fate. As she watched, in horror, with the machine guns systematically mowing down everyone that stood there and knew that there was no escape, she survived by jumping onto the bodies and lying still.

Her story was reported by Hugo Martin, staff writer for the *Los Angeles Times*, in an article dated September 30, 1991, during the commemoration of the 50th anniversary of the Babyn Yar Ravine Massacre.[1]

As related by Yevgeniva, she was able, with the cover of darkness, to dig herself out from the pile of bloodied, lifeless bodies and escape. She was able to spend the remaining years of her life in freedom in Los Angeles but with the haunting and most painful memories of Babyn Yar Ravine.

In 1995, President Bill Clinton visited this ravine and stated:

"Never forget that the forces of darkness cannot be defeated with silence or indifference. Never forget that we are all Jews and Gypsies and Slavs. Never Forget," the President said. "May God bless this holy place."[2]

---

1. Hugo Martin, "Sad Reminder of Slaughter Is Unveiled: Holocaust: About 700 people gather in West Hollywood for dedication of a monument to the victims of a Nazi massacre at Babi Yar in the Soviet Union," *Los Angeles Times*, September 30, 1991.
2. The White House National Archives, "Remarks by the President Honoring Those Who Died at Babi Yar," The White House Office of the Press Secretary (Kiev, Ukraine), May 12, 1995, https://clintonwhitehouse6.archives.gov/1995/05/1995-05-12-president-remarks-at-babi-yar-kiev-ukraine.html.

CHAPTER 2
MY ESCAPE

A TINY DIRT CRAWL SPACE

Although we didn't stand at a dugout awaiting a machine gun execution as described in the "Babyn Yar" story, Mom knew the imminent fate that was awaiting us. There was nothing she could do to try and save me, except rely upon her faith and tell me to run quickly and not glance back.

Adhering to Mom's instructions, by weaving my way through the dense forest of bare bony knees and legs of the vast number of people crammed inside that cold and awful-smelling building, I scurried toward the far edge of the enclosure. I couldn't have been more than about three and a half feet tall, skinny as a twig, and with all that anguish occurring at the time, I doubt anyone even noticed me. Sure enough, just as Mom had stated, hoped, and prayed for, I had no trouble finding a small dirt crawl-space at the base of the wall, barely big enough for my wee, tiny body to wiggle through—like a frightened little mouse.

Once on the outside of the wall, I instantly turned to my right, and without wasting a split second to scan the area around me, my skinny little legs propelled me into an adrenergic flash of speed—a kind of power that surprisingly came out of nowhere, totally amazing me. Like a scared wild rabbit trying to outrace a pack of coyotes in hot pursuit of their next meal, I also didn't slow down, not even for a second, keeping in mind that I had to put as much distance as possible between me and that horrific place of hell behind me—that awful place which separated me from my helpless weeping mom.

Every time I think of the Bible story of Sodom and Gomorrah, I'm reminded of my mom's similar warning for me to keep running away to safety as fast as possible and not look back.

According to the Bible, God's angels had clearly explained to Lot, his wife, and to their daughters that Sodom and Gomorrah would be destroyed by fire—that they should quickly run to safety and warned them to not look back. In defiance of the angels' instructions, however, his wife chose to look back at the burning city from which she and her family had just escaped. In an instant, she turned into a pillar of salt while the rest of her family continued their escape to safety. Even her husband, Lot—who chose to obey God's instruction—knew better than to even glance back for his missing wife. "But his wife looked back from behind him, and she became a pillar of salt" (Genesis 19:26).

Was it because I was so tiny and undernourished, or so quick and low to the ground? Or, perhaps the armed guard at that particular spot chose to look the other way? It really doesn't matter—for in my heart I believe that the Lord temporarily blinded the guard and gave me the power to keep running.

With every ounce of strength within me, I continued running at full speed, only looking straight ahead toward open fields, bushes and trees. Though I eventually became totally exhausted, I would repeatedly stop just long enough to gulp some fresh air into my lungs and resume my run to freedom. Soon, I was unable to run anymore. So I began to walk, then crawl on my hands and knees, until I couldn't move another inch.

My entire body ached from exhaustion. My heart was beating ever-so-fast and loud like a machine gun. Even with my mouth wide open and panting rapidly, I still found it difficult to get enough air into my lungs.

Breathless, hungry, and thirsty, with darkness slowly devouring the sun, I decided to crawl under a low-lying bushy tree, curled up close to the tree-trunk, and covered myself with a blanket of dry brown, yellow, orange, and red leaves from head to toe. I felt secure, warm, comfortable, and happy that I had carried out my mom's instructions to a tee, as everything fell into place so perfectly. The euphoria and hope of a bright and wonderful world awaiting me from the next day forward, allowed me to temporarily take my mind off the miserably hopeless and fearful place I had just left behind. Since I was totally covered with leaves, no one would be able to find me. I felt very safe and peacefully fell into a sound and restful deep sleep.

FOUR-EARED MONSTERS

In the quiet early dawn, while still enjoying the restful, cozy sleeping accommodations under the blanket of autumn leaves, I began hearing faint and totally unfamiliar sounds in the distance. Very gingerly, I brushed aside the dry loose leaves that had covered my face, thinking that I would be able to hear much better if, in addition to concentrating on my keen sense of hearing, I would also quit breathing and with my eyes wide open, might be able to determine what those noises might be. The grass around me felt damp from the early morning dew and the visibility was obscured by the hazy mist. Sure enough, those eerie sounds seemed to be getting louder and closer.

I became very concerned. Through the mist, I began to see a group of about ten gigantic four-legged and four-eared monsters—some black ones, some brown ones, and some two-toned. Very slowly, they were all heading toward me with their heads low to the ground. Should I quickly get back under the cover of leaves, play dead, and quit breathing? Maybe they hadn't yet seen me? Or, perhaps I could outrun them? I couldn't decide.

Before I knew it, I was trapped. They surrounded me and stared at me with their huge black eyes. I shut my eyes tightly and held on to the tree trunk for safety just like I was clinging to my mom's leg the day before. They were sniffing and snorting, some of them touching my skin with their cold, wet, slimy noses and even licking me with their rough sandpapery tongues. Despite my assurance to Mom that I wouldn't be afraid of anything, here I was—only one day later—so frightened, expecting the inevitable end to my short-lived freedom, that I lost my bladder control.

My mom's final words flashed before me, "Don't be afraid; God will always be with you and protect you."

At that moment, to my complete surprise, the monsters, one-by-one, slowly began to turn and lazily walk away, all in the same direction, leaving me totally unharmed, still hugging the tree. In a deep sigh of relief and thankfulness, as my eyes followed them, I marveled at their enormous size and surmised that the reason all their heads were so low to the ground was because they were all continuously eating the grass directly in front of them. But what would prompt them all to leave so suddenly? The longer I watched them, the more my stomach began growling and hurting because I hadn't eaten anything in a long, long while. I concluded that since none of those monsters had any appetite for me and instead, preferred eating the grass, then it must be very nutritious. Why not give it a try? Surely, it would relieve my growing hunger pangs, regardless of the taste, and renew my energy.

I yanked a tuft of fresh grass in my fist, placed some into my mouth, and began chewing. Yuck; what a horrible idea that was! After spitting it all out, I picked some of the dry leaves from around the base of the tree and even attempted to chew a piece of loose bark, only to spit everything out. Now I was feeling sick, famished, and feeble, but I knew better than to give up and lie down. I just had to keep moving forward, even if I had to crawl. Surely, something good was bound to appear soon if I just keep forging ahead.

"Will God or an angel find me out here?" I wondered.

MANNA FROM HEAVEN

Continuing to wander aimlessly through fields of dirt, mud, brush, and weeds, I eventually came upon a dilapidated old house. For a minute, I thought that I must have found my way home. Well, it may have been someone's home at one time, but now, it was just a pile of decaying old wood and trash. While exploring the adjacent yard, what must have been someone's garden long ago was now tall prickly weeds. However, my eyes caught something protruding above the weeds.

There stood a bright, tall, golden sunflower plant with its happy face looking directly at me. In contrast to everything I'd seen thus far, it appeared to be beckoning me to come closer. Convinced that an angel must have planted it there specifically for me, I joyfully admired it and began touching the neatly arranged rows of black seeds in the center. Some ripe ones, with their shells partially split open, fell right into my hand. Without hesitation, I peeled back the shells and began eating the nutty delicacies inside. Ah—they tasted so good! I helped myself to as much as I wanted. It was like manna from Heaven. Soon my stomach stopped growling and my strength was renewed enough to continue my escape to freedom.

IN THE MIDDLE OF A BATTLEFIELD

In my continued effort to just keep going, even with hardly any strength left, I found myself in the midst of an active battlefield. Big brown and green-colored trucks and huge tanks appeared from nearby bushes causing unbearable, deafening, ear-piercing booms, explosions, smoke, and the most awful burning smell.

Awakening from the dazed effect of shell-shock, I found myself curled up in a fetal position at the bottom of a deep dirt trench, wondering what was causing all that ear-shattering noise. Towering above me was a soldier peeking over the upper rim of the trench, holding the butt of his gun tightly against his chin and shoulder and frantically firing it as rapidly as possible toward an advancing enemy shooting back toward us. The deafening explosions and continuous gunfire convinced me to just remain still. With his heavy boot on top of me, the soldier was doing his best to shield me from shrapnel and flying rocks while continuing to shoot. In spite of all that was happening, I felt a sense of comfort and protection.

There were many more soldiers toward each end of the trench, all continuously shooting their guns in the same direction. Some of them would bend down, pick up an egg-shaped grenade and other explosive devices with attached handles, and throw them as far as they could toward the enemy which was firing at us.

Having spotted me in the middle of the active battlefield in a dazed and wandering stupor, this brave soldier, risking his own life to save mine, had dashed out into the open fire to scoop me up and race back to the trench holding me tightly under his arm like a football.

During a brief lull in the gun-fire exchange, he bent down, smiled, and sat me on his knees. Assuming that I was probably dehydrated and hadn't eaten in a long while, he reached into his pack to share some of his food and water with me and began softly and gently conversing with me in Ukrainian, making me feel very safe.

Just being in the company of a real armed soldier in the midst of an ongoing battle aroused my curiosity. So, I carefully touched his helmet, his uniform, and his heavy gun, wondering what would cause it to be so loud and powerful. After switching his gun to safety mode, he gently took my hand and guided my index finger against the trigger. Then, he gave me permission to pull the trigger which released a tiny hammer above it, followed by an audible "click" but no "bang." I just had to touch that magical miniature hammer—so, when the trigger was pulled again, I put my right index finger on it, which pinched me unexpectedly, ending my curiosity for the time being. I felt so safe and comfortably good just being protected by this new friend of mine that I would never want to leave his side.

Suddenly, much more repetitive shooting and loud explosions from tanks and grenades erupted all around us. All the soldiers quickly resumed their prior firing positions and shouted commands to each other. The enemy fire seemed much closer to us this time. Noxious, choking smoke filled the air. The smell of burning gunpowder was nauseating, causing me to rub my burning eyes while coughing profusely. The bottom of the trench was filled with empty ammo shell casings. Pieces of burning metal landed all around us and the ear-splitting loudness of so many explosions at close range caused my ears to cease functioning, as all I could feel was a steady high-pitched ring in my head.

My soldier friend motioned for me to lie down low and, as before, he straddled over me to keep me safe. I began to think that this ferocious battle would never end. But I felt safe, cupped my ears with my hands, shut my eyes real tight, and didn't move. I knew that my friend, hovering above me, would not allow anything to happen to me. He was my Guardian Angel.

When the shooting and loud explosions finally ended, my new friend, that brave, kind soldier, my Guardian Angel, now lay motionless next to me with blood all over him. He was completely unresponsive to the efforts of his comrades.

I cried out, "No, No, you can't leave me now, not out here all alone."

I just sat in the trench next to him and continued sobbing until a big army truck slowly rolled its way to our trench to pick up all the dead and injured. Someone reached down, pulled me up from the trench and hoisted me up into the back of the truck with all the casualties and injured soldiers.

Thanks to the protection of my soldier friend (my Guardian Angel), I came through without as much as a scratch on me. The image of that kind soldier, comforting me and shielding me in that deep dirt trench while fighting off the enemy would have a profound effect on me for years to come. His kind and soothing demeanor and his display of fearlessness provided a sense of safety when I needed it most and gave me the courage to carry on. In such a short period of time and amid such dangerous circumstances, he made me feel like I was his baby brother.

Caught in the middle of a war zone between two murderous empires (Germany and Russia) created an unthinkable state of chaos for the Ukrainian people. Would the German Army beat back the ruthless

Soviets and liberate Ukraine from their on-going oppression? Such wishful thinking led thousands of Ukrainian men to fight alongside Germany hoping that it would achieve their country's freedom in the process. Hitler understood the Ukrainian people's fear of communist Russia and used that fear to his advantage in his pursuit toward Moscow. As it turned out, Ukraine paid the heaviest price per capita in terms of casualties of any other European nation during World War II.

After a long, bumpy trip toward a military medical post, with dozens of soldiers bleeding, moaning in pain, some in tears and sobbing, and also those, like my friend, who didn't make it, lying there motionless, the army truck eventually came to a slow crawl just to drop me off, before immediately resuming its medical mission. As the truck began moving away, the driver leaned out his door, glanced at me briefly, and pointed toward a building down a side road, yelling, "Over there," and drove off.

CHAPTER 3
MY FIRST ORPHANAGE

Surrounded by a high iron fence, the building stood behind a playground where about three dozen boys and girls were kicking a ball around, chasing each other, yelling, and some even fighting. As I walked toward the gate, I was met by a stern-looking, portly woman who motioned for me to follow her past the playground into the main orphanage building. Most of the kids just ignored me—others gave me a disdainful look, laughing and pointing their fingers at me. I felt so ashamed and belittled because I knew how dreadfully dirty and ragged I must have appeared. I wished that I could have stayed in the trench with my friend and learned how to be a soldier just like him. But, if this was where my road was meant to lead me, then I'd make the best of it—convinced, in my heart, that the best was yet to come.

A tiny fold-up cot along with a small blanket as a cover for sleeping was assigned to me. There were about three dozen similar cots, neatly lined in a row on a dirt floor in the sleeping quarters. Since I was the newest resident, my cot was placed closest to the entry door. A bit later in the day, everyone was ordered to wash their hands at an outdoor water trough and then proceed to the dining hall for a mid-day meal. Sitting on wooden benches along either side of a big old wooden table in the dining area adjoining the kitchen, we were all provided with a spoon and a small round bowl for our food.

With the feast about to begin, the wonderful, heavenly aroma of cooked food began to drift toward me from the kitchen. I didn't recall when I may have tasted or even smelled cooked food before. Since I'd been starving for so long, this meal would be so extra special for me. I could barely contain my appreciation of the anticipated joy about to unfold. At last, my continuous stomach pain would vanish and I would begin feeling healthy and strong again.

THE SOUP EXCHANGE

A tall and portly woman, wearing a somewhat soiled apron from her neck down to her ankles, carefully carrying a big steaming pot of soup, made her way around our table and with a long-handled ladle, filled each of our bowls with a warm, creamy-white fresh potato soup. No one said a word!

Before taking my first taste, I did my best to control my eagerness of just gobbling the soup down. Instead, I encircled my bowl with both hands, closed my eyes in thanksgiving, and inhaled its blessed aroma several times deeply into my lungs, knowing that my hunger pangs and the growling in my stomach would finally end.

As I picked up my spoon to take my first taste and begin this long-awaited feast, everyone seated at the table around me began grumbling and complaining louder and louder. Then they proceeded to bang their spoons and fists on the table in a defiant act of belligerence and mutiny. I looked around the table and was shocked to witness them all beginning to spit into their soup. I was horrified in disbelief and moved my bowl as close to me as possible, still shielding it with both hands to guard it. Apparently, they'd been given potato soup every day and this was to be a final show of rebellion.

That portly lady, still clad in her long apron, returned from the kitchen carrying a big wooden stick. Witnessing the spitting and spoon-banging, she became furious. Her face turned bright red in anger as she began yelling and cussing. Then, she lifted her big stick and, in a most threatening manner, slammed it with full force across the table and ordered everyone to exchange their soup (spit and all) with the person sitting across the table.

When she approached me, still hugging my bowl, I tried to explain that I was very, very hungry and would never defile this wonderful meal. Still in her angry mood, she merely lifted her stick over my head, then grabbed my bowl, and exchanged it for the one across from me. I would never forget the cunning grin on that fat kid's face as he looked at me, cleaned up my precious meal, and watched me have to eat his. I was so hungry that I consumed everything in the bowl, spit and all. Well, it sure beat the taste of grass, leaves, and the bark off a tree. Above all, it suppressed my on-going hunger and pain in my stomach.

The day-by-day routine at the orphanage was a far better existence than running aimlessly away from that evil place where I left my mom. I now had a cot to sleep on and food to eat. With each distant sound of explosion, I was reminded that the war was on-going. Fortunately, we were not in the line of fire and there were no soldiers or artillery near us.

Time dragged on and on. With each passing day, the feeling of sadness, abandonment and hopelessness began to grow within me. I thought to myself that if God was to care for me, as mom had promised, then He must surely be very busy with the many other children needing His attention.

AN EERIE TRAIN RIDE

Early one morning, all the children at the orphanage were told to get ready for a long train ride. Everyone was happy to leave the orphanage, even though no one had any idea or cared where the train was going. We waited by the tracks and soon could hear the distant chugging of the locomotive engine. The black smoke billowing from its smoke stack engulfed many of the freight cars in its tow. As it got closer, it began slowing down with much less smoke. While the train was still slowly moving, several armed soldiers jumped down from the train cars and walked alongside until it came to a full stop. Steel pipes protruding from the hot steam engine would continue to hiss and release a little steam while the smoke stack was lazily emitting very small puffs of black smoke—awaiting signals to start up again.

Several soldiers, with guns drawn, opened the heavy metal door of the last box car and commanded all of us to quickly climb aboard, where we joined a group of people and some children already crammed inside. One of the soldiers hoisted me up because of my small stature. Once the large metal door was slammed shut and locked from the outside, the darkness, foul odor, eerie atmosphere with fearful people moaning, and young children crying reminded me of that old warehouse from which I had recently escaped.

It seemed like we were in the unlit box car half the day with the steel wheels of the train thumping against the track joints at a steady pace. Several hours later, as most everyone aboard needed to go potty and perhaps the guards did too, the train slowed and came to a stop next to a remote grassy area. The soldiers, again with guns drawn, unlocked the heavy metal doors of our freight car as well as several other cars in front of ours. They surrounded the entire train and ordered everyone to quickly jump down to relieve themselves in a patch of tall weeds and grass a few steps from the train, then to promptly return. When the door opened, I was blinded by the bright sun, since it was still daylight and it had been so dark in the train car. For privacy reasons and being rather shy and timid, I went just a bit farther than the rest of the people, where the grass was taller and found a place "to do my business." In a threatening position, with their guns drawn, the soldiers scanned the area and kept close watch to ensure that everyone returned to the train when so ordered.

After a few minutes, I heard the repeated shouting commands of the soldiers to return to the train quickly. I took my time since I wasn't quite done—thinking that by the time all those other people, especially the older ones, got back onto the train, I could outrun them all and be there in plenty of time. I heard the repeated loud commands of the soldiers for everyone to quickly get back into the train.

Then suddenly, I heard the sound of the locomotive engine beginning to build up steam. There was a loud sound of a whistle followed by its slow chug-chug and heavy black smoke puffing from its smoke stack. Everyone had been accounted for. The metal doors were locked and the train began moving.

Realizing that I would not be able to make it back in time and that I would be left out here all alone, I frantically began running as fast as I could, shouting and waving my arms, but no one heard me as the train picked up its speed very rapidly, and all I could do was watch it get smaller and quieter, until it, along with its black smoke, totally disappeared into the horizon.

I believe that the soldiers were being extra careful to account for all the adults and bigger kids and didn't notice my absence, since I was the tiniest one of all. Or could it be that the same Guardian Angel distracted them as it did when I first escaped from the warehouse? By simply following the rail tracks, I was certain that I would eventually arrive at the same destination, only somewhat later.

The roughly hewn wooden railroad ties were too far apart for me to use as steps and the surrounding gravel was too sharp to walk on with my bare feet. So, with my arms extended to my side, I managed to balance myself along the cold iron track and just kept going until I came upon the joining of two sets of rails—like a "Y." "What now?" I pondered. "Oh well, what's the difference? They both seem to be heading in the same general direction."

I chose the tracks to my right and with the warm sun in my face, continued skipping along, balancing myself on the metal tracks and making pretty good time. I would always wonder where that train was taking all the people in those freight cars and how different my subsequent journey would have been had I not missed getting back on —or if I had chosen the other set of tracks. Toward late afternoon, with the sun shining lower to the ground and my shadow behind me getting longer, I was getting very tired and hungry, wondering why it took me so long to catch up to that train or to the place where it was headed. I began thinking about where I would spend the night once it got dark.

CHAPTER 4
A GERMAN OFFICER

As I was wondering where I would find safe shelter for the evening, I heard the sound of a far-off motor which caused me to stop and search the horizon to identify its source. About a half mile to my left, I observed a motorcycle racing directly toward me. Obviously, I must have been spotted walking all alone on the railroad tracks. Within a minute or two, a German officer was directly in front of me. Remaining on his motorcycle seat with one foot planted firmly on the ground to keep his rumbling motorcycle from tipping over, I couldn't understand what he was asking me.

Very excitedly, I pointed into the direction of the departed train down the tracks and tried to explain how I was left behind during a brief stop. He must have understood me. Without another word, he just hoisted me up with one hand, sat me directly behind himself, pulled my arms tightly around his waist, and away we zoomed down the highway and into the golden sunset.

Comfortably seated behind the officer made me think I was on wings of angels flying across the wide-open terrain to a better part of the world. What a thrilling, most exciting experience for any boy, just to be on a speeding motorcycle seated directly behind a uniformed army officer! The scent of the soft and rich black leather seat, the smell and sound of the purring rumble of the powerful engine, and the overall sense of such wonderful adventure would last a lifetime for me.

Recalling the Ukrainian soldier who rescued and protected me back in the trench, this officer looked totally different. His helmet was designed to also protect his ears, his green uniform was clean and his highly-polished black boots were knee-high. He had a wide black leather belt around his waist which crossed diagonally to the right side of his waist-belt. His pistol fit snugly inside a black leather holster by his right hip and was secured by a narrow black leather belt from his left shoulder.

We continued traveling at a high speed, non-stop late into the night. Whenever I slackened my grip, he would gently reach back and guide my arms tightly around his belt so that I wouldn't fall off. Eventually, we approached a road closure manned by several armed German guards. When we got closer, the officer reduced his speed to a crawl, but didn't stop. He raised his right arm toward the guards and shouted, "Heil Hitler." The guards, likewise, returned his salute, then opened the gate, allowing us to continue our journey into Poland.

A POLISH ORPHANAGE

We would soon arrive in a city where he located a large house behind an iron gate. Since it was the middle of the night, the officer led the way to the front door and knocked repeatedly until an elderly lady opened it to greet us. After a very brief conversation with her, the officer sped off on his motorcycle, leaving me in her care. This would now be my new home—a Polish orphanage.

With her flickering lantern in hand, I was led to the boys' quarters. She raised the lantern above her head to reveal a room full of sleeping boys on individual small cots covered with blankets. Reaching behind the door, she unfolded a spare cot that was leaning against the wall, gave me a blanket, and walked away, closing the door behind her. The room was dark and quiet, since everyone had been asleep for some time. As I lay in my new bed, I was so thankful for my new sleeping accommodations, but even more for the kind officer who rescued me and brought me here on that wonderful motorcycle, so very far away from the terrible and dangerous war zone in Ukraine. Surely, he must have been an angel chosen by God to bring me here. After all, I felt so warm, comfortable, and safe behind him on his motorcycle, as though I were on the wings of angels.

At daybreak, the stillness of the night began to give way to the unruliness of many of the kids in the room. The kids were yawning, chattering, laughing, and yelling which led the bigger kids to pillow-fight in the room. I remained under my blanket until the lady that admitted me the night before came in to restore order. Everyone then had to rinse their hands and faces at a large wash basin by the kitchen and sit at a wooden table for a quick snack of dark bread and a cup of water. This orphanage was bigger and much busier than the previous place I was at. As before, I was the smallest among the other kids, and no one paid any attention to me. It was wise of me to stay out of everyone's way and strictly adhere to the orders and protocol.

A couple of weeks after my arrival, all the children, including me, became infested with head-lice. I started scratching myself more and more vigorously and in frustration, even trying to kill them with my bare knuckles. Those tiny pests made life at the orphanage most unbearable, especially at night-time. The overall unsanitary situation of the place seemed hopeless. We were all dirty, with sores and cuts on our bodies, long, shaggy hair, and many of the girls were in tears. We wore old, hand-me-down raggedy clothes from other kids that had outgrown them. All of us were bare-footed, revealing our black and bloodied stubbed toes.

After enduring these horrible conditions for several weeks, we were elated when a truck took us all to a nearby river for the afternoon. I had never experienced the refreshing thrill of playing in water— jumping, splashing, laughing, and at the same time becoming squeaky clean from head to toe. This was a very popular water recreational spot in the area because there were many other people there to enjoy the water. I even saw some horses and dogs in the water with us. A number of adults swam into deeper water, and I felt I could do the same and, in the process, get extra clean and hopefully drown those pesky lice. Well, as easy as it looked, I certainly didn't have a clue how to swim and the river current just swept me up like a floating leaf.

With all the fun and high-pitched laughter that was going on, no one noticed or heard my plea for help as I frantically began thrashing the moving water with both arms and legs. Trying repeatedly to scream only allowed the water to fill my mouth and lungs, causing me to cough profusely. Panic began to set in and I was certain that I was going to drown. As the current swept me around a curve, some tree branches floated alongside, which I desperately grabbed onto for dear life. Within a few minutes, I was sitting in mud by the edge of the river, along with some smelly dead fish lying there upside down with their exposed white bellies and swarms of flies upon them. But what a welcome sight, when I'd feared that my life was almost over. I quickly ran back to join the group, which was still in full enjoyment of the water activities—ever-so-glad that I was still among them and didn't drown. This time, I remained sitting on the shore with only my toes touching the water. After the truck brought us all back to the orphanage, we felt very clean and happy.

CHAPTER 5
AN ELEGANT LADY ANGEL

I t is my belief that angels symbolize protection, courage, love, purity, harmony, happiness, hope, and faith. I have heard that angels are mentioned in the Bible 273 times, and I have experienced coming across many references of angels when reading the Bible. I believe that angels are spiritual beings created by God but are not meant to be worshipped.

LADY ELIZABETH

Toward the end of 1942, when I was nearing four years old and the world was halfway into the ongoing war, there seemed to be an air of excitement at the orphanage. The floors were hurriedly swept clean, our faces and hands were washed, and our hair was combed. All the children were quickly assembled in the main room with the smallest ones (which included me) standing in the front line, the mid-sized ones in the second row, and the tall ones in the last row. The staff also appeared unusually clean and friendly—all of them smiling for the first time since my arrival.

A horse and carriage pulled up close to the front door which had been left wide open in anticipation of this special visitor. The most regal-looking lady elegantly stepped down from the carriage and came inside. None of us, not even the staff, had ever seen such grace, beauty, and charm.

I observed a real rust-colored fox resting comfortably on the lady's shoulders and curled around the lady's neck. Its mouth was neatly holding on to its own tail, while its wide-open shiny dark eyes kept a steady, protective watch over its awesome master. She also wore a dark brown fur hat with a slightly curved multi-colored feather protruding from the side of the hat. With my eyes and mouth wide open, I was in a frozen state of wonder, disbelief, and amazement. Pacing slowly back and forth in front of us, she carefully studied each one of us. I could smell the heavenly scent of flowery perfume surrounding and following her.

All eyes were upon this special lady. She introduced herself as Elizabeth and explained to the staff that she had a little girl back home, in the city of "Lodz," located west of Poland's capital city of Warsaw. Her hope was to find another little girl so they could grow up together as sisters.

Lady Elizabeth was born in Lithuania and her husband, Nikolai, was born in Latvia. They were both in their late forties, without children of their own, living in their lovely estate in Lodz, Poland. In 1939, when the war broke out in Poland, Nikolai enlisted in the German Army and because of his higher education and command of over half a dozen European languages, including German, Ukrainian, Russian and Polish, was commissioned as an officer to serve as an official interpreter to the commanding general. With the high speed in which Hitler advanced the war from one country to the next, Nikolai, on his motorcycle, was constantly on the move—unable to spend any time at all at home.

She found her home alone a bit too quiet and empty. On a Sunday afternoon, in 1939, following church service at the local Lutheran Church, she decided to visit the cemetery next to the church to pay her respect and pray for a relative that had recently been buried there. Upon entering the cemetery, she noticed an odd-looking bundle of newspapers and decided to take a closer look. What a startling discovery! Wrapped inside the abandoned bundle of newspapers was a baby girl—still alive.

She immediately picked up the bundle and ran to the Red Cross facility, only to be told that with all the turmoil caused by the war, that their resources and time were stretched to the limit and suggested that it would be best if she could take the baby to her home. So she took the baby girl home and named her Irma.

Lady Elizabeth seemed happy that there would be no problem selecting the right young girl to bring home with her. Knowing that for one very lucky girl at the orphanage to be chosen, and that today may very well turn into a hope-filled opportunity for freedom and happiness, all the girls, especially the older ones, put forth their brightest charm with adoring smiles, gleaming eyes, and perfect posture. Continuing to pace back and forth, looking closely at each one of us, she surely must have observed that most of the little tykes in the front row, including me, had no shoes and that our feet were somewhat bruised and not very clean. She took a second look at all the girls. All of us continued to stand at attention, looking straight ahead, not making a sound, and like me, we probably stopped breathing.

Then, the most unexpected and most phenomenal thing occurred. She stopped directly in front of me. I felt totally paralyzed but my heart was beating so fast and loud, I thought it would explode. She bent down and asked my name. That fox around her neck was mere inches from me and stared right at me. With my mouth still wide open in disbelief that she would ask for my name, I tried answering, but no sound would come out. I was in a total state of shock.

Again, she asked, "What's your name?"

"Alex," I replied quickly.

"Do you have a second name?" she asked.

"No, just Alex—that's all I know."

When she asked how old I was, I just smiled and shrugged my shoulders. The head lady confirmed that there were no records of me or of most of the children at the orphanage.

"Alex is the youngest and the most recent to arrive here and is fluent with the Ukrainian language," said the lady. "A German officer brought him here on his motorcycle in the middle of the night, but with the on-going war, there is just no way of locating his family, especially since he doesn't know his last name."

This elegant Lady Elizabeth asked me one more question. It would be the most profound, heart-throbbing, wonderful question ever—one that would reverberate within me the rest of my days. With her warm, angelic smile, she stooped down, very close to me and said, "Alex, would you like to come home with me, far, far away from here?"

I wanted to scream and jump up and down with jubilation and thanksgiving and hug her, but my jaw and my entire body remained in a state of shock and wouldn't move.

"This couldn't be real!" I thought to myself. "It must be a wishful dream—I must be hallucinating!"

Before answering and possibly making a fool of myself in front of everyone, I quickly glanced to my left and right and especially behind me to be certain she was really addressing me and not one of the big girls in the back row. I also distinctly remember her telling the head lady when she first arrived, that she was hoping to find a girl. Lady Elizabeth moved even closer to me, put both her hands tenderly on my shoulders, looked deep into my eyes, and repeated, "Alex, would you like to come home with me, far, far away from here?"

The word "yes," such a simple, short word in any language, couldn't be uttered more quickly and emphatically by anyone. With the broadest and happiest smile, I responded with a resounding, "Yes, oh yes," and immediately followed with a couple more "yeses" along with the widest grin from ear-to-ear that would remain on my face for the longest time while repeatedly nodding my head. My heart was about ready to explode from sheer excitement.

"But we thought you were interested in finding a girl and as you can see, we have plenty to choose from," said the head lady.

"Yes, I know," responded Lady Elizabeth, "but my heart tells me that this little boy needs me much more. There's something special about him that's tugging at my heart to bring him home with me. He's also about the same age as my little girl back home."

(Compassion is a feeling so strong that it compels one to take action to meet another's need. If I were to search for the meaning of the word compassion, I would surely find Lady Elizabeth's picture next to it.)

FREEDOM AND ELATION

It was just a little over a year since my mom sent me off from that deadly Ukrainian warehouse and into God's care. But, wow! What a miraculous, fast-moving year it had been! Who could ever have imagined such a divine response to a desperate mother's deep faith. Now, I was in a new country— Poland, and my life was transformed into a new creation. An angel had come to take me away, up and over the clouds to freedom and happiness—away from all the sorrow, pain, loneliness, hunger, danger, and evil.

Hand-in-hand, as if on a puffy white cloud in the sky, Lady Elizabeth, God's special angel and I, floated magically out the door of the orphanage toward her waiting horse and buggy. She lifted me up, sat me on its wooden floor, and wrapped me in the softest, sweet-smelling warm blanket imaginable. Holding a long, thin leather rein in each hand, she gently moved her wrists slightly to which the horse instantly responded, leading us on a journey, far, far away. I didn't even glance back for a final look. Now, I felt like a prince, adorned with my royal robe, riding in a golden chariot. The bright sunny day with a wintry chill in the air and the soft hint of snow atop the gentle rolling hills ahead appeared ever so heavenly, picturesque, and welcoming.

As our horse, with the rhythmic clippety-clop sound of its hoofs, snorts, and puffs pranced along to take us to my new home, Lady Elizabeth reached into her picnic basket and gave me a bread roll with butter and honey inside it. I took one bite, and "Ooh—wow!" It was unbelievably and out-of-this world tasty. It must be what angels normally eat! That sweet, heavenly taste would always be a reminder to me of how fortunate and blessed I truly was. My entire body tingled with happiness and thankfulness.

As she watched me holding that sweet, precious bread roll between the palms of my hands, inhaling its wonderful aroma, a small crumb fell onto the wood floor, which I instantly picked up and put into my mouth. I looked up and saw her smiling back at me.

For a moment, my thoughts took me back to that first orphanage in Ukraine, when I held my soup bowl with both hands, inhaling its delicious aroma only to have it snatched away from me in a threatening manner—never again!

Filled with sheer joy, in total safety and comfort, being transported in a private horse-drawn carriage with its gentle rocking motion, and guided by a special angel, my eyes to get heavier and heavier. Wrapped in that cozy warm blanket, with the white, puffy distant clouds looking back at me from up in the sky, I curled up in the corner of the rocking wooden floor and with a smile on my face, fell into a deep sleep, dreaming that I was sailing among those big clouds. It was the kind of sleep that every child should experience, filled with blissfulness, contentment, love, warmth, and just the most wonderful overall feeling imaginable.

CHAPTER 6
MY HEAVENLY NEW HOME

MAJOR SCRUBBING AND DEEP-CLEANING

Slowly awakening out of a deep sleep and somewhat still groggy from the very long trip leaving the orphanage, I found myself seated on a wooden bench with my head bent over a table that was totally covered with sheets of newspaper. I hadn't felt a thing, but my long curly black hair had just been cut very, very short and lay there before me. I couldn't believe that so much hair could have all come from me. As I stared at the pile of hair, I was startled to see hundreds of the tiniest black critters scurrying about on the newspaper. Lady Elizabeth gasped at the sight of the vast number of lice and quickly gathered them along with my hair in the newspaper, crumpling everything into a tight ball and burning it all in the furnace. She then placed a metal pan under my chin and washed my scalp two times with a special kerosene-smelling shampoo, then rinsed it clean and applied a very small amount of fresh-scented lotion over my scalp. From that moment on, those pesky head-lice would never, ever, come near me again. They were gone for good and in no time, my clean, new crop of hair would grow even thicker and curlier than before.

Next, she lowered me up to my neck into a bathtub filled with soothing, perfume-smelling warm water covered with a fluffy blanket of suds and bubbles. Not only was this my first ever time experiencing what warm water felt like, but I truly thought I was floating in the midst of those soft, puffy white clouds up in Heaven. After a thorough scrubbing from head to toe, I felt squeaky clean for the first time in my life. She gave me a new pair of pajamas to wear, then hoisted me up into a huge puffy bed—fit for a prince. For a minute, I hesitated—not knowing what to do with the large soft down-filled pillow next to me. Lady Elizabeth smiled and instructed me to place my head on it, covered me with a huge, puffy cloud-like soft quilt and after watching me dozing off, whispered softly, "Good night," then disappeared.

Before falling asleep, I thought to myself, "What a dramatic change from only yesterday, when I tried sleeping on that tiny fold-up cot at the orphanage, fighting off those nasty, blood-sucking lice." I felt like I was born anew, as though my past life was just scrubbed away like a bad dream.

A GLIMPSE INTO HEAVEN – CELEBRATING CHRISTMAS (1942)

Early the next morning, I awoke to the sound of the most heavenly, spine-chilling music I could ever have imagined. It was truly out-of-this-world and sounded like an angelic chorale. Come to think of it, this was the first time I had ever heard music of any kind. Where and how could such a beautiful sound be created? I sat up in bed, with eyes wide open, when that dear angel, Lady Elizabeth slowly opened the door, came in, and cheerfully greeted me with a beaming warm smile, saying, "Frohe Weinachten Alex [Merry Christmas Alex]." I didn't know what that meant. She took my hand and slowly led me down the stairway toward the main room of this palatial estate. With all the unbelievable wonders occurring around me at such a rapid pace, I felt that I was given a glimpse into Heaven—a place of non-ending joy and blessings—more than anyone could conceive. My eyes just couldn't absorb it all. I was drowning in amazement of all the unbelievably overpowering sights and sounds.

At the far end of the room stood the most beautifully decorated, tall pine tree reaching up, almost touching the ceiling, with silver icicles hanging down from nearly every branch with countless tiny burning candles delicately fastened near the tips of the branches. Upon closer observation, I noticed dozens of miniature golden and silver toy drums, trumpets, flutes, and harps suspended below the branches. Attached to the very top of the tree, almost touching the high ceiling, was a large silver star and around the base of the tree were a number of boxes, all wrapped in bright colorful shiny paper with bows and ribbons.

As I came closer to this astonishing Christmas tree, a cute golden-haired baby girl (about the same age as me), wearing a bright multi-color dress, was busy unwrapping one of the pretty boxes. Her name was Irma. I just assumed that she was a baby angel because she kept addressing Lady Elizabeth as "Mommy." Since I no longer had a mom, I asked if I could also call her Mommy. She smiled, gave me a big hug, and said, "Why, of course you can and Irma can be your little sister."

That warm hug was the first since my escape from Ukraine a year ago and in a way, felt like an extension of my mother's final embrace. God did indeed answer her prayer by arranging this miraculous new path to freedom and happiness. Everyone was full of joy and merriment, greeting one another with hugs, kisses, wishing each other a Merry Christmas and blessings for the coming New Year. Little Irma, at the prompting of her mom, picked up a gift from under the tree and gave it to me. I wouldn't dare rip that nice wrapping paper, so she did it for me, revealing a red toy truck that would be all mine. To everyone's surprise, an old, long-bearded man with a large sack over his shoulder made a brief appearance and left more presents by the Christmas tree, then secretly disappeared.

As if all this celebration wasn't already more than enough to last a lifetime, the most unbelievable aroma began drifting in from the kitchen as several ladies continued to bring out to the dining table an endless array of the finest, most delicately-prepared food I could ever begin to dream of. My eyes zeroed in on a heaping silver tray filled with colorful candies and freshly baked cookies topped with chocolate and white powdered sugar. Within minutes, the entire dining table was completely covered with trays on trays of the most tantalizing baked delicacies imaginable. Between compliments to the hostess (Lady Elizabeth), for such a memorable Christmas feast, everyone began tasting and eating a bit from each tray to their heart's content. Although we were in Poland, they all communicated in German as well as in Polish, both of which I learned very quickly.

I kept thinking that all this display of joy and celebration must be a dream. My attention turned to that beautiful little gingerbread house next to the piano in the main living room. As I got closer to it, a man came over, sat at the bench facing the piano, and began playing the most beautiful music imaginable. It sent chills through my spine. Everyone in the room walked right over, surrounded the piano, and began singing along with the popular "Stille Nacht, Heilige Nacht" ("Silent Night, Holy Night"), followed by "Oh Tannenbaum, Oh Heiliger Baum" ("Oh Christmas Tree, Oh Holy Tree"). I just gazed up at the people—all singing together in perfect harmony—and wondered at how wonderful they sounded with the piano music.

The graceful movement of the pianist's hands and fingers across all those shiny black and white piano keys fascinated me. Unable to resist my urge, I slowly eased my way to the bench and sat next to the piano player to closely study all his fingers touching different keys as the music continued to flow through the whole house. Observing my keen interest, he was kind enough to replay Silent Night several times, very slowly, using only his right index finger and prodding me to follow him. After a couple of tries, I was able to get through the first few lines on my own. I glanced over to my new mom, who beamed with pride and approval. After the pianist played his last song, she asked him to help her arrange music lessons for me. I recall a man coming over a couple of times to show me some basic finger movements and reiterate the importance of continued practice on a daily basis, if possible, by following some basic instructions he left for us.

My awe-struck joy and wonder of the Christmas celebration was difficult for me to comprehend and absorb. On a small end table, next to the tree, was a miniature display of the Biblical manger scene with baby Jesus, his mother Mary, and Joseph. Mom explained that the manger scene represents the birth of Jesus, to whom we all pray and sing. In a short passage of the Bible, my reaction was described very accurately:

In the First Letter of Paul to the Corinthians, chapter 2, verse 9 it reads, "But as it is written: "Eye has not seen, nor ear heard, Nor have entered the heart of man. The things which God has prepared for those who love him."

LIKE A HAPPY DREAM

Deep in my heart, I would always believe that this was God's promise in answering my real mom's faithful prayers before she sent me off into His care.

What a happy, joyful, most wonderful life sprang up before me—like the happiest dream. For the first time in my life, all my senses were activated: the sense of sight, sound, smell, taste, touch, feelings, and happiness were not only filled to the top, but overflowing.

Just as I'm sure my new mom had envisioned when she decided back at the orphanage to select me, Irma and I filled her home with laughter. Each day, Irma and I played in the large garden-like orchard, climbing up cherry, apple, and pear trees and tasting samples from each tree to our hearts' content.

While balancing myself atop the cherry tree, I found it interesting that all cherries hung on the tree in perfect pairs. I looped one pair over my right ear and another over my left, displaying to Irma my creativity in making my own earrings. We also enjoyed playing with the friendly free-roaming domestic animals: holding on to the horns of the goats— like handlebars of a bike—or running after the chickens until they would simply squat down, allowing us to pet them. Mom showed us how to milk the goats, feed the chickens, and where the hens laid their eggs.

It didn't take long, however, before I got myself into trouble—literally, up to my ears. While playing in the orchard, Irma and I located a very unusual bush. It was covered with thousands of silver-colored fuzzy little ornaments. As I admired them and felt their irresistible silky softness, some came loose in the palm of my hand. I tickled my nose and cheeks with them and placed one inside each of my ears, like ear plugs. I dared Irma to do the same, but she always acted more mature and more cautious than me.

Upon our return to the house, just in time for lunch, I was anxious for mom to see my clever use of the pussy-willows in my ears. She went about her work and then said, "Alright children, lunch is ready. Wash your hands—and Alex, you have to remove those pussy-willows from your ears."

Well, the more I tried, the deeper they wedged into my ears. Mom gave it a try and even with tweezers was unable to dislodge them because the fuzzy nap was smooth going into the ear but trying to pull them out against the nap, caused the pussy-willows to expand and resist. Right after lunch, we gave it another try, but to no avail. A few minutes later, my head started throbbing with rapidly mounting pressure, like it was about to explode. Without further delay, hand-in-hand, mom and I were off to see a doctor.

HEIL HITLER!

The minute we walked into the front waiting area of the doctor's office, Mom, facing a large portrait of Adolph Hitler hanging on the wall, fully extended her right arm and audibly declared, "Heil Hitler." About six or eight waiting patients who were sitting in the room, all responded, as if on cue, "Heil Hitler." Mom then taught me how I was to greet people in public places and show my respect to Adolph Hitler, by standing straight and tall, with my chin up and shoulders back, extending my right arm, clicking my heels together, and at the same time proudly declaring, "Heil Hitler."

She also instructed me to always stand and give up my seat to an elderly person whenever seating is limited. Since every seat in the waiting room was taken, I stood at attention by her side until we were called into the doctor's office. He put a few drops of clear medicated oil into each ear, which softened the wedged-in pussy-willows. After a minute or two, using small tweezers, he was able to remove the pussy willows bit-by-bit.

"Oh, what a relief," I sighed, as I vowed to never put anything in my ears again. Our walk back home was pain free and much more enjoyable. Mom didn't need to reprimand me because she knew that I had learned my lesson by the sheer pain inflicted from placing foreign objects in my ears.

One sunny afternoon, Mom took Irma and me into town to just stroll leisurely along the sidewalk, while she chatted with many of her friends and eyed the latest ladies' fashions which were colorfully displayed on life-size mannequins in the large windows of department stores next to the sidewalk. We also passed by several extra-large windows displaying real German army tanks, armored vehicles, motorcycles, an array of artillery, and soldier mannequins, all adorned with the Nazi swastikas. That's where most boys, including me, wished to spend more time. Invariably, small groups of armed soldiers would march past us, while overhead, dozens-upon-dozens of roaring airplanes flying in formation would prompt everyone to stop, look up, and marvel at Germany's show of air power.

On Sundays, Mom generally took us to the local Lutheran church, and since Irma had previously been baptized, it was now my turn to experience the baptism tradition and follow the teachings of the Christian Lutheran Faith.

CHAPTER 7
HITLER AND STALIN

HITLER'S MILITARY PARADE

A very special military parade was to take place in the city center and Mom knew how happy it would make me to watch it up close. When we reached the wide main street, there were swastika flags hanging from every building and light post. Hitler's posters were affixed to most of the store windows. Countless people were already gathered along both sides of the street, and hundreds more were drifting in from every direction, cheering excitedly for the parade to begin.

As we made our way closer to the edge of the sidewalk, several dozen marching trumpet players very loudly played a German marching song for a huge regiment of German soldiers, all marching so close to us that we could almost touch them. They didn't make eye contact with the spectators but marched in perfectly timed precision with the music, stepping high and then forcefully stomping down on the cobblestone street with their highly polished black knee-high boots. Each step sounded like a sharp, reverberant clap of thunder. With their crisp, green uniforms, gleaming green helmets shaped to partially cover their ears (like the one I saw on the soldier that had picked me up from the train tracks in Ukraine), and powerful-looking polished guns held against their right shoulders at exactly the same angle by all of them, it was a most unforgettable show of pride and military might.

Suddenly, the loudest cheer imaginable roared through the city as the moment everyone waited for unfolded before us. There, in the midst of the marching regiment, was Adolph Hitler, standing proudly and regally inside a big, black, slow-moving open-top automobile, with his right arm outstretched in the direction of the cheering crowd. By repeating their deafening and emphatic, "Heil Hitler," the people continued to emphasize their respect and admiration. When he neared our location, Mom reminded me to greet him as she had taught me.

Shop-keepers, common folks of all ages, and little children were magnetically drawn to witness this historic moment—for here, before our very eyes, was the most powerful figure in the world. The entire city appeared to be in a state of glee. Mom was smiling with extra pride, since her husband Nikolai, fluent in many European languages and well-educated, served as an interpreter in the German army. Mom didn't seem concerned about where all those soldiers were headed, what Hitler's true motives were, or question the deadly fear he invoked throughout Europe and the whole world.

WHO IS HITLER?

Adolph Hitler was born in Austria-Hungary on April 20, 1889, which today is known as just Austria. By most accounts, Hitler led a troubled life from an early age and was exposed to antisemitic ideology in his early years. Not long after he moved to Germany, World War I began. Even though Hitler wasn't a German citizen, he joined the German-Bavarian Army and fought in the infantry. The war pitted the Central Powers against the Allied Powers, between 1914 until the war ended in 1918, with the Allied Powers prevailing in victory. But Hitler's dismay over how the war ended and the rise in German antisemitic views further fueled his drive toward his destiny.

Several years after the war ended, Hitler renounced his "Austrian" citizenship in 1925 when he was approximately thirty-six years old, so he would be able to run for political office when he became a citizen.

The process took roughly seven years, but now, as a German citizen, he could move one step closer to achieving the power he so desperately desired.

Hitler finally achieved his rise to power in 1933 when he became chancellor of Germany and began accumulating power, driving him further toward becoming the "Führer!"[1]

In 1939, Hitler invaded Poland that led to the beginning of World War II, which subsequently became the deadliest war in history.[2] There have been many estimates of the war casualties, but generally the estimates have been between 70 to 85 million deaths with approximately half being civilians, including over an estimated six million Jews.[3, 4, 5]

When the Allied Forces began to close in on Hitler, he chose to commit suicide instead of falling into his enemies' hands and being made a spectacle, as was the case with his Italian counterpart, Benito Mussolini, who was summarily executed and hung upside down for all to see.

Soon after Hitler's death, the German forces surrendered and that day became known as V-E Day or Victory in Europe. World War II officially ended in September when the Japanese finally surrendered.[6]

---

1. Antony Beevor, *The Second World War* (New York: Little, Brown, 2012).

2. Wikipedia, "Invasion of Poland," Wikipedia, accessed August 2025, https://en.wikipedia.org/wiki/InvasionofPoland.

3. United States Holocaust Memorial Museum, Washington, D.C.

4. Wikipedia, "World War II Casualties," Wikipedia, accessed August 2025, https://en.wikipedia.org/wiki/World_War_II_casualties#:~:text=External%20links-,World%20War%20II%20casualties,-37%20languages.

5. Wikipedia, "Victims of Nazi Germany," Wikipedia, accessed August 2025, https://en.wikipedia.org/wiki/Victims_of_Nazi_Germany#:~:text=External%20links-,Victims%20of%20Nazi%20Germany,-13%20languages.

6. Wikipedia, "World War II," Wikipedia, accessed August 2025, https://en.wikipedia.org/wiki/World_War_II#:~:text=External%20links-,World%20War%20II,-234%20languages.

A DEVIL'S AGREEMENT OF FRIENDSHIP

Although Germany and Russia were historic enemies, Hitler, just prior to launching World War II, in 1939, used his mastery of slyness and craftiness to convince Stalin (leader of the Russian Soviet Union) to a non-aggression treaty. This treaty, in my opinion, was a devil's agreement of friendship, cooperation, and demarcation. By securing this agreement, Hitler had free reign to invade most of the European nations in order to carry out his plan for world dominance through terror, horror, and systematic ethnic cleansing.

With his trained, armed soldiers exceeding 1.5 million, 2,500 tanks, over 2,000 planes, and his well-planned element of surprise, Hitler, on September 1, 1939, swept through Poland, then immediately proceeded through Belgium, the Netherlands, the Balkan countries (Lithuania, Latvia, and Estonia), Luxembourg, and France without any significant resistance.[7]

When in Paris, Hitler proudly took extra pleasure by triumphantly parading with his army down the renowned Champs-Élysées and through the historic Arc De Triomphe which put all the European nations and the world on notice. The most powerful nations were reluctant to mobilize and stop him. However, the invasion of Poland caused Russia's leader, Joseph Stalin, to begin planning his own invasion of Poland.[8]

OPERATION BARBAROSSA (THE CRUSH ZONE) - 1941-1944

This was exactly the area and period of time during my escape.

Hitler's grand prize would be the defeat of Russia. Although the German army advanced very quickly through the Crush Zone (from Poland through Ukraine and into Russian territory,) it grossly underestimated the harsh winter weather and the grit and

---

7. Antony Beevor, *The Second World War.*
8. Wikipedia, "Adolf Hitler," Wikipedia, accessed August 2025, https://en.wikipedia.org/wiki/Adolf_Hitler?wprov=srpw1_4.

determination of the Russian people. Four million German soldiers were killed in this battle, but Russia's losses amounted to a staggering twenty-seven million—the largest human sacrifice of all. It stopped Hitler and forced the German retreat.[9]

JOSEPH STALIN (DICTATOR OF U.S.S.R.)

Looking back at an article written on September 30, 1993 by Patrick J. Buchanon that was published in the *Santa Ana Orange County Register*, pg. 26, Santa Ana, California it reads as follows:

Stalin's Terror: The Forgotten Holocaust[10]

This September, one of the great horrors in history, Stalin's "Terror Famine," in which one in four of the men, women, and children of rural Ukraine were starved to death, as a matter of state policy, is being memorialized.

In that terrible winter of '32—'33, 60 years ago now, Malcolm Muggeridge, then a dedicated young socialist, had come to Moscow to cover the brave new world in which he had come to believe. Hearing of starvation in Ukraine, disbelieving the Party would tolerate such a horror, he bought a train ticket and traveled to Kiev and Rostov.

What he saw terminated his affair with Communism.

"The famine," Muggeridge wrote in shock, "is an organized one." More than that, it is "a military occupation; worse, active war."

Stalin's objective: Break Ukraine. His strategy: requisition all grain, send in troops to search cellars and remove hoarded food, make certain the peasants did not escape their famished towns and villages. With the Russia-Ukraine border sealed, the starving could not escape the barren land, and food to save them could not get in.

---

9. Wikipedia, "Operation Barbarossa," Wikipedia, accessed August 2025, https://en.wikipedia.org/wiki/Operation_Barbarossa.

10 Patrick J Buchanan, "Stalin's terror: the forgotten holocaust," *Santa Ana Orange County Register*, September 30, 1993, 26, accessed August 2025, orangecountyregister.newspaperarchive.com/santa-ana-orange-county-register/1993-09-20/page-26/.

Stalin's motives for this crime of the century: He was paranoid about the nationalities, especially Ukrainians. His party nourished a class hatred for "kulaks," i.e., "rich" farmers who owned 25 acres or three cows; he needed scapegoats for his failed harvests. Despising the peasantry for their attachment to old ways and old values, he wanted to collectivize all food supplies, to guarantee that the army and urban proletariat he feared, and needed to defend and industrialize his state, were fed. As the dying Roman emperor told his son: Pay the soldiers, the rest do not matter.

So began what historian Robert Conquest would call "The Terror Famine" and the world's "Forgotten Holocaust."

In *Stalin's Apologist*, biographer S.J. Taylor describes the reaction of Muggeridge and Arthur Koestler:

"In Kuban well-fed troops were being used to control and coerce peasants who were in many cases starving to death. The supplies of grain sent into the area were being used to feed the troops who, along with Party activists, were still searching barns and cellars for hidden grain or hoarded food. Meanwhile, Muggeridge reported, there were 'fields choked with weeds, cattle dead, people starving and dispirited, no horses for ploughing or transportation, not even adequate supplies of seed for the spring sowing'."

To Koestler, who spent the winter in Kharkov, then Ukraine's capital, the children looked like "embryos out of alcohol bottles." Traveling by rail was "like running the gauntlet; the stations were lined with begging peasants with swollen hands and feet, the women holding up to the carriage windows horrible infants with enormous wobbling heads, stick-like limbs, swollen pointed bellies."

Koestler found the local press asking, "What was the reaction of the West to the deliberate starvation of millions?" Dead silence. Reports about industrial progress, but "not one word about the local famine epidemics, the dying out of whole villages .... The enormous land was covered with a blanket of silence."

What was the reaction of the West to the deliberate starvation of millions in Ukraine, Kazakhstan, and the Caucuses? Dead silence.

Why did America not protest? Why did we not help?

Because America did not know. And high among the reasons we did not was that *The New York Times*'s Walter Duranty, dean of correspondents in Moscow, lied for Stalin. Duranty was a "fashionable prostitute" who "covered up the horrors and deluded an entire generation by prettifying Soviet realities," said Joe Alsop. "He lived comfortably in Moscow, too, by courtesy of the KGB."

For fourteen years, Duranty was the most authoritative voice from Moscow. When editors asked if there was starvation, he wrote back, "There is no actual starvation or deaths from starvation but there is a widespread mortality from diseases due to malnutrition."

"The famine is mostly bunk," he wrote a colleague.

Duranty's work won him a Pulitzer in 1932 for "dispassionate interpretive reporting of the news from Russia." Fifty years later. *Time* put the total number of deaths from the terror famine Walter Duranty had covered up at between 8 million and 10 million souls.

On this 60th anniversary of the Forgotten Holocaust, *The New York Times* would do well to renounce Duranty's Pulitzer, apologize to the people of Ukraine, and admit on page one what the world now knows: Its famous correspondent Walter Duranty was, to borrow from Khrushchev, nothing but the "cur and toady" of Joseph Stalin. Mr. Buchanan is a syndicated columnist.

What was the reaction of the West to the deliberate starvation of millions? Dead Silence.

CHAPTER 8
AIR RAIDS AND BOMB-SHELTERS

From the very beginning of World War II (September 1, 1939), people in Poland were used to seeing formations of German military planes "Luftwaffe" (Hitler's "Air Force") flying overhead. But from 1941 to 1944, the formations were growing in size very rapidly—all heading eastward to Soviet Russia—so many that at times they would block the sun, like a dark storm-cloud. Wailing air-raid sirens at any given time, day or night, would alert everyone to hurry for cover in their designated neighborhood underground bunkers. Air-raid sirens at night also meant that all lights throughout the city had to be turned off at once until the "all clear" signal was given. I clearly recall Mom waking us at night so we could all race to the underground bunker about two or three city blocks away.

With the sirens blaring more and more frequently, it was obvious that the war was intensifying very rapidly and getting closer to us. We began hearing whistling sounds of flying rockets. Large buildings were being bombed and razed to the ground in smoke and fire. Whenever a big factory got bombed, the only thing still standing would generally be the tall brick chimney, which puzzled me until I learned that the taller the chimney, the wider and more secure the base and the stronger and more efficient the upward draft. Understandably, most everyone feared that their homes and even our bunker may get hit at any time. However, the fearless and naïve boys (me included) were excitedly watching the fireworks (bombardments) on display so close to us.

Upon our return from the bunker one night, we were met by about a dozen German soldiers waiting in front of our house. They didn't look at all like the ones we saw marching in the parade a while back. These were frightened looking soldiers in retreat—dirty, unshaven, torn and filthy uniforms, and muddy boots. Mom invited them in, fed them, and quickly made sleeping arrangements for them in the living room on couches and on the floor. I marveled at the ingenuity of one young soldier who moved two sofa chairs together, facing each other, thereby creating a comfortable-looking enclosed bed—similar to a baby's crib.

One of the soldiers explained to Mom that during their company's attempt to retreat from the overpowering Russian Soviet Army, they were the only ones able to evade capture and that the rest became prisoners, possibly including her husband Nicolai. He went on to explain that the Russian Army was so evil that they even started killing some of their prisoners. They cautioned Mom that all of Poland would be invaded and overrun by the Soviet Army by the early months of 1944, as they had already broken through the German line of offense. These retreating soldiers gave her a lot of information to help her plan her most important decision. In the morning, they were all gone but Mom's demeanor changed dramatically. With the look of fear and anxiety clearly written on her face, she nervously paced the floor without saying a word.

THE RADIO MAN

By late evening, after Irma had already gone to bed, I watched Mom move her chair very close to a wooden cabinet next to the sofa— listening very intensely to a man's scary speech. Her eyes began to well up with tears, and her jaw dropped in disbelief. She unfolded a white hankie and began dabbing her eyes and wet cheeks. The more she listened, the more her tears began running down her face. I got chills through my body because it brought back the memory of my real mom's fear and tears back in that evil Zhytomyr warehouse. Would I again be told to run to safety alone as before, or would we all try to escape together?

That wooden cabinet (about four feet tall) was a high-quality radio, and having never heard of, seen, or understood anything about a radio, I truly believed that there was a real man hiding inside, especially when Mom hushed me to be still so she could hear what the man in the radio was saying. With her ear almost touching the radio, the man's voice from inside the cabinet very clearly instructed Mom to leave her home as soon as possible, as the Soviet Russian Army was marching toward the city and would be at people's doorsteps within days. At this late hour, Irma had already been asleep for some time, but I stayed up—fully aware of the life-threatening danger closing in on us. Realizing that I was standing close behind her and also listening to the radio, Mom told me to immediately go up to my room, go to sleep, and that everything would be fine in the morning.

I did as I was told, but how could I possibly sleep now? My mind was racing and trying to make sense of all that had transpired that day and thought to myself that time was of the essence. This was not a time to sleep and pretend that it would all go away by morning. I couldn't get that radio out of my mind:

"How dare that mean little radio man, hiding in that cabinet, threaten us and tell Mom to leave her home and cause her to cry in fear?"

Based on the size of that wooden cabinet, I figured that in order for him to fit inside it, he couldn't be any bigger than me and that I could probably take him on. So, I devised a plan to help resolve the stress that he created for us. I stayed in bed under the covers with my eyes wide open and nervously waited until I heard Mom retreat to her bedroom and shut the door behind her. Then, most cautiously and quietly, I crept downstairs and headed straight toward that cabinet to teach that mean radio-man a lesson he'd never forget.

I slowly eased myself behind it, ready to challenge that midget-sized man hiding inside. To my surprise, all I saw were about eight to ten small glass tubes. They were neatly arranged on a flat metal shelf, all pointing upward. After carefully inspecting the entire cabinet without finding any sign of a hidden man within, I concluded that those tubes must have something to do with him and all I needed to do was take them out one by one and smash them. Then, Mom and the rest of us wouldn't be worried or afraid any longer.

With my heart beating ever-so-rapidly, I gathered enough courage and attempted to pull out the largest tube first, hoping that the man wouldn't mysteriously jump out and attack me. To my horror, when I grabbed the tube, it was burning hot and as much as I wanted to scream, I was wise enough to bite my tongue and remain silent. Otherwise, mom would've been startled and I would've been in deep trouble. So, I quickly and quietly ran back up to my bed, licking my singed fingers and eventually fell asleep.

CHAPTER 9
OUR EXODUS FROM POLAND

THE END OF A WONDERFUL, HEAVENLY HOME

How quickly my joyful year passed! In early spring of 1944, that wonderful place in Poland—our dream home—the heavenly place where God's angels had brought me, was coming to an end, not just for me but for all of us. It was quite cold, with a trace of snow still on the ground. I was now about five years old and on the run again but no longer alone. With my angel mom guiding us, I had nothing to fear. Feeling as secure and joyful as when she rescued me from the orphanage, there was no doubt in my mind that our adventurous voyage would take us far away from evil and fear to freedom and security.

In spite of my young age, Mom was aware of my overly-inquisitive mind, my fearless and positive nature, the value of freedom, and also of my escape from a death camp in Ukraine. She felt that I was strong enough to understand the potential danger facing us.

In the frosty cold middle of the night, Irma and I were again rousted from our sleep, but this time we didn't go to the bomb shelter. Mom explained that we had to make a very, very important decision: Either we stayed here in our lovely home and submitted to the invading

Soviet Russian Army which was already en route toward our city, or we'd leave everything behind and immediately try to escape far away, where we would be much safer. Mom had heard many horror stories about the ruthless and evil Soviet Army and the horrible things their soldiers did to the women, especially if the women's husbands were soldiers or officers in the German Army. As for me—I would most likely have been sent back into a Russian orphanage and eventually undergone training to fight in the Soviet Army.

That familiar horse and buggy, which had transported me to that wonderful place a year ago, was now waiting out by our front door, ready to take us all away on the longest trip imaginable—westward—across Europe.

Mom had always looked very stylish and wore expensive jewelry. Her private closet was filled with beautiful clothes, furs, hats, shoes, and gloves. Adjoining her closet was her husband Nicolai's closet, which was filled with the latest menswear, an array of new-looking dark suits, white dress-shirts, high-polished black and brown shoes, as well as a number of officer uniforms, boots, hats, caps, and helmets which remained untouched as he was off fighting in the war. For Mom, freedom was most precious regardless of the cost. Her faith would guide us there.

Daylight was about to break and there was a winter chill in the air. Mom had already packed several blankets, baskets of food and water, plus several precious pieces of jewelry and just a few of her most memorable photos. Once Irma and I got settled and covered with the blankets, Mom climbed aboard and with that familiar clippety-clop sound of the horse's hoofs against the cobble-stone street, our daring journey began. There was no hesitation, no tears, and no glancing back at what was left behind. For a minute, I felt like my life was being unwound two years—back to Zhytomyr, Ukraine, from where I initially escaped. There was also no hesitation or glancing back from me.

Could this determined brave woman, with only a horse and buggy and two orphan tots, without any road map or assistance to guide her, flee the advancing ruthless Russian Army closing in on the city? She would rely totally on her unshakeable faith, hope, love, and complete trust that God would be her guide and bring us all to safety and freedom (identical to my birth mother's conviction). Without a doubt, she must have been chosen by God to be His assigned angel and carry out another rescue mission—the most challenging imaginable.

Although Mom had told Irma and me to remain under the blankets and stay warm, for me, that only lasted for about two minutes. Like a co-pilot or back-seat driver, I sat up to observe everything and if needed, provide aid. Recalling my escape from that horrible warehouse in Ukraine, I knew that we had to get as far away as possible to safety. How fortunate for us that we had a comfortable wagon and a horse and didn't have to run like I did. Irma, as usual, remained safely tucked under the blanket as instructed. As we approached the main road leaving the city, Mom and I glanced to her right, then to the left and gasped in disbelief when she saw an endless line of thousands upon thousands of people heading in the same direction out of the city in an attempt to escape the imminent arrival of the Soviet Russian Army. The road was totally filled as far as we could see, making it difficult for us to cut in. Mom anxiously snapped the reins on the horse's back, urging it to squeeze into the tight traffic lane on the right.

Like most two-lane roads, the left side of the road (the fast lane) was for motorized vehicles (cars, buses, trucks, and motorcycles). I found it exciting to observe such a variety of cars, motorcycles with sidecars, huge trucks, and even small three-wheeled trucks. Our lane was for slower-moving, non-motorized traffic, including foot-traffic, bicycles, wheelbarrows, horses, or oxen-pulled carts, carriages, and wagons of all sizes. No matter what means of travel, however, many people by nature (except for Mom) brought along much more than needed for the long perilous journey ahead. The caravan in the slow lane moved along at a crawl—a snail's pace, ever-so-slowly, making Mom quite anxious and concerned that we would not be able to make much headway to escape in time.

OUR FIRST OBSTACLE

About a quarter mile ahead, to our left, Mom focused her eyes on a narrow dirt trail leading away from the main road. At the entrance to the trail was a barbed-wire gate manned by an armed soldier. Glancing over her left shoulder, she suddenly commanded the horse to veer across the fast lane away from the caravan, heading straight toward the soldier guarding the gate. She pulled the horse to a brief stop, stepped down from the wagon and, leading the horse by the bridle, walked directly, without hesitation, toward the soldier.

In my curiosity, I sat up and watched the soldier raise his gun, pointing it at Mom, sternly commanding her to turn around and rejoin the caravan. Fearless and determined, she defied his warning and kept walking briskly toward him until the muzzle of his gun was at her chest. Recalling how deadly those guns were when I was in the trench back in Ukraine and the result of the gun-battle, I feared that this would surely be the end for Mom, as well as for Irma and me—that we would all be shot.

However, to my surprise and unbelief, in less than a minute, as though under her magical spell, the soldier lowered the barrel of his gun, opened the gate to let us continue our lonely journey, then immediately closed the gate behind us and resumed his post. I watched all this in awe that angels possessed that kind of power.

Understandably, because of the chaos and upheaval throughout the European nations, money would have been of no value with which to win his favor. She could have bribed him with one of her favorite pieces of gold jewelry or impressed him with an official document of her husband's rank within the German Army.

Most certainly, the hordes of people in the caravan watching us would assume that Mom was crazy to be leaving the main highway and the protection of the organized exodus—slow as it was. Yes, she was indeed crazy—crazily committed and focused on saving her two little orphans and pursuing freedom at any cost, even at the risk of her own life.

In our subsequent lone journey, we could hear the distant sounds of war with artillery fire, bombings, rumbling tanks, and whining sounds of fighter planes and bombers, while its destructive black smoke began to fade into the horizon behind us.

As it turned out, by day's end, the Soviet Army overtook the long caravan and quickly sealed off all roads, forcing most all escapees back to their homes where they would henceforth be subjected to live under Soviet Communist rule. By the next day, the entire country of Poland would be overtaken and sealed from the outside world.

OUR MEDIEVAL BUT WISEST CHOICE

Considering the humble and medieval mode of transportation with just a lone horse indiscriminately pulling a small buggy through the countryside, we wouldn't attract anyone's attention. However, the people in the long caravan were totally helpless. Though much, much slower and certainly much more daring, our medieval method of travel had the best chance of succeeding. By avoiding all roads and villages, we continued traveling cross-country through forests and uninhabited and undetectable areas. For many, many days, very often by night, we were able to remain out of sight and inconspicuous.

Mom knew quite well that we would encounter many dangers along the way. Many a time, low-flying fighter jets would whiz by, above our heads, at such a rapid speed that they would disappear into the horizon before the deafening sound reached our ears. The motor noise from regular planes and big bombers, however, gave us ample time to take cover.

In order to lessen the burdensome weight of the buggy, Mom would often-times choose to walk alongside the buggy and guide the horse by its bridle, especially through rocky, uneven, or up-hill terrain. Although it was very cold and windy at times, Irma, always the wiser one, would remain under the cozy warm blanket but I felt it was my duty to be Mom's watchman—to keep a keen eye out for any sign of danger.

While walking next to the horse for an hour or so, a very cold and icy wind with snow began blowing across our wagon from our left—the perfect conditions for frostbite against tender young skin (generally the nose or ear lobes). Mom had wrapped a large warm shawl around her neck and kept walking, while my head was still extended over the buggy, like a periscope on a submarine, in order to continue my self-assigned watchman's duty. She turned to glance back at me, then suddenly stopped the horse and ran to me with a worried look on her face.

Without saying a word, she quickly yanked me off the buggy, grabbed a handful of snow off the ground and began rubbing my nose very briskly with the icy snow. I was totally confused—is this her way of punishing me for not staying under the blanket? Surely, she must have appreciated my vigilant intent. A minute later, she did scold me to remain under the blanket, especially during extreme cold, windy weather like this, but also proceeded to explain that my nose had already turned white from frostbite and that the best remedy was to rub it with snow as soon as possible. As a constant reminder of that incident, the left part of my nose would remain somewhat sensitive and turn red during extreme cold weather or exposure to the sun in summer.

Through much of our voyage, we followed very narrow nature trails created by animals roaming freely through the uninhabited parts of the countryside, over hills, and alongside creeks and rivers. But how anyone could avoid getting lost and disoriented and continue to pursue the intended final destination can only be described as an ongoing miracle. Whenever we heard any suspicious distant sounds, Mom would immediately lead our horse behind trees or bushes. Always with the utmost attention to remain out of sight, Mom would plan our nights' respite and sleep times by unhitching the horse and camouflaging our wagon with leaves and branches.

Her extra-careful hiding routine rewarded us immensely on several occasions as each time we avoided being spotted by low-flying single-engine planes and a couple of times by soldiers on motorcycles.

An occasional owl would bid us good night and during the day the lonely echoing song of a cuckoo and the woodpecker's staccato percussion accompaniment high up in the trees would provide us with a comforting signal that all was safe and peaceful from high up on their lookout posts.

Mom had been rationing our food supply very thoughtfully during our endless days of travel and at no time did Irma or I experience any hunger pangs. Though our food basket at times was near bottom, it was never completely empty. We didn't have to worry at all about our horse's nourishment since fresh grass and drinking water from creeks and rivers was plentiful. Even when snow covered the grass, our horse would scrape the snow away utilizing its front hoof and eat the frozen grass beneath.

Crossing a number of rivers—horse and wagon included—on flimsy wooden barges operated by river dwellers and stopping at small hillside farms along the way for brief rests and any bits of food they could spare, was becoming an ordinary routine for us.

A TIMELY REAPPEARANCE

Very early one morning, waking from a restful, uninterrupted, and well-deserved night's sleep, with our horse close by lazily enjoying its early morning fresh grass breakfast, I began hearing a very familiar sound. Our wagon was still hidden behind a bush next to a wide lush grassy meadow and a creek. As I listened more intently, I clearly recalled hearing those identical strange sounds back in Zhytomyr. Yes, those four-eared monsters must have followed us all the way here! I stood up to alert Mom, but she was gone. Fearing that the monsters may have attacked her and dragged her away, I jumped down from the wagon, ready to spring into action and save her. To my surprise, however, I observed her not too far away—very slowly and cautiously closing in on those monsters and softly talking to them. In her right hand, she carried a metal pail.

"This is crazy," I thought to myself. "What in the world would she be thinking of doing with that metal pail?"

Those monsters just stood there, swishing their tails to and fro and watching her as she reached out and gently stroked several of them, while continuing to talk to them with her comforting soft voice. Then, very slowly, she stooped down with her pail and began milking one of them. She brought the milk back to our wagon to share with Irma and me. Fresh and warm milk would never, ever taste this good again. My whole body felt so warm and content. I was instantly re-energized and happy. What unique angelic power—to turn a four-eared monster freely roaming about into a provider of such a delicacy in the middle of an open field such as this!

Mom used that moment as an opportunity to teach Irma and me about God's providence to mankind in His creation of cows, goats, pigs, chickens, geese, turkeys, as well as a variety of vegetables and even fish from the rivers and sea, all for the nourishment of people around the world. Her poignant and timely explanation meant a lot to me. It was only two years earlier, when my feeble body couldn't go on any longer and I came upon a yellow sunflower plant, my "manna from Heaven." It was just enough to re-energize me so I could continue my escape and search for freedom.

Then, after Mom (Lady Elizabeth) had rescued me from the Polish orphanage and provided an endless source of delicious food and delicacies, I didn't give much thought about its source and simply assumed there would always be an endless supply.

"FLORENCE OF THE ELBE"

When we left our home in Poland, Mom had planned to travel westbound all the way to West Germany (a total distance of perhaps 1,000 miles). She had counted on going through the historic city of Dresden in Eastern Germany (about 300 miles from our home in Lodz, Poland). Regarded as one of the world's most beautiful cities in Eastern Germany, Dresden was located along the Elbe River which was one of the major water tributaries stretching from the Czechoslovakian mountains across four European countries and emptying into the

North Sea. Dresden had been an easy access for refugees fleeing the aggression of Communist Russia (a.k.a. the Red Army).

Mom had thought about a temporary layover at a relative's home in that city—perhaps even long enough for the war's intensity to subside or, hopefully, come to an end.

However, as we slowly got closer to the German border, with the sound of war in the far distance ahead of us intensifying, Mom's sixth sense kept urging her to abandon the idea of a stay-over in Dresden altogether because we could end up getting trapped there by the Red Army.

She followed her instinct, choosing instead to continue in a more west-south-westerly direction toward Czechoslovakia and later continued toward Western Germany by way of Austria (both countries were under German control). Although this would be a much longer route, she believed it would be much safer since it would not be in direct exposure of the on-going conflict.

Her fears became reality when, between February thirteenth and fifteenth, 1945, the city of Dresden was completely destroyed by the worst barrage of Allied firebombing. Over 700 British aircrafts, followed by a wave of American bombers dropped more than 3,900 tons of bombs decimating the entire city. Up to 25,000 people were killed.[1, 2] We may well have been among them had Mom not followed her sixth sense.

At some point later, I overheard my mom mentioning that one survivor reported seeing the entire sky aglow in fiery, bright-red colors and watching people and horses running indiscriminately through the streets, screaming as though it was the end of the world. The inferno was so intense and sudden that he saw a burned shell of a bus filled with dead charred soldiers, all sitting perfectly still in their seats like dolls. They didn't even have a chance to move out of their seats.

---

1. Antony Beevor, *The Second World War*.
2. Wikipedia, "Bombing of Dresden," Wikipedia, accessed August 2025, https://en.wikipedia.org/wiki/Bombing_of_Dresden.

There were several reasons why, of all the many German cities, the Allied Forces decided on totally destroying this particular beautiful city of Dresden. This horrific assault occurred about a month after some 19,000 American troops were killed at the Battle of the Bulge and Dresden was the major center of Nazi Germany's railroad network and transportation hub. The Allied Forces were committed to stopping Hitler in his own country in order to end the Nazi atrocities and the mass murders at the Auschwitz Concentration Camp.

It continues to amaze me that there are people like Mom, regardless of their national, political, or social association, people of such noble, supernatural character, yet most compassionate and God-fearing, sacrificing their all—including putting their own life on the line, just to help others that may be in imminent, life-threatening danger.

Although her home in Poland was in the direct path of the most brutal war and her husband was taken prisoner by the Red Army, she knew, in her heart, by faith, that God had placed Irma and me into her care and that He would guide us all to safety and freedom. Had she not possessed such deep faith, compassion, commitment, love, and devotion, she could have chosen a much easier, less-stressful, and certainly much less dangerous route by simply taking Irma and me to the Red Cross for care and safety (since we weren't hers to begin with) and just fended for herself much more easily.

AN AUSTRIAN REFUGE

(Austria had been an independent, sovereign nation until Hitler, in 1938, forcefully annexed it to German control. Right after the war, it returned as a federal republic to its neutrality.)

After approximately six months on the run through never-ending forests, over steep hills, down narrow trails, and across several rivers, Mom was so relieved when we finally entered Austria's countryside. She felt that since Austria took a neutral position and was not an active participant in the war, the fighting and bombardment would bypass us completely. She wasted no time locating a suitable temporary dwelling location for our layover with an elderly farm couple in exchange for working for them in their field until the end of the war.

When Mom and the farm couple (Friedrich and Helga Bergen) first greeted each other, rather than a normal handshake, they extended their right arms and in unison, declared, "Heil Hitler!" As soon as we entered the main room of the house, I observed a large portrait of Hitler hanging on the wall—very similar to the one I saw in the doctor's office back in Poland.

Their two-story house would provide ample space for us all and the adjacent big garden would grow an abundance of fresh vegetables. There were a dozen or more chickens roaming about the yard to provide a daily supply of fresh eggs for all to enjoy, and even a couple of cows for milk, butter, and cottage cheese. In short, we all had everything we needed to sustain us in comfort and safety. It felt so wonderful to once again be able to sleep in a regular bed, eat cooked food, run and play in the grass, and even interact with neighborhood kids.

(Born in the town of Braunau am Inn, Austria, Hitler, although having renounced his Austrian citizenship in 1925, remained an idol to most Austrians until the end of World War II.)[3, 4]

Near the end of the day, we all sat down around a large wooden table covered with a tablecloth to a wonderful meal that Frau (German for Mrs.) Bergen and Mom prepared together. After such a long and grueling cross-country escapade, Mom, Irma, and I were ever-so-grateful for this feast of thanksgiving. The mouth-watering aroma through the house was heavenly. It brought back memories of my first taste of such delight when Mom first brought me out of the orphanage to her home in Poland. What a delicious dinner, with freshly baked dark pumpernickel bread, roasted beef and potatoes with gravy, and a variety of freshly-cooked vegetables from the garden. I attempted to chew a small bit of tough white gristle in the meat and was about to set

---

3. Ian Kershaw, "Adolf Hitler: Hitler: 1889–1936" *Encyclopaedia Britannica*, (Hubris 1998).
4. Wikipedia, "Adolf Hitler."

it aside when Mom quickly turned a potential embarrassing situation into a positive one by explaining to me that by chewing and eating the gristle, I would always have the nicest and curliest hair of anyone throughout my life and that I would never go bald—and how right she proved to be, as I would often remind myself over time.

Through the harvest season of 1944, Mom assisted Herr (German for Mr.) Bergen with the field work, while Irma and I tried our best to pitch in by gleaning any left-over stalks of grain. Although we felt much safer here on the Austrian farm than on our journey fleeing through the deadly war zone, we continued, by habit, to take cover every time we heard a plane passing overhead. We had no idea whether those planes were heading to the battlefield or escaping their adversary. I'm sure Mr. Bergen and Mom had a pretty good idea where they were all going but they didn't express any concern. Although I was only five, I wished that they would have shared some of their thoughts with me because I was well aware that the war was still ongoing and that the Red Army may very well be closing in on us, ready to occupy Austria.

CHAPTER 10
END OF WAR IN EUROPE
(V-E DAY)

On a bright sunny Tuesday afternoon, May eighth, 1945, about a dozen local farmers and their children gathered in front of our place, which was situated along a regularly traveled dirt road normally used by these Austrian farmers. Our location provided a convenient gathering spot for sharing the latest gossip and news—mostly about the war. I thought it seemed odd, as I watched the adults, including Mom, all huddled together in tight formation, chattering nervously accompanied by erratic hand-gesturing. With the exception of Irma and me, the kids, totally unconcerned about the events of the war, continued playing, laughing, and chasing one another as most kids normally do. Curious, as I've always been, I wondered why the adults acted so strangely and decided to inch my way next to Mom so I could listen in. They were all trying to speak at the same time, getting louder and more anxious.

I overheard them saying that they heard on the radio that the war had just ended and that all fighting had ceased. The moment I heard the words "war" and "radio," I recalled that it was the radio that made us flee from Poland and now, here in Austria, the radio was telling us that it had all ended.

"How would the radio know so much?" I wondered. "And also, be able to make everyone obey without question?"

At first, everyone was very happy and relieved that the six-year long war with all the killings across Europe and Russia was finally over. We assumed that Adolph Hitler, with his vast war machine, prevailed in driving his enemies, especially the Soviet Red Army, out for good. Mom just listened without saying a word, when one man ran over and very excitedly reported the most shocking news imaginable—that the German army had been totally defeated by America and the Soviets.

Another man jumped in with even more shocking news—that Adolph Hitler was dead. We were all in shock, looking at each other in sheer disbelief. What should we do now? Who would be coming after us— the Russians or the Americans? Everyone, especially Mom and I, were aware of the Soviet ruthlessness and oppression but knew very little about the Americans.

"Don't tell me that our daring cross-European escape was all in vain," I thought. "Doesn't Mom realize that we will end up being ruled by the Russians! Has she so quickly forgotten what we've gone through?"

I was unable to comprehend all that was happening, and no one cared to take the time to explain anything to me because of my young age. Until now, my life was focused around escaping and fleeing from death, fear, war, and evil. My faithful Ukrainian mom's final words assured me that God would protect me and guide me to safety. I had wholeheartedly believed that my home in Poland was God-sent, only to see it vanish. I wondered, "So, where will we go from here?"

I had understood, and to a degree witnessed, that the brutal war and the millions of lives lost on and off the battlefield was carried out between two empires: Russia and Germany, so what's all this about America? Who are they and where did they come from? Are these Austrians all nuts? How could anyone just appear and claim to have defeated the most feared mighty German powerhouse? But if it is true that the Americans really did defeat the Germans and that Adolph Hitler was dead, then they must surely be even more dangerous than the Russians.

THE AMERICANS ARE COMING

Leaving a cloud of dust behind them, the deafening roar of dozens of American tanks, trucks, and jeeps rolled past our place heading back to their base in West Germany. One truck, full of American soldiers, veered away from the procession and stopped in front of our place where the local villagers were huddled.

Frau Bergen quickly ran into the house to remove the large portrait of Hitler from the wall, shoving it under the sofa, then scurried through the rest of the house hiding any memorabilia and photos relating to Hitler or Germany in order not to reveal their loyalty to their family's former idol.

Since everyone was just standing around and no one was doing anything to defend us from what I assumed was an American invasion, I quickly ran upstairs to retrieve a rifle tucked behind Herr Bergen's bedroom door.

Holding the heavy gun tightly against my right shoulder (just as the soldiers did in the trench back in Ukraine), I stood at the top of the stairs, pointed the barrel of the gun directly at the front door, and placed my index finger on the trigger—ready to fire at the first American that dared to enter.

Nervously, shaking with fright and trying to control the vibration and unsteadiness of the heavy gun, I was startled when one of the live shells became dislodged from the chamber, fell out, and noisily bounced down the wooden stairwell toward the front door. Not knowing how to reload it, I quickly put the gun back, ran out the back door, and locked myself inside the smelly outhouse a short distance behind the house—thinking that the Americans would never think of looking for me there.

Somehow, I had to get Mom's and Irma's attention to join me inside the safety of the outhouse. I could see them and cried out to them by name, but they either couldn't hear me or simply chose to ignore my desperate plea. Expecting, at any moment, to hear guns blazing and people screaming, I heard, instead, everyone cheering, applauding, laughing, and just having a great time. Slowly, I opened the outhouse door, and to my surprise, saw everyone happily waving to the Americans and shaking their hands. For a moment I thought that these must be German soldiers who reclaimed their power and drove the Americans as well as the Russians back; so, I ran over to join everyone.

To my amazement, all the soldiers standing in the back of the truck were black-skinned with big, pearly-white teeth exposed by their broad smiles. They were indeed Americans, not Germans. Since I had never seen an American or a black person before, I assumed that all Americans must be black.

But why were all the local Austrians so cheerful and friendly to these strange Americans? Did they forget so quickly what had just occurred —that they'd even colluded with the Soviets, defeated the Germans, and also killed Hitler and may now be planning to capture and kill us? Was I the only one that could clearly see what was happening? Why wouldn't Mom, who understood better than any of them, speak up and explain the facts to them? Nothing made any sense to me.

Well, I got my answer loud and clear: The American soldiers were throwing packages of Camel cigarettes out to the Austrian men and dark chunks of chocolate candy bars to the children and women. When one piece of chocolate landed right in front of me, I picked it up and stared at the smiling soldier's face that had tossed it to me. His face was the same color as the chocolate. Like everyone else, I bit into the chocolate and wow—the most wonderful, good taste imaginable! Immediately I picked up another piece, thinking to myself that if Americans can so freely toss out such mouth-watering delicacies and precious cigarettes to total strangers, they'll certainly be loved by everyone around the world, young and old.

Within minutes, all previous loyalty to Hitler and fear of Russia evaporated. Old habits, protocol, and fear came to an end. The former "Heil Hitler" greetings were instantly stopped and forgotten.

Young soldiers who had survived the carnage of this bloody war were now coming home to the waiting arms of their families and loved ones. Sadly, however, there were millions who would never see their homes again—they gave the ultimate sacrifice.

Mom enjoyed watching the jubilation of everyone, mostly Irma's and mine, as we joyously laughed and played without another thought about any fear. But her heart would never cease to ache for some news about her beloved Nikolai—hopefully alive somewhere in a Soviet prison. With renewed determination, prayer, and unfailing faith, the end of her daring journey would still be a long distance away, but without the danger and stress of our journey thus far.

CHAPTER 11
WEST GERMANY—OUR FINAL DESTINATION

(Nikolai and Mom had a prearranged agreement, that if the German army were to be defeated by the Soviets or if he was captured or delayed for any reason, then she should quickly flee Poland and make her way to West Germany to a small town between Augsburg and Munich, called Schwabmünchen, where he would hopefully locate her.)

The iconic love story in the heart-warming 1965 film, Doctor Zhivago, makes me think of Mom's deep love for Nikolai. In that story, Lara (Dr. Zhivago's love) was arrested in 1949 in a Russian Siberian labor camp, which makes the connection to Nikolai even more compelling. The music and its lyrics remain in many people's hearts around the world, including mine.

DEPARTING AUSTRIA

With the war officially over, our time in Austria had served its purpose. The prolonged layover of approximately eight months in Austria now seemed like an extended vacation to me, with a happy, uplifting ending. By the grace of God, we evaded the direct path of the brutal war and escaped the evil claws of the oppressive Soviet Communist Regime.

Although the Soviets took control of Poland, Czechoslovakia, and Eastern Europe, including East Germany, Austria regained its independence and West Germany would be stabilized under America's Marshall Plan.

In the absence of continued fear, Mom's attention would now turn to the resumption and completion of her planned venture to West Germany.

In early May 1945, only a few days after the war ended, we again prepared, hopefully for the last time, to travel cross-country. As before, Mom packed our food basket, blankets, and the barest of essentials into the little wagon, and hitched the well-rested horse to it for the final leg of our long venture. She took a moment to gently stroke the horse's face and its velvety soft nose in appreciation of its priceless service. After loading a generous supply of food into our wagon, Herr Bergen and Frau Bergen gave us big hugs and away we rode, heading in a W-N-W direction to West Germany.

But what a big difference from our exodus out of Poland a year earlier! We would now be going through the most beautiful and scenic area from Austria into the Bavarian region of Southern Germany which resembled the scenes from the *Hansel and Gretel* fairy tale or *The Sound of Music* story. Compared to the daring and desperate experience out of Poland, Mom wouldn't have to lead the horse or walk alongside, and she now had the choice of traveling on any road and resting anywhere she pleased. I didn't need to be on the lookout any longer, except to just drown in the peaceful pleasure and wonders of nature. The weather was pleasant and warm as the scent of pine trees and wildflowers continued to lead the way along with the music of a variety of birds, including the familiar cuckoos and woodpeckers.

SCHWABMÜNCHEN

The closer we got to our final destination, Schwabmünchen, the more evidence of the war's destructive remnants lay before us. The once pretty little town was a far cry from what Mom remembered when she and Nikolai had visited at one time in the past. Huge piles of red bricks now lay along torn up streets where schools, hospitals, department stores, apartments and factories stood only months ago. Even churches with adjoining gravesites lay in ruin, surrounded by scattered white human bones and skulls. But the resiliency of the enterprising German people and the refugees from neighboring Eastern European countries that settled there immediately embarked on rebuilding and quickly returning Schwabmünchen to its former flourishing and vibrant town.

Mom chose a remote little house on St.-Rochus-Straße and was able to negotiate renting one of its rooms overlooking its lush grassy backyard, perfect for Irma and me to play in. That would now be our new home—our new beginning in the free world of West Germany.

The room, with its wooden floor, was spacious enough and adequately furnished with a wood-burning stove (which also provided heat during cold spells), a small wooden table with four chairs, and a set of bunk-beds with a tiny narrow ladder leading to the upper bed.

After emptying our wagon, we went for our very last short ride out of town to sell our beloved horse, including the wagon, to a farmer. With tears in her eyes, mom tenderly hugged the horse's head and stroked its soft mouth for the last time, whispering softly into its ear—thanking it for its devoted, unconditional loyalty throughout our long miraculous journey.

We were all smiles as Mom prepared our first home-cooked meal in our new little home. It was most delicious, satisfying and very special. After our meal, Mom took us by the hand as we leisurely walked toward the white wooden fence at the far end of the yard, where a hedge of bright-colored purple, pink, and white lilac bushes welcomed us with their sweet-smelling perfumed blooms. She then snapped a tiny branch off the white lilac bush and began tasting it, coaxing Irma and me to try some. Irma was somewhat hesitant and unsure, but I immediately joined Mom, thinking that it'd also make me smell sweet.

After gaining permission from the owner of the house, she wasted no time in turning a small section of the grass yard into a garden. Watching Mom lift each shovelful of sod and turn it upside-down, I eagerly pitched in with a spade and a hoe. Within days, we were rewarded with tiny new shoots of growing vegetables springing out of the dark fertile soil.

A few days after our arrival, Mom began working at a wood assembly factory so she could pay our rent and provide for our meager necessities. The following Sunday, we also resumed attending church on a regular basis by going to the Lutheran church nearby, where I soon became an altar boy. These were very hard times for Mom, but in spite of it all, she wanted to teach Irma and me some early financial responsibilities and saving habits by giving us a very small allowance to put into our little individual piggy banks. At some point, she asked us to empty our piggy banks by removing the rubber plug from the bottom and counting the amount we had saved up. Irma and I each had a whopping 10 German Reichsmarks, which encouraged us to place the rubber plug back in and continue our saving habits.

A few weeks later, however, before we were able to add much more to our savings, Mom heard an announcement on the radio that Germany would be conducting business under a new monetary system and that everyone should bring their old Reichsmarks to the bank in exchange for the new ones. When we each opened our piggybank and presented our savings of twelve Reichsmarks to the bank teller, we were only given back one new Mark and twenty Pfennigs (representing a ten-percent return). The new money was no longer identified by the swastikas like the old ones.

LOOKING FOR NEW FRIENDS

With Mom at work all day, I said to Irma, "Let's go for a short walk into the village and just look around for a few minutes, maybe meet some new friends."

"No, I'm not going with you," she said, "because we didn't ask Mom first."

So, I went without her and soon came across a group of older boys attempting to play soccer by kicking a strange-looking white round object toward each other. I became curious as to why, after each kick, it made such an unusual clackety-clank-clunk sound and realized that they were using an old white-colored human skull as a football. The skull must have come from a cemetery which had been blown up during the war.

One of the bigger boys approached me and asked, "Bist du ein Jude [Are you a Jew]?"

I didn't know what he meant or how to respond. Then, reaching inside the back of his pants and pretending to throw something bad at me, he said, "Ja! Du bist ein Jude [Yes! You are a Jew]."

The hatred radiating in his eyes and his demeanor toward me was startling. I just ran home without saying a word to anyone, especially not to Irma or mom, because it would have infuriated her and caused her more stress.

RATION COUPONS

Because of the war's devastating destruction and collapsed economy, each head-of-household was issued a meager amount of ration coupons for the bare necessities of survival. I recall Mom telling us that only one pair of shoes was allowed per household each year, so we were taught to take very good care of whatever we had or go barefooted.

As hard as she tried to make ends meet in providing for us by working at her factory job, Mom realized that it would simply be inadequate. So, on weekends, she and I would venture into the countryside without Irma and randomly stop at a number of farmhouses asking if they could spare an egg, a cup of flour, or a slice of bread (which would usually be home-baked black pumpernickel).

By adding those items to the fresh vegetables from our garden, the three of us could enjoy nourishing and tasty meals, usually preceded by a short prayer of blessings and thankfulness. Her short prayer taught me and reinforced the importance of thanking God for all our provisions, even the most basic ones.

PITCHING IN

I was about six years old when I felt eager to contribute to our daily needs. As the man-of-the-house, I convinced Mom that I could venture out alone and bring home enough food for us so she could stay home, rest a little, tend to her garden, and spend time with Irma. Determined to become proficient in my new job as a reliable provider to the family's food supply, I honed my natural, God-given skills of projecting a joyful, positive attitude, always with a happy smile at every stop. I also studied the more lucrative routes and made quick friends with most everyone along the way. Invariably, I brought home more than enough for all of us. There were many small orchards by the roadside—usually guarded by German shepherd dogs from within the fenced enclosures, but I could always find a few trees with their heavy branches laden with ripe apples or pears hanging over the fence, begging to be picked, and some over-ripe ones already fallen to the ground, ready for my immediate consumption.

During one of my food excursions, one farmer put two generous scoops of yellow gold powder into my satchel. I recalled Mom showing me some of her expensive gold jewelry back in Poland. This powder was the identical yellow color. With my mouth and eyes wide open in disbelief, I thanked them over and over and ran home as fast as I could to show Mom, excitedly telling her that she wouldn't have to work so hard anymore because we had struck it rich. Well, my scoop of gold powder turned out to be yellow cornmeal, which Mom used to bake a loaf of cornbread. She hugged me, smiled, and began to cry, realizing that this lifestyle couldn't continue much longer.

On my very last food excursion, a farmer gave me enough potatoes to totally fill my satchel. Oh, I knew that Mom and Irma would be so proud of me because that would be enough to last a couple of weeks or longer. On my way home, the bag of potatoes seemed to be getting heavier and heavier, and soon I began experiencing a very sharp pain in my lower right abdomen. I sat on the ground, resting a minute, then tried walking again, but the pain was unbearable, forcing me to lie down, unable to sit up or even cry out for help.

As I lay there helplessly, the warm sun was slowly giving way to an early evening chill. Knowing that Mom would begin to worry if I didn't get back soon, I tried repeatedly to get up and resume my homeward trek but to no avail. Daylight turned to dusk when a farmer in a small three-wheel truck stopped to pick me up and drive me home.

Mom had to rush me to a hospital right away. The kind, Good Samaritan farmer volunteered to drive us there. Due to the limited cab space, Mom jumped into the bed of the truck. We arrived at the hospital in the nick of time as I had acute appendicitis and required an immediate appendectomy.

After a few short days, I was back home—good as new, except for the healing scar. But Mom didn't allow me to resume my food excursions. I couldn't understand why, since I became pretty good at it—greeting all the kind and generous folks, supplying our food needs, and even befriending some of the German shepherd guard dogs which would wag their tails rather than threaten me. Instead of idly sitting by, another contributing opportunity presented itself to me.

On the outskirts of town, not far from home, I wondered why there was always a smell of sour milk around a certain big white building. Mom explained that it was a commercial dairy processing facility producing a variety of milk products like regular whole milk, skimmed milk, buttermilk, cottage cheese, and butter. She went on to explain that the least expensive item would be buttermilk, because it was the byproduct in the making of the very expensive butter and that buttermilk could also be used in the making of cottage cheese at home.

"Well, I could just take a small pail," I said, "and go bring some buttermilk home for us."

"You'd have to be there very early in the morning," she said, "right at the end of the butter-churning process."

So, early the next morning, before sunrise, she gave me one mark and two small metal pails (one liter each). It all went well for a few weeks, until one particularly cold, icy morning, after stepping out with my buttermilk, I slipped on a patch of ice in the street and fell down, spilling all the buttermilk. I just sat there sobbing—not because I was hurt, but because I had spent the one hard-earned mark Mom gave me and I couldn't bear the feeling of coming home empty-handed. I understood how hard Mom had to work for each mark and how she had counted on this fresh supply of buttermilk for the three of us.

A construction worker carrying a shovel over his shoulder on his way to his job, seeing me sobbing and sitting in the puddle of milk, reached in his pocket and handed me one mark so that I could go back in and get a fresh supply. How quickly my sobbing stopped. I looked up in disbelief and saw him smiling back at me. With a big smile, I thanked him and went back to refill my empty pails.

When I approached the cashier the second time with my empty pails, milk over my clothes, and presented my money, he looked at me somewhat puzzled but then realized that I must have slipped and fallen. After refilling my empty pails, he winked at me, smiled, and gave me back my money. His act of compassion, as well as that of the construction worker, brought back my real mom's last words that God would always watch over me. It also reinforced in me that in spite of so much evil and suffering around the world, there is a lot of love and goodness in people's hearts regardless of having to endure endless hardships themselves.

MOM'S DIFFICULT DECISION

Being fully aware that now, at age six, both Irma and I needed to be enrolled into school, Mom was faced with making some hard decisions. The decimation of most every German city and town caused by the war would continue to make life most difficult for all, especially for a single woman like her, trying to raise two young children. Although she was glad to have found a job at the wood assembly factory, her take-home pay was barely enough to eke out a living for the three of us.

I would often find Mom in tears and praying for us and for her husband's survival, safety, and eventual return—praying that his life would be spared, that he would not be tortured or confined to the harshness of hard labor in the dreaded Siberian labor camps from where most prisoners never returned. Her continued perseverance and hope rested on his promise that somehow he would find her in this little place of Schwabmünchen and also on her faith that God would answer her prayers in bringing Nikolai back to her someday.

One beautiful Sunday afternoon in spring, Mom took me aside, away from Irma, and said, "Alex, let's go for a long, long walk, just you and I, and talk about school."

Hand-in-hand, we started out down a somewhat familiar road leading out of town—past some of the farms I had visited before. We continued to walk farther and farther for a couple of hours, during which she began to explain that since school was about to start, she wondered if I would like to live on a farm near a small farming village, where I would be able to attend school in a smaller and much better all-round environment.

"Oh, yes," I replied very excitedly. "Wow, when can we move there?"

Slowly and ever so thoughtfully, sincerely and methodically, she laid out her plans before me and began to explain, "You must know, Alex, that I want what's best for you and will do everything within my power to provide you a life filled with freedom, happiness, and opportunities, so that you can grow up to your full potential. I have to stay at home and keep working at the factory. Irma is not as strong, brave, and adventurous as you. So, I must always be close to her. I gave it a lot of thought, Alex, and was wondering how you would feel about living on a farm with a nice German farm family, away from us for a while?"

For a brief moment, my thoughts and memory took me back to the Ukrainian warehouse where my real mom peeled my tight grip from her and commanded me to quickly run away to safety under the watchful eye of God and His angels. She assured me that God would lead me to a wonderful and happy new home, which He did. Now, my new mom, Lady Elizabeth, was also preparing to send me off. This time, however, I was three years older and not running away or escaping the past. Instead, as a farm boy, I would be pursuing a more wholesome life. I looked at it as a gift from Heaven.

Despite my young age, I sensed the tenderness and agony in Mom's voice and completely understood and agreed with her vision and hopes for me. Without dwelling on my response, I said, "Oh, thank you, Mom! That'll be so exciting—living on a farm! Don't you worry about me! I'll be a good boy, help with the farmwork, and do well in school—you'll see."

Thinking about my quick response, I would later wonder if she felt hurt that my answer expressed no feelings of love or closeness to her or that I would even miss Irma and her, or, if she felt relieved that her plans for me were so well presented and received? As for Irma, I totally understood why a similar arrangement for her would have been out of the question since she was a permanent member of the family and much more fragile and dependent. Together, they would continue to provide love, comfort, and a priceless companionship for each other. Mom, no doubt, took into account my endless displays of fearlessness, positive attitude, and hunger for adventure, regardless of circumstances, hoping that this temporary arrangement would work out well for everyone's benefit.

CHAPTER 12
A NEW HOME—A NEW NAME

A NEW HOME—A NEW NAME

Mom must have searched hard for some time to find that great place so far from home. Perhaps someone at church or at the factory where she worked recommended it. As we continued to walk, we approached a cute two-story farmhouse she had selected for me. The owners, Herr Ludwig Ott and his wife, Frau Ott, came out and greeted us cheerfully and welcomed me as the young new member into their home.

With tearful eyes, Mom gave me a big, long hug and kissed me several times before rushing back home. That tearful hug, kiss, and goodbye instantly took me back to my departure and escape from my real mom back in Ukraine, and I wondered if it would also be the last time I would see her, except that this time I didn't have to run through the war zone to save my life.

Frau and Herr Ott were very kind-hearted and humble middle-aged German farmers whose three sons had been forcefully taken at gunpoint by German officers at the beginning of the war in 1939 to fight on the front line in the German Army. Frau Ott pleaded in vain for the officers to leave just one of her sons to help her husband run the farm. Two sons never made it back and the third, the oldest—also named Ludwig, was fortunate to survive and return home without any visible injuries. Frau Ott explained that she was so thankful that the Lord brought one son back to her because many of her friends and neighbors lost all of theirs. She went on to explain that when the war finally ended, her son had to walk for several days to reach home, totally exhausted, dirty, unshaven, and very hungry, but ever so glad and thankful to be alive.

"The first thing he asked for when he came home, after cleaning up a bit," she said, "was my home-cooked meal, before crashing into his own comfortable bed for a long-deserved and best sleep of his life."

Sitting around the small kitchen table in the main room of the house with Herr and Frau Ott, I knew right away that I would love it there and was anxious to learn all about my new home and its surroundings. After exchanging some basic questions and answers, I felt a sense of warmth and trust in their demeanor and knew that this bond would be a happy and rewarding part of my life, no matter how long it would last.

Leading me up a short, narrow stairway, Frau Ott opened the door to show me my own small bedroom located between theirs and their son's.

When we came back down, Herr Ott, still sitting at the kitchen table, smoking a pipe, introduced me to his son, who had just arrived in time for dinner and was anxious to meet me. He was tall, with blond hair, muscular, and very handsome. Just like his parents, he was kind and began patiently teaching me and explaining to me as much as I was eager to absorb about himself and his parent's farm, treating me almost like his little brother. However, he preferred not to discuss his time in the army or anything about the war, and I also preferred to leave my war memories behind me.

Ludwig had been dating a beautiful lady prior to his service in the army and resumed their romantic relationship upon his return from the war. Within a few short weeks after my arrival, he left us to marry her and settled in their new home near Augsburg. Ludwig would periodically come by to visit us, spend time with me, and help his dad with field work, especially at harvest time.

Herr Ott proudly showed me around his meticulously laid-out domain. I marveled at every detail he had taken into consideration with its layout. It wasn't at all like the small farmhouse in Austria. Leading me from the main room of the house through two sets of doors, we walked through the storage section where sweet-smelling clover and hay for the cows was kept. As we proceeded toward the next part of the same building, he opened another door and, "Voila!" we were inside the barn which didn't smell so good.

"You see, Alex," he explained, "by having a sweet clover smell between the barn and the house, we're able to separate the two within the confines of one building. We also have a couple of cats happily residing in the hay to keep the mice in check."

The interior of the barn was also well-designed and very clean, considering that it was the winter home of a half dozen cows, a pair of oxen, and about a dozen big geese. A narrow trough next to the center walking aisle allowed for the liquid waste to empty into an underground storage tank behind the barn. I asked Herr Ott what happens when the tank gets full.

"In springtime," he explained, "we pump it out and spread it into our field as fertilizer. We also spread the solid waste, mixed with straw as fertilizer."

What appeared to be a rather large home from the outside, turned out to be a three-in-one, all-inclusive efficient farm house (somewhat similar to homes with attached garages).

Having raised three boys, he kept the most interesting part of our tour to the end, knowing that I, too, would find it most thrilling. With a bit of youthful excitement in his voice, he raised his arm and pointed to a structure down the street, explaining, "Look down there, Alex, where the road and the river meet—that odd-looking building is a very old watermill where my boys and their friends played together tirelessly for days on end when they were young. The old wooden structure was built before my time and is still operational as a functioning mill, turning wheat seeds into flour. My boys also swam and fished in the river next to it."

I knew right away that it was also going to become my favorite place to play and make friends.

Frau Ott enrolled me as "Alex Ott" into first grade at the local school near the farm, thus giving me the surname of her family. I found my first exposure to school-learning very interesting and earned good grades. Since all first, second, and third grade students were in one classroom, I would habitually listen in on the teaching of the other grades. My classmates were all very friendly and eager to include me in all their games.

On weekends and at times after school, I would meet some of them by the river to swim and also to try our luck fishing with our improvised fishing gear. With a pair of pliers, we cut a safety pin in half, bent the sharp end into a hook, tied a long piece of black sewing thread through the eyelet of the pin and the other end to a stick, then attached a worm to the hook and let it out into the water. Between the worms wiggling loose and escaping from the hook, or the fish simply stealing the worm, it took many, many tries before we had a bite. Eventually, we landed a very small fish, which we released back into the river. With time, however, we kept improving our method with better results.

As we all played around the old watermill, I became ever-so-curious as to what made that big wooden wheel turn, so I kept watching the many cup-shaped buckets around the circumference of the wheel getting automatically filled from the river water above the wheel, then, on their way down, spilling back into the flowing river below. It was, in my opinion, a fascinating invention. A few days later, during a milling operation, Herr Ott made arrangements to take me inside to witness the huge grinding stone wheel crushing the wheat into flour. All the power for the entire milling operation was derived from the water wheel.

Every Sunday morning, Frau Ott would hustle the family off to the

Roman Catholic Church, where I would soon be baptized again and become an altar boy.

When I tried to explain that I had already been baptized in a Lutheran Church in Poland, Frau Ott and the priest both replied that the protestant baptism would not be recognized by the Catholic church or the pope and that we'd have to do it the right way.

As months passed, I was enjoying my new life and began to accept that my stay here may very likely become permanent, especially since I was now known to everyone as Alex Ott. So, I thought that the best thing for me to do would be to honor Frau and Herr Ott, and in appreciation for their care and kindness to me, begin calling them, "Mama and Papa Ott"—for they certainly filled the role, as far as I was concerned. Between school, helping Papa Ott run the farm, and playing with my school friends during the warm summer days and in the fluffy winter snow, I didn't have time to dwell on the past or think about the future, but instead, joyfully made the most of each new thrilling day.

Without any coaxing or prodding, I anxiously jumped at every opportunity to help with the farm work (gathering stones and pulling weeds off the field, cleaning the barn, feeding the geese and livestock, raking the dried hay and clover into small mounds for subsequent hauling to the barn as fodder for the livestock). However, as everyone who has lived on a farm knows quite well—the all-important harvest season takes precedence over everything else. Young and old, everyone pitches in to gather the grain.

Once the wheat in the field ripened and turned to a rich golden color, indicating that it was ready for harvesting, Papa Ott, would sharpen the long blade of the odd shaped scythe and ever-so-skillfully cut the wheat into neat rows. A few days later, after the wheat became crisp and dry, we would all take a wide wooden rake, making small piles to be bundled, tied, and taken home for milling. Since the rake was much too big for me, I was, instead, given a large burlap sack to search the field and glean what the reapers left behind so not one wheat stalk would be left behind.

An electric threshing machine separated the wheat kernels from the straw. I got the job of untying each bundle and placing it on the wide conveyor belt with all kernels facing in the same direction. The end result produced a pile of straw to one side and the grain into a wide barrel to be taken later, as needed, to the watermill for grinding into flour. The straw would be used in winter as bedding for the animals.

At the end of each busy day, we would each soothe our tired and bruised feet in a deep pan of warm water. My tender feet would be much more bruised and sore because of the more tender skin. Farm kids, in general, went barefoot all summer long, even to school and church.

For total relaxation and enjoyment, Papa Ott would fill one of his smoking pipes with a sweet-aromatic tobacco and leisurely sit in his personal padded chair until his eyes seemed almost shut with his head continuing to droop down to his chest, at which time Mama Ott would prompt him to head upstairs to bed.

Tucked into the corner of the main room was an old spinning wheel with a foot-pedal. I was very curious what its function was. During the long, cold winter days, Mama Ott demonstrated the entire process to me. Placing a large bundle of fluffy wool (the size of a puffy pillow) on her lap, she carefully pulled and twisted a small amount of wool making it look like a string and wrapped it around the wheel that began to turn as she operated the foot pedal. Following her instruction, I took the finished end of the yarn and began winding it into a ball until it was as large as a soccer ball. The next day, she produced two eighteen-inch long, pointed metal knitting needles and began to create a wool sweater. I was just dumbfounded with this entire magical demonstration.

When I tried to point out to Papa Ott how ingenious his wife was, he would only give me a brief glance, before continuing reading the newspaper and puffing away at his old S-shaped pipe hanging from his lips, down his chin. The aromatic smell of pipe-smoke was like sweet licorice. I thought to myself that when I got to be older, I would also get a pipe like that.

Like a gust of wind, an entire year quickly passed by! I was now about seven years old and ready to return to school into second grade. Walking through the school playground, I reconnected with most all my friends—all of us excitedly sharing our summer's fun.

Frau Himmel, the same teacher as before, greeted me in the hallway and took me aside to talk to me privately. She complimented me on having been most attentive during my first year in her class and noticed that I had also paid close attention to her second-grade lessons. She went on to explain that my good grades, good behavior, and perfect attendance record were the best during my first year and since first through third graders were again in her class, she recommended to the Superintendent to have me skip second and advance to third grade. I was elated and vowed to work even harder.

My time on the farm was truly enjoyable; filled with fun, work and school. I had no further contact with my mom, Lady Elizabeth, or Irma as they were too far away. As Alex Ott, I didn't have time for sadness or loneliness or even to think about the past. Too many exciting and adventurous things filled my life each day in my new home.

WOW; WHAT A SURPRISE!

With another harvest season upon us, I was no longer a stranger to the work awaiting us and considered myself an experienced and much more helpful farmhand. One Sunday afternoon after church, as I began chasing our big white and grey-colored honking geese around the yard and down the lane, they all decided to abruptly turn on me.

With their long necks extended and their yellow arrow-like beaks aimed directly at me, they began honking and screeching very loudly while half-running and half-flying, intent on attacking me mercilessly. As they continued to flap their powerful bony wings against my bare legs and viciously bit my buttocks with their sharp beaks, I mustered up one more burst of energy to outrun those angry geese.

After turning sharply at the next curve of the dirt lane, I glanced behind me to see if they gave up their menacing chase and, in the process, ran full-speed right into the arms of a lady walking toward me.

I looked up to apologize, when, lo and behold, I was literally in the arms of my Angel mom from Schwabmünchen. Wow! That was the biggest surprise of all. By now, I had pretty much lived past such expectations. After a long hug, we proceeded to update each other with news of the past year. Very excitedly, I asked about Irma's well-being and her school and tried to tell her all about my busy year. Mom's glowing smile revealed her happiness in seeing me so healthy, tall, and full of energy. As I continued describing some of the highlights of my life on the farm, that I was now in third grade in school, had been baptized as a Catholic and that my new name was Alex Ott, she didn't seem to be too impressed.

But, as she studied me from head to toe, her smile abruptly stopped. With her mouth agape in disbelief, she couldn't take her eyes off my feet. I guess they were dirty, a bit swollen, scratched, and even with some visible dried blood on them, which was normal for us farm-kids.

"Good heavens, Alex, look at your feet!" she remarked. "Where are your shoes?"

"I don't have shoes," I answered. "None of the kids around here wear shoes in the summer months, not even to school or to church. We do, however, all wear rubber boots in winter."

"But, just look at your feet," she remarked. "They're filthy and totally covered with deep scratches, bruises and dried blood."

I explained that I help out in the field at harvest time with the hay and wheat and that in the evening we soak our feet in warm water which helps to heal it up pretty fast (I'm sure her thoughts must have turned to the orphanage where she first observed my dirty and bruised feet).

Again, she asked, "And you don't ever wear anything on your feet out there in the field?"

"No, it's fine. I'm used to it," I replied.

She was furious! Rather than confronting Frau and Herr Ott, she grabbed my hand and, shaking with anger, said, "You're not going back to live at the Ott farm any longer, not even for another minute. You're coming home with me, right now, back to Schwabmünchen. Somehow, we'll manage."

I would never see Frau and Herr Ott again, and I knew better than to argue with Mom or even mention their names in the future. In fact, my newly-acquired name disappeared from use just as quickly as the greeting of Heil Hitler did when the war ended.

That sudden departure would bother me for a long time to come as I didn't feel that it was fair to that nice farm couple. In fact, I felt that it was akin to a kidnapping. This was, after all, my home, where I was happy, learned a lot about life on a farm, did well in school, never went hungry, made many friends, and even had my own bedroom as well as some of my homemade toys.

I'm sure that my sudden disappearance created a deep concern and worry for Frau and Herr Ott as well as for my teacher, Frau Himmel. Perhaps they even searched for me near the river or by the watermill.

In my heart, however, I understood that Mom loved me deeply and was only looking out for my well-being. It was only three years ago when she sacrificed everything to save me and get me away from the Soviets all the way here to West Germany. Her current act was a natural reaction, an extension of her continued protection of me—like a lioness protecting her cubs.

The long, long walk back to Schwabmünchen took most of the afternoon and was mostly in silence because of Mom's lingering anger toward Frau and Herr Ott. I kept wondering, with my naivete, why so many people had to die and suffer and watch their homes and entire cities get destroyed during the war and then had to endure the long road of recovery without food, shelter, or resources, when the farmers, on the other hand, not directly affected, remained on their farms with plenty of food, as evidenced both on the Austrian farm and the farm we just left. Why wouldn't more people choose to live on the farm?

Back in our tiny place in Schwabmünchen, nothing much had changed. Irma had grown a little taller, the bunk beds, table, and chairs were in the same spot as the day I went away, and Mom still had her job at the wood factory. In the morning, I went back to the dairy to fetch buttermilk for us like before. However, I could tell that she seemed much more nervous and stressed out than before and this latest "Ott" episode certainly didn't help.

However, in spite of everything that Mom had endured, she never deviated from her faith, prayers, and hope that her husband would someday be freed from Soviet confinement. I overheard her telling a neighbor that even if he had met a good Russian woman to care for him, she would be content in her heart, just knowing that he was alive and well.

As before, I joined Mom in the garden, which she meticulously nurtured all summer-long. It was filled with a variety of vegetables in neat rows—some bearing fruit above ground, such as peas, cucumbers, beans, and tomatoes; and some below ground, like carrots, beets, radishes, and potatoes. Mom pulled out a couple of carrots from the ground and a few pea pods from the next row, handing them to Irma and me to taste.

Among the rows of growing vegetables were small weeds that seemed to spring up overnight, which Mom regularly cleared with her well-used gardening hoe. Since I now considered myself an experienced farmer, I took the hoe from her, hoping to impress her with some of my acquired farming skills, promising her that I would keep the garden free of weeds on a regular basis.

On my first morning at school, Mom accompanied Irma and me, where Irma had been attending in Schwabmünchen. This school was far from the smaller school I had been attending near the Ott's farm. She was in second grade and I would be enrolled into third grade under a new name, "Alex Marcel," which mom selected for me without explanation. Although the curriculum was similar to that of my former class near the farm under Frau Himmel, the size of this school and the large number of students per class caused a more uncontrollable, disruptive, and misbehaved atmosphere, where bullies were plentiful and close friendships rare.

CHAPTER 13
AN ANSWERED PRAYER

AN ANSWERED PRAYER

Approximately six months after my return to Schwabmünchen, with the winter snow now hastily retreating from the warm spring sunshine, Mom and I began to prepare our garden for a new crop of vegetables. The lilac bushes along the fence anxiously began blooming again and the birds joyfully sang, as if to announce that God hadn't forgotten us—that a bright future filled with hope and blessings awaited us all. Within days, Mom was again admiring her planted garden, deeply inhaling the fresh scent of the brightly colored flowers around its perimeter and the perfumed scent of surrounding wildflowers and lilac bushes. In keeping with my promise of maintaining our garden free of weeds, the garden tools were my constant companion whenever I stepped into the backyard. I was happy to see Mom with a smile on her face again.

There she was—in deep thought—with the warm sun on her face and eyes half-shut, looking up to Heaven, then slowly scanning the horizon in order to rest her eyes. With her elbows and shoulders stretching back to straighten her spine and with eyes wide open, she scanned the horizon one more time. All of a sudden, she stopped breathing. I looked up and noticed that her face was pale white. She had a very mysterious, almost frightening look on her face—like she was about to faint. I asked her what was wrong, but she totally ignored me and kept staring with her eyes intently focusing on something across the distant field.

I tried to touch her and noticed that tears began to fill her eyes and her lips began to quiver. Inching slowly closer toward the far-off image in order to get a clearer view, there in the distance, I saw a tiny image of a man slowly walking closer and closing in toward us.

There was something very familiar about the man's gait. Unable to wipe her eyes quickly enough, even with the use of the palms of both hands, her heart was beating so fast that it was about to leap out from within her bosom—she knew it was her beloved Nikolai and took off running faster than a deer while hysterically screaming:

"NIKOLAI, NIKOLAI, MEIN NIKOLAI; OH MEIN GOTT, DANKE, DANKE." [Nikolai, Nikolai; Oh my God, thank you, thank you.]

God did, indeed, answer her endless prayers and, with her profound faith, after eight long years, He rewarded her by guiding Nikolai home all the way from a Russian war prison. They fell into each other's arms, both continuing to cry uncontrollably with joy—never to be separated again for the rest of their lives, not even for one day.

Racing after Mom, as fast as we could, Irma and I were so excited to meet our war hero—our dad—Mom's love of her life, whom we've heard so much over the years. What a blessing! What a miraculous divine gift! Finally, we were all together, as a complete family. Mom's strength, faith, prayers, perseverance, and hope had finally been fulfilled. She was, once again, able to openly display her true joy and love. This had been her dream all along. Finally, gone for good, was the stressful, worrisome, sleepless, and fearful existence in keeping it all together inside her.

I would never cease to wonder how much this very special angel had endured and accomplished against all obstacles and dangers through the entire deadly war and beyond! Neither she nor Nikolai lamented over the loss of their former lifestyle and the comfort of their estate back in Lodz, Poland. Just being alive, free, and together was all that mattered.

Mom had so much to tell Nikolai—all about our escape from Poland, about finding baby Irma in a graveyard, and also locating me in an orphanage. Nikolai took a closer look at me and asked mom at which orphanage she found me.

When she told him, he was stunned. With his eyes and mouth wide open, he said, "I can't believe this! Come closer, Alex."

He stooped down, put his hands on my shoulders, looked deep into my eyes and said, "Do you remember walking along a railway track all by yourself and getting a ride on a motorcycle when you were very, very young? Was that you?"

"Yes, I remember getting a ride on the back of a German officer's motorcycle. That was so exciting! He wore a helmet and had a revolver strapped to his side and left me at an orphanage in the middle of the night," I responded.

"Well, Alex, guess what!" said Nikolai. "That was me with my motorcycle."

Wow! That was unbelievable!

"In my wildest dream, I could never have imagined seeing that little kid again."

I was speechless! To think that the kind-hearted German officer on his motorcycle, spotting me wandering alone on the railway track in Ukraine, would end up becoming my dad is unexplainable.

Mom was even more shocked because of all the available children at that orphanage, where she had hoped to find a little girl, she had selected me!

We all huddled together, realizing that each one of us was immensely blessed by God's mercy, love, and faithfulness in a most miraculous way.

This called for a celebration! Our little room was suddenly filled with happiness and dancing. Mom prepared a wonderful meal of fresh vegetables from her lush garden, some home-baked biscuits, and buttermilk that I brought home from the local dairy. She set a bouquet of fresh colorful flowers on the table, lit a candle, and our reunited family of four sat down for our first meal of thanksgiving. We all joined hands as Mom led us in prayer, thanking God for this miraculous event.

I hadn't seen Mom this happy since that heavenly Christmas celebration in her palatial home in Poland. God used this special angel, Lady Elizabeth, to faithfully carry out His plans, reuniting us in freedom and renewed hope. Without a word, I closed my eyes, recalling my real mom's tearful send-off from the warehouse in Ukraine and into God's care. She must be smiling from Heaven to see all four of us celebrating our freedom together. Our family of four continued to live in the little one-room house in St.-Rochus-Straße, and within days of Dad's arrival, he also began working in a factory.

Since the strict rations in Germany and throughout most of Europe continued to be in effect, I would watch him early each morning, preparing to walk to work by meticulously wrapping his bare feet with pieces of rags prior to stepping into his old battered boots with which he had walked the long trek home because he wasn't even able to buy a pair of socks or shoes.

In my small mind, I had it all figured out. From here on, with Dad the additional breadwinner and provider, my buttermilk deliveries, plus the fresh produce from our lush garden, Irma and I continuing with our schooling, we would all enjoy a perfectly happy family life ever after just like in those happy- ending children's story books (*"And they all lived happily ever after"*).

Because of his former service in the defeated German army and his time as a Russian prisoner, Dad registered his new address and his place of employment with the American authorities who now controlled all of West Germany's legal, political, and military affairs.

Most German officers were being sought out and questioned regarding their position and involvement with the former German Reich. Since Nikolai was able to prove that he had strictly served as an isolated interpreter, not a member of any regiment, the Americans had no interest in questioning him any further.

When Dad came home from his long, extensive meeting, he explained to Mom that the Americans were very respectful and considerate, and that they would provide an opportunity for me, a war orphan, to be transported to America as a Displaced Person (DP). He also shared with her that the Soviets were planning to locate and bring back all the young boys that may have left or escaped from their controlled area in order to raise them and train them as future Russian soldiers. He went on to explain that it would only be a matter of time for them to locate me, since I was born in Zhytomyr, Ukraine, which would continue to be under Soviet control. I knew, without a doubt, that Mom would never let that happen—not after all she had done to rescue me from their grasp.

Mom and Dad very tactfully explained this to me, not wanting to frighten me, but laying out the ruthlessness of the Soviet mindset so that I would keep my personal background as my own secret and not share it at school or with anyone.

I assured them that I would keep this strictly between us.

However, I wasn't concerned at all and completely trusted that all would turn out well, especially now that the war had ended and, thanks to Mom, that we were now so far removed from that dreadful evil Soviet tyranny.

I've often placed myself in Dad's position of having to understand Mom's profound devotion and sacrifices for my safety and well-being but also advising her ever-so-thoughtfully and tactfully not to be a clinger and to look ahead. With his wisdom, life experiences, and humanity, he understood better than anyone that the future facing us all was going to be very, very difficult. He could clearly see that it would take a whole generation to rebuild Germany, and that a young boy would have to endure many hardships to survive and hope to have an opportunity to develop his talents and ambitions in such a war-torn environment.

Everything Dad had ever owned, in addition to his dreams and hopes had been taken away, leaving him penniless and broken. Now, at the age of fifty, he had to start building a new life, in a new country, for himself, his wife, and their adopted little girl. He certainly must have placed himself in my position—to have the option of restarting, as a young boy, in the vast, world-renowned free land of America with endless opportunities. But would Mom look ahead and agree?

Dad's wisdom brings to mind a famous quote attributed to Richard Bach,

"If you love someone, set them free. If they come back, they're yours.

If they don't, they never were."

Mom openly laid out her sacrifices and love for me before Dad and explained to him that she would do anything in her power to continue guiding me through these trying times. Dad patiently listened and then expressed to Mom that she may end up harming me in the long run.

"You and I were there for Alex when he needed us the most," he explained to Mom. "We literally saved his life. You have so bravely fulfilled your calling the best you possibly could and he'll never forget it. Let's not hold him back. He's bright and adventurous and will thank us later when he grows up."

Admitting and agreeing that Dad's wisdom overcame her passion to continue struggling and sacrificing and clinging at all costs just to be together, she relented but laid out one final point of assurance. "I want to ask Alex directly how he would feel about such a big decision."

One evening, at an opportune time after dinner with the four of us sitting around the table, Mom and Dad were discussing America and its attempt to bring about a sense of stability in Germany following the end of the war. They spoke very highly of that great country and the vast number of European people choosing to emigrate there to start a new life. Observing my keen interest in their discussion, Mom looked deep into my eyes and asked if that would be a place I'd like to live in, without them, far, far away across the ocean, where peace, freedom and opportunities were boundless and where the Russians would never, ever be able to find me. There would be no more running with fear from evil.

Aware of my fearless, adventurous spirit and my past history, Mom knew in her heart what my answer would be and prepared herself that her tender heart would be broken beyond repair.

I recalled a somewhat similar situation back at the Polish orphanage when she stooped down, looked deep into my eyes and asked if I'd like to go with her far, far away. I also remember the time she asked if I'd like to live away from her on a German farm. In both instances, the immeasurable blessings, joy, adventure, and life-changing experience remained priceless.

With a resounding response, I jumped up from the table, both arms in the air, "Oh yes, I'd love to go to America. That sounds so exciting!"

CHAPTER 14
D.P. (DISPLACED PERSON)

D.P. (DISPLACED PERSON)

I was about seven or eight years old when Dad prepared all the necessary paperwork and arranged for my departure. It felt like a high-stakes kidnapping (similar to the kind you'd see in a thriller spy movie) when two American officers in an Army jeep arrived at our home to take me away. Mom knew that she wouldn't have been able to watch those final moments. So, she and Irma went for a long walk beforehand. With the engine idling, Nikolai put me in the back seat behind the American officers and, as Dad and I exchanged our final goodbyes, the jeep revved up its engine and, in a flash, there would be no more St.-Rochus-Straße or Schwabmünchen for me.

I would again be all alone, looking for a new home far, far away and would always think of the awaiting agonizing, non-ending pain in Mom's heart upon her return to the house without me there, knowing that I would not be coming back again.

Of course, I was very excited about a new life awaiting me in America, even though I knew absolutely nothing about it. However, the farther away the jeep traveled, the tighter my throat began to feel—as though a rock was wedged in it. Before long, my eyes began welling up, then flooding with heavy tears as reality set in—that this irreversible event would be a permanent separation from that very special angel that sacrificed her life to save me, nurtured me back to health, and brought me out of the grasp of Soviet Russia to freedom and safety. It was most difficult to remain tough in the presence of the two American officers sitting in front of me. I was now a big boy, so I was determined to not let the soldiers see me as a seven or eight-year-old sniffling crybaby. So, I held it together as best I could, by continuously trying to swallow my tears.

After a couple of hours on the road, the officers led me inside an American military D.P. control center in Munich where they handed a completed document to a clerk and left me there to be questioned and screened. I was given a number with instructions to wait my turn. Looking around me, inside the extra-large room, I was among a large group of youngsters just like me, all waiting our turn to be called.

When I heard my number announced, I approached an area where a couple of American military ladies in tan-colored uniforms were seated behind a table with a stack of official-looking files and documents in front of them.

They began with three simple questions: My name, birth-date, and place of birth. I'm quite certain that Nikolai had already provided all that information about me beforehand and that my answers today would merely confirm the accuracy of their report. I hesitated for a moment about my surname and wondered if I should give them all the ones I had been using.

"The most recent surname," I answered, "is Marcel, but I don't know my real name or birthday. I think I'm about eight years old."

Time dragged on for days, with more questions, interviews, medical examinations, shots in my arm and buttocks, and then a series of X-rays. Standing naked before several examining doctors who were looking for any signs of disease or abnormalities, the entire process almost came to a complete stop when another doctor came in with a large grey-colored X-ray image of my chest and pointed to a tiny shadow—indicating a touch of tuberculosis (TB). Each doctor took turns examining the X-ray more closely, then touching my bare chest and back repeatedly with their cold fingers and a stethoscope, asking me to take deep breaths and cough several times. After they all agreed that the slight shadow on the X-ray was too small for concern and that my new life in America, far away from the war and all the turmoil and devastation caused by it would, in a short time, clear up the tiny TB spot in one of my lungs, I was medically cleared.

Thanks to Nikolai, all my documents and medical tests were stamped for approval by the American D.P. program and I would soon be sailing to America as Alex Marcel with an assigned birthdate of March 28, 1939—March 28 being the date the documents were completed and 1939 representing my approximate age of eight.

A bus transported our entire group to the city of Bremen—the port of departure. There would be another long wait here. To help pass the time, the staff at the port announced that everyone was to come inside the waiting room for a special treat. When we got inside, we all began lifting our heads and deeply inhaling a wonderful, mouth-watering aroma that none of us had ever been exposed to before. As soon as we were all seated, the staff passed out small paper bags full of hot buttered popcorn. Everyone began digging into the most delicious-tasting treat, creating a combined crunching sound like a hailstorm against a tin roof. A few minutes later, the staff announced that the special treat would now begin.

The lights were turned down very low and I saw my first ever movie—an American show, starring Roy Rogers—king of the cowboys—and Dale Evans with their beautiful horses named Trigger and Buttermilk and also their German Shepherd dog named Bullet. I was so completely taken by the show, truly believing that it was a live production.

As soon as the show ended, the staff passed out small bags full of salted, roasted peanuts—again my first ever taste and every bit as good as the popcorn. Oh my goodness! Now, I couldn't wait to get to that wonderful place called America. Maybe I'd get a chance to actually meet Roy Rogers and Dale Evans in person?

ANOTHER BIG SURPRISE

Finally, the long-awaited moment of departure arrived and I became even more excited. We all boarded another bus early in the morning for a short ride to the Bremen shipyard. Upon our arrival, as I stepped down from the bus, I got the surprise of my life again.

Who should greet me at the bus stop but my angel mom, who made the long journey from Schwabmünchen, all alone, by train, just to share one final good-bye and to reassure me how good my new life in America would be. Between hugs and kisses and tears, we had so much to talk about. I wanted to tell her how excited I was to see America, tell her all about Roy Rogers and that I wished she could come with me. My excitement was interrupted by a couple of short, loud blasts from the ship's horn, indicating that all passengers were to begin boarding the ship for departure across the Atlantic Ocean to America and continuing to Canada.

For a brief moment, my thoughts took me back to a very similar surprise when this angel mom appeared at Frau and Ludwig Ott's farm. It made me wonder if she would again grab my hand and take me back home with her to Schwabmünchen.

The pressure of excitement within me was building up like a steam locomotive. Hand-in-hand, we walked up the long boarding ramp. As Mom prepared herself to give me one final hug and walk back down, I observed that there were still many passengers lining up with their suitcases and rope-tied boxes waiting to board. So, I said to her that I had plenty of time to escort her down and share just one more moment together. My dear sweet angel mom embraced me one final time, holding me real tight, and kissed me goodbye with an avalanche of tears running down her cheeks. Sobbing and dabbing her eyes with her white handkerchief, she kept reassuring me that my life in America would be so much better and safer, that I would forever be free and that I would be adopted into a good family home with opportunities to see all my dreams come true.

I gave her a big hug, kissed her wet cheeks, and told her not to worry about me—that I was really looking forward to this most exciting new America, reassuring her that it would all turn out well.

This final send-off felt so similar to my previous permanent separation from my real mom back in Ukraine—that there would be no turning back.

The ship's loud horn sounded the final call for boarding. So, after a very short hug, I raced up the ramp and edged my way to the railing for a good viewing spot to wave back. The lump in my throat felt like a German tank from the war was lodged in it permanently. Had I lingered a few more seconds with Mom, I would have broken down and acted like a scared wailing baby, which may have prompted Mom to whisk me away—back to Schwabmünchen.

Mom's final instructions prior to my imminent departure, in a way, resembled the scripture passage in Deuteronomy:

"And the LORD, He is the One who goes before you. He will be with you, He will not leave you nor forsake you; do not fear nor be dismayed" (Deuteronomy 31:8).

"Fürchte dich nicht! Gott wird dich leiten und schützen [Do not be afraid! God will guide and protect you.]"

Those, her final words, though in a different language and a different country, were very similar to those given to me prior to my biological mom's send-off from that awful warehouse back in Zhytomyr, five years earlier, including the hugs and tears. Now, this loving mother, Elizabeth, God's chosen special angel, through whom His gift of life in a world of death had been so faithfully carried out, had resulted in me sailing to America. The fast-moving, life-changing events over the past five years had been racing by with such speed that the pain from my real mother's departure had been temporarily abated. But now, that scar would not only be torn open anew, it would be twice as deep with this additional permanent departure. Both separations would remain wedged in my heart and soul the rest of my days. These two most devoted mothers of such profound faith and love gave their all. Then, in their final act of love, chose to let go. By doing so, they both set a little boy adrift into an unknown world, pleading for God to continue caring for him. The first departure, by far the most dangerous one, was through an active war zone and this one, across an ocean, the most promising one.

By continuing to look back at Mom and watching her sobbing and waving her soggy, tear-filled, wet white handkerchief, it started to affect me a lot more because now I understood the finality and non-ending heartaches awaiting both of us. Perhaps she made this quick trip not only to see me off, but to give me the opportunity of reversing my decision and returning home with her.

Standing down there, heart-broken, was that Godly lady—the angel that God had chosen to save me and carry me on her wings through the bloodiest war of the twentieth century, across Europe. And now, believing that her divine duty was fulfilled and that another angel on the other side of the ocean would be taking over, she willingly let me go. I would never see her again! I continue to be in a state of continuous awe, realizing just how much I've been blessed—that I could be the recipient of such deep love from God and from two faithful, loving mothers.

With so many people crowding along the ship's railing as well as those on the dock below, all cheering, waving, some with both arms extended as high as they could, yelling, crying, and whistling, the combined noise was deafening. As the boarding ramp was moved aside, the deep, loud, lingering blast of the ship's horn told everyone that we were officially on our way to the new free world. As the ship began inching away from its berth, its loud horn went off several more times in succession and my throat was now so tight and painful that I couldn't even swallow my tears.

I doubted that Mom would be able to see my little waving hand amongst the many people around me, but it was easy to spot Mom's white handkerchief continuously waving. I looked down at the water and realized that the ship had now moved too far for me to consider jumping off. I caught one more glimpse of Mom's waving white handkerchief fading into the hazy grey shoreline of West Germany. It would always represent a white dove with a message of hope, love, and blessings.

Making its final turn to head out to sea, the ship's engine revved up and the horn went off one more time—louder, longer, and deeper than before, assuring everyone that there was no turning back. That final blast tore my heart in half. I raced to the nearest doorway, away from everyone, and burst out crying uncontrollably, as though my heart was being pulled out from inside me. The sound of that deep, eerie, lonely horn would repeat itself in my mind and heart for the rest of my days. Thankfully, Mom did not witness that, or I'd surely have been on the train with her back to Schwabmünchen.

CHAPTER 15
TADEUSZ (TED)—MY TRUSTED POLISH COMPANION

S trolling leisurely along the ship's narrow aisle and scanning the German coastline as it slowly faded into the grey horizon, a much older boy (perhaps around seventeen to twenty years old) spotted me, and reacting to my obvious distress, hurried over and knelt down beside me. With his compassionate and soothing mannerism, he gently placed his right hand on my left shoulder, gave me a warm smile, looked deep into my teary eyes, and like magic, I immediately felt as though an angel had just touched me.

Reaching into his pocket, he produced a small soft plastic pack of Kleenex, handing it to me. Realizing that I was just staring at it, he pulled out a couple of tissues with which he dabbed my wet cheeks. When I asked how I could wash the wet tissues, he smiled and explained the meaning of "disposable." Ever-so-understanding, wise, and physically strong looking, he immediately transformed me from a cry-baby to a smiling happy boy who found a new and caring friend.

With his comforting strong hand still on my shoulder, he said, "My name is Tadeusz Martica, just call me Ted. And what's your name?"

"Alex Marcel," I responded while sniffling.

"Are your parents here on the ship with you?" he asked.

I explained that I'd been designated as a D.P. and placed on board this ship heading to America, hopefully to be adopted by someone there.

"I'm also alone," said Ted. "I escaped from Poland during the war after both my parents were killed. I'm going a little farther—up to Canada— where I will live with my older sister."

Both of us were fluent in several languages, but since he also attended a German school recently, we continued conversing in German, spending most of our time on the ship exchanging our stories of escape and survival.

In an effort to evade the Soviets, Ted was able to connect with relatives in West Germany, where he attended school and waited for his family to arrange sponsorship by his Canadian sister.

When I inquired about his disembarkation in Canada and his plans, Ted proudly explained, "For a little while, during my stay at my sister's place, I'll learn the English language. Then, I'll become a Royal Canadian Mounted Policeman (RCMP) with my own horse and a police dog. I'll have a big black bear as a pet and live in a log cabin next to a winding river in the middle of the forest. I will fish and hunt for my own food and enjoy the peaceful freedom and boundless natural wonders of the vast Canadian Rocky Mountains."

Then, like a magician, he produced the most beautiful full-color glossy brochure revealing every detail he had just described to me. I was so impressed and wished that I could be like Ted and become an RCMP as well—wearing that bright red serge and riding my horse.

I tried to explain why I was really looking forward to living in America because just prior to boarding the ship, I had seen Roy Rogers—King of the Cowboys—and his wife, Dale Evans, as well as his horse, Trigger, and learned that they lived in America. Ted said that he also saw the same show and then proceeded to explain all about the make-believe world of cinematography and the art of acting, which is creating all kinds of life-like movies in a place called Hollywood. I didn't understand what he was telling me. It was like trying to tell a youngster that there's no St. Nick or Santa Claus.

A few days out in the open sea, the ship began dipping, rising, rolling, and heaving with the huge, black-colored mountain-high waves, causing chairs and tables to get tossed around like toys. Water from the ocean flooded the decks with high waves crashing over the ship's bow. Hanging onto a metal railing for dear life, I feared that the ship may sink and that we would all perish. A steward came by to offer his help, assuring me that we would be okay. I looked up and saw a man in a white uniform with a big happy smile revealing his pearly white teeth against a black face and who looked very similar to the black soldier back in Austria that had previously tossed me a piece of chocolate.

Reaching into a large burlap bag hung across his chest, he said, "Here, son, eat this orange. It'll make you feel much better."

Having never seen an orange before, I just held it in my hand with a puzzled look, until he signaled, with his hand to his mouth, to just eat it. So, I bit into it as I would an apple, expecting a sweet taste. Instead, it tasted like vinegar.

At that moment, Ted came by, weaving and stumbling like a drunkard, hanging on to every metal post and railing along the way. The steward also gave him an orange before moving on.

The mere presence of Ted made me feel a little better. He proceeded to teach me how to peel the orange. My pale-looking face indicated to him that I was affected by motion-sickness. He told me not to look out at the rising, dipping, and churning sea but to lie flat on my back. Sure enough, I began feeling better right away. Eventually, the turbulence began to subside and I wondered why so many people took the storm in stride, as if it were a common occurrence.

Fortunately, the sea remained relatively calm the rest of the trip. In fact, once the warm sun turned the dark sea into a beautiful blue, everyone on board was in for a special show as a school of dolphins came ever-so-close to our ship, swimming alongside us for the next few minutes, jumping in groups a few feet above the water and glancing at us with their smiling faces.

The transatlantic ocean voyage turned into a valued educational experience as Ted, so patiently, listened to all my concerns and explained to me in detail—sharing his knowledge with me and preparing me for the challenges and opportunities in the free new world ahead. Above all, he stressed the all-important task of learning the English language as quickly as possible, including the right spelling, pronunciation, and sentence structure in order to assimilate into the new world. Furthermore, he explained that he had been studying English over the past year and warned me that it's much more difficult than the languages we had come to know in Europe. Together, we spent time studying the translations of commonly used words and phrases from German to English from a small handbook he constantly carried in his pocket.

After approximately a week at sea, with no land in sight, except for an occasional far-off ocean-liner heading in the opposite direction, Ted thought that we should be nearing America's coastline soon and told me to keep looking to our left, just like many other passengers (some with binoculars) were doing. About two to three hours later, with a bit of excitement in his otherwise calm demeanor, Ted extended his right arm, pointing to the distant, hazy-grey horizon, and excitedly declared, "Look, Alex, way over there to the left—that's America."

I strained my eyes, hoping to see something, but all I could see was a very faint grey line which blended into the ocean. In a short time, more and more folks joined us on the port side of the ship, all expressing their happiness in various languages that the week-long journey was about to end.

We continued to watch, that hazy grey line become clearer by the minute, and soon we could make out some buildings. As the horizon began to transform into endless tall buildings, we could feel the ship slowly decreasing its speed. Ted again extended his right hand to point out some of the tallest buildings we could ever have imagined, referring to them as New York's skyscrapers.

Heading toward Ellis Island for disembarkation, the attention of everyone on board turned to the Statue of Liberty and its historic significance of welcoming people from the far corners of the world seeking freedom, opportunities, and the fulfillment of dreams. For me, however, it meant that I would soon have to get off without Ted and be alone. The closer we got to the end of this long cross-Atlantic voyage, the closer I stayed at Ted's side. Not wanting to be separated from him, I let him know how much I'd rather continue my trip to Canada with him.

Earlier in our journey, Ted had shown me pictures of New York City, my intended destination, and also many colorful brochures of Canada's beautiful majestic scenery with the mounted police, which I much preferred. Since Ted's destination was Canada, I would do anything to stay by his side regardless of any consequences I could face if I were caught.

Before the ship came to a complete stop and got secured at Ellis Island, the anxious passengers, like a herd of cattle, were beginning to bunch up in front of the exit sign with their children, suitcases, and boxes of personal belongings, chattering loudly in many foreign languages. While most everyone was watching the ramp for disembarkation slowly being moved into place, Ted helped me find a good hiding place on the opposite side of the ship.

At his suggestion, I quickly slipped under one of the upside-down lifeboats secured along the edge of the ship. He then whispered for me to lie on top of one of the narrow seats inside the lifeboat and remain totally still until we were far out at sea heading to Canada. Ted promised that he would be close by to distract anyone getting too close to me. I remained hidden under the inverted lifeboat, totally relying upon his watchful eye. From an inconspicuous nearby spot, he continued to keep watch until all the American-bound passengers disembarked and the ramp was moved away.

I could feel the ship's movement and after the final loud blast of the ship's horn, Ted came by to tell me that it was safe for me to come out. I was elated with the renewed hope and joy of continuing to be with him. We were on our way to Canada. Following close behind Ted, like a little puppy, we disembarked in Halifax, Nova Scotia, Canada, along with everyone else. What an odd feeling of dizziness, as I attempted to walk on land after having been at sea for over a week. The walkway seemed to be swaying and rolling similar to the ship's movement out in the ocean.

Ted's sister had arranged for transportation from the dock to the train station and on to Hamilton, Ontario. Sitting next to the window of the train's luxurious passenger car was very uplifting for both Ted and me, as we watched the serene landscape roll by without any bombed-out buildings or signs of destruction. I thought about my previous train ride during the war back in Ukraine—that armored, smelly freight car —and how miraculously God's angels were able to get me from there all the way here, onto that modern train heading westbound, deep into that beautiful land.

Everything here looked so clean, orderly, colorful, and exuberant with tall buildings, countless shiny cars, and big trucks traveling along endless stretches of smooth highways. Vast rolling green hills and colorful patches of farmlands, sparkling blue lakes, herds of cattle, and horses freely grazing in the lush green meadows all added to the anticipated new life of freedom, boundless opportunities, and joy welcoming us.

A CANADIAN CONVENT AND ORPHANAGE

Our final short car-ride from the train station through the city of Hamilton, Ontario, revealed a clean bustling city—full of energy and happy people greeting one another with handshakes and happy faces. The beautiful, bright colored flowers along the streets magically erased all those sad, dark, grey images that represented the destruction and sadness of the world we left behind. We arrived at a private estate outside the city limits and slowly proceeded through a decorative high black wrought iron gate with the name, "MOUNT MARY IMMACULATE CONVENT," affixed across the top of it.

This impressive 100-acre estate, which had been functioning as a Ukrainian Catholic convent, was also designated as an orphanage to help in processing the high volume of European orphan children that survived the devastation of the war. About three or four dozen nuns, all multilingual, wearing their traditional long black habits (robes) and white starched linen wimples which framed their faces by covering their foreheads, ears, and necks, were busy with a variety of duties. An elderly nun introduced herself as Mother Superior and led us to our room.

After washing our hands, we were asked to join about thirty other orphans and sit at a long wooden table in the dining room for a delicious meal. My thoughts briefly took me back to the long table back at the orphanage in Ukraine and the soup exchange. But this Canadian orphanage was a delightful experience in comparison. Everything was exceptionally clean and orderly.

Before we were allowed to begin eating, Mother Superior introduced Ted and me as the newest members and then asked everyone to bow their heads as she led us all in a short prayer to thank God for providing all our daily needs.

Mount Mary Immaculate Convent and Orphanage was a sprawling wooded sanctuary with hiking trails, a huge orchard and garden, a large chapel, a school, children's sleeping quarters, a large playground, living quarters for the nuns, an administrative office, a big dining room, and a kitchen. Every day was bustling with activities as children of all ages from around the world were either brought in for adoption or picked up to become members of new families.

As usual, this orphanage also had its mix of friendly, well-behaved kids as well as some rowdy ones. The nuns, however, didn't put up with any nonsense and would regularly exercise their disciplinary methods, including that feared, but most effective, old-fashioned leather strap in order to maintain a harmonious and well-run atmosphere. Daily chapel attendance was mandatory as were English classes taught by the nuns. Similar to Ted and me, most of the other kids were multi-lingual in several European languages but not in English, which, as Ted had warned me before, would be most difficult to learn.

About two weeks after Ted and I arrived at the convent, his sister came to pick him up. I had totally forgotten that when I first met Ted, he had told me that he would be living with her and her husband in the city of Brandon, Manitoba. Standing by motionless and totally disheartened, I watched Ted hug her and the driver of the car who must have been her husband. After placing his few personal belongings into the car's trunk, he saw me standing back with a sad, blank look on my face. With his warm smile and wide-open arms, he rushed over for a final farewell, picked me up, and gave me the longest bear-hug that would last a lifetime.

"Goodbye Alex, my dear brother and beloved friend. I will never forget you. Be brave and remember what your mother told you—that God will watch over you wherever you go. Maybe we'll meet someday, riding our horses up in the Canadian Rockies," Ted said.

"You won't be hard to find," I replied, "wearing your bright red serge and riding your horse with your German shepherd police dog close behind. I will surely miss you, Ted. Thank you for being my guardian angel during our long ocean voyage and bringing me with you all the way here."

As I struggled to contain my tears, Ted climbed into the back seat of the waiting car, and before closing the door, gave me one more big brotherly smile. Big Ted, my dearest and only friend, my hero, that kind-hearted giant that protected me from the moment we set sail from Germany, could not contain the tears in his eyes either. We continued waving to each other until the car exited the gate and vanished from sight. One of the nuns came over, placed her hand on my shoulder to console me, and led me back to join the other kids in a game of soccer.

Mother Superior asked if I'd like to be an altar boy at the chapel, which I gladly accepted. In addition, I volunteered for every opportunity to assist the nuns with general cleaning and yard work in order to stay busy. For several nights, before falling asleep, my mind would replay the exciting times I experienced with Ted, including his teaching moments. Several weeks slowly passed by with a steady stream of visitors coming to choose an orphan. They would generally select the young, cute, outgoing, and healthiest looking. Also, girls, by far, were preferred to boys. I didn't openly display any of these qualities and I surely wasn't a girl.

How clearly I remember that same scenario back in Lodz, Poland, when I was four years old and the miraculous outcome of that time. Now, as an eight-year-old boy, I was in the least likely group to be considered for adoption and it would become even more difficult with each added year. I began thinking that if I didn't get adopted by someone within a reasonable period of time, I could become a priest and stay right here the rest of my life.

After the war's end, every nation and its people, especially the ones that had been directly affected by the cruelty of the evil dictators (Stalin and Hitler), were devoted to rebuilding their country and their lives. By the grace of God, I was there, safe and sound and far removed from having to look at all the destruction and misery that I left behind in Europe.

Now, this vast, beautiful land of freedom and opportunity, where all my hopes and dreams were to be realized, had welcomed me with its outstretched and compassionate arms. I suppressed my loneliness and accepted the hand and temporary circumstances before me, knowing that this wasn't the end of God's plan for me and that another angel would appear at a proper time.

I always think of that moment whenever I sing or hear the song, "I Have A Dream" because of its inspiring, happy, positive outlook, and belief that goodness and good people are all around us even in times of adversity.

CHAPTER 16
ANOTHER MOM
AND DAD?

The Ukrainian Catholic Churches of Canada had been circulating a plea to its many parishioners across the country to contact Mount Mary Immaculate Convent and Orphanage and to consider adopting one of the orphans in their care from Ukraine and Poland. One Sunday afternoon, after having heard the adoption announcement at their local church in the city of Hamilton, Ontario, Mr. and Mrs. Bill Gorda, an elderly Ukrainian-Canadian couple in their late sixties, felt a tug in their heart to at least drop by the convent on their way home to become more informed.

Mother Superior was glad to show them around the facility, as she had done countless times, and answer all their questions. They explained that since their two grown children had moved out, they were open to bringing one of the orphans, preferably a boy—not too old or too young—to live with them. Mother Superior must have sensed that they hadn't given it too much thought but appreciated their desire to give it a try. She also observed that Mr. Gorda appeared more motivated than his wife and came up with a win-win solution.

"We have a bright eight-year-old Ukrainian orphan boy who recently arrived here," said Mother Superior. "He has been an orphan since he was three, attended school in Germany, and currently serves as an altar boy in our chapel. Would you like to meet him?"

"Yes," replied Mr. Gorda.

This would be my first face-to-face interview with a potential new family. I had a chance to, again, have a mom and dad and maybe even some brothers and sisters. My thoughts took me back to my previous two bonding attempts: my angel mom—Lady Elizabeth, rescuing me from the Polish orphanage, followed by Mr. and Mrs. Ott, the elderly German farm couple. Both provided an immeasurably positive, joyful, and life-changing experience for me, especially Lady Elizabeth.

When Mother Superior introduced me to Mr. and Mrs. Gorda, I stood at attention, smiled, and prepared myself to answer all questions. Mr. Gorda was a big, burly man. His friendly and somewhat jolly demeanor, sincerity in his eyes, and warm smile put me at ease. In spite of me being young enough to be his grandson, he gave me the impression that he was looking for a meaningful father-son relationship. His wife sat by his side without uttering a word, allowing her husband, as head of household, to do all the questioning. It seemed like a carbon copy to my relationship with Mr. Ott in Germany, except that this time I would be living in an older part of the city of Hamilton, Ontario. There would be no language barrier between us. Instead of German, I would be communicating in Ukrainian and simultaneously becoming more exposed to the English language because the Gordas were fluent in both.

Mr. Gorda glanced at his wife. Her smile sealed the agreement to have me move in with them. Although I had no idea whether this would be a temporary or a permanent arrangement, I fully embraced that new chapter in my life with bold certainty that it was part of God's planned journey for me. Since my stay at the orphanage was rather short and the number of boys and girls steadily moved in and out of the facility, I hadn't developed any friends with whom to share my departure. So I said goodbye to Mother Superior and left with the Gordas.

Riding in the back seat of their green Dodge sedan, I felt like a V.I.P. as Mr. Gorda maneuvered his car through the busy city streets, down a narrow back alley, and into a tiny backyard—just big enough to accommodate his car. We were greeted by a flock of pigeons noisily fluttering their wings in unison, ascending rapidly from their cote tucked in the corner against a wooden fence.

"Oh, I hope we didn't scare them off," I remarked.

"Not at all," replied Mr. Gorda. "They'll all return in a short while because this is their permanent home and we feed them every morning."

As I followed the Gordas toward the back door of their small two-story tract house, I observed an old bicycle leaning against the cote and a clothesline on a pulley extending from the porch along the wooden fence to an eight foot high post near the back alley. After walking up four wooden steps that led into the kitchen, Mrs. Gorda asked me to follow her upstairs to my room.

"This used to be our son Bill's room," she said. "He has his own place now."

Wow! What a coincidence, I thought. This is like going back in time when Mrs. Ott led me up the stairs and offered me her son Ludwig's room because he had also recently moved away. Mr. and Mrs. Gorda were very friendly, kind, and seemed elated to have me as an added member to their household. She was very mild-mannered, soft-spoken, and a great cook. Mr. Gorda proudly introduced me to his neighbors on both sides of their house and across the street.

Like the Gordas, most of the neighbors were bi-lingual immigrants from Ukraine. Most of the homes in the neighborhood, including ours, looked very similar in size and style with a few steps down from the front door facing a narrow grassy yard, set back from the sidewalk and street.

The next day, Mrs. Gorda enrolled me into the nearest city school as Alex Gorda. She explained to the principal that I was an eight-year-old orphan and had attended fourth grade in Germany but that I spoke no English.

"No problem," said the principal. "We'll put him into fifth grade and he'll do just fine."

Like most Europeans, I was fluent in several languages. Attending school in Germany was a breeze, but although the English and German alphabet was very similar, the word structures and non-phonetic pronunciations threw me for a loop, such as: "ph, th, sch" or the letter "c" being pronounced in some instances as "k or s," in addition to the very many words where some of the letters are silent, some words were spelled exactly the same but had different meanings, and some words sounded exactly alike but had different spellings as well as different meanings.

Sitting in the back row overlooking my classmates, I knew that I was in for an uphill challenge. With my clothes so different from what other students were wearing and unable to even utter one English word, I completely understood and accepted the reasons for being shunned. When the recess bell rang, the classroom quickly emptied out as all the students from the entire school scurried out into the playground. I simply followed them and watched a crowded yard full of similar-aged children as me engaged in various games—soccer, baseball, or volleyball—or simply chasing each other. The sound of everyone laughing, yelling, or shrieking with excitement reminded me of the scene back at the Bremen dock when I boarded the ship heading to America.

Unable to understand any of the teacher's lessons and instructions or comprehend any of the oral or written tests administered by the teacher, I flunked all except for mathematics and creative art, both in which I received a rather high grade. The teacher was simply too preoccupied with the duties of her large class size to devote any special attention to me or offer any tutorial or after-school aid.

Not being able to understand what the students were saying or the games they were playing during recess, I could only stand there trying to make sense of it all. It caused me to think of my near-drowning desperation back in that Polish river where I was saved by grabbing on to a floating branch. In a similar way, I would again be on my own in a "sink or swim" situation. A saving branch, God willing, may again appear.

Ever-so-slowly, I began to feel a bit more confident with the English language in class by concentrating, memorizing, and studying the language extra hard. I also carefully listened to the use of each word spoken by others, especially the teachers.

After a few weeks, the school principal came into our classroom to make an announcement. With a surprised look on the teacher's face and the sudden dead-silence in the classroom, we all assumed that someone was in deep trouble and that some kind of punishment was imminent.

The suspense lingered for a few seconds and based on my poor test results, I braced myself that he was very likely here to confront me, humiliate me in front of everyone, and remove me from class. Comparing my sense of fear to the innocent victims of the ugly war I left behind and my survival, this would be just another small bump in the road of my overall journey, no matter how serious the punishment. So, I sat up in my seat prepared to face the inevitable.

Sure enough, the principal called for me to step forward to the front of the classroom. My legs felt a bit weak and wobbly, as I proceeded to face both the principal and my teacher. In front of the whole class, I thought of my mom's assurance of God's protection and how it had brought me through the many insurmountable obstacles to date. This was no life-or-death situation, but I surely could benefit from a decent way out of it.

With the entire class breathlessly watching, the principal, holding an official-looking document in his left hand, smiled, placed his right hand on my shoulder, and addressed the class.

"Last month, I welcomed Alex, this young lad, who had very recently arrived here from Germany, to join this class. Although he's fluent in three or four European languages, he's working hard to learn English from the ground up. His recent test scores revealed high marks in math and exceptionally high in creative art. Our school submitted several pieces of artwork to the Hamilton City Art Festival, including several from Alex."

Holding up a certificate, the principal continued, "Today, I'm proud to announce that Alex's watercolor landscape and his charcoal drawings received the highest award in the entire Hamilton City School District."

Was I dreaming, or was this for real? I was in shock and speechless. He shook my hand, congratulated me, and presented me with the official certificate bearing my name, Alex Gorda, in large letters together with an embossed gold-colored City of Hamilton School District emblem. Yes, my mom was right again—that God would watch over me, guide me, and protect me.

Suddenly, I was everyone's friend. My classmates helped me with my English vocabulary and pronunciations and included me on their teams during recess. Some also asked me to make drawings of them. Even the teacher pitched in with some helpful remedial assignments. By the end of the school year, I acquired a passing grade on all my tests and proudly brought home my diploma, advancing me to sixth grade. Mr. and Mrs. Gorda were extremely proud and happy of my accomplishment.

MY FIRST DOLLAR

Within a few short blocks from home was a movie theater where some of my classmates and neighborhood kids would gather and attend the Saturday matinee movies for a dime.

Each time I walked by that theater, I would admire the large colorful posters by the entry describing the movie being shown at the time, but I was unable to see any of the shows because I lacked the required ten cents to purchase a ticket. One Saturday afternoon, as I strolled past the theater, I observed a newly displayed poster and—lo and behold— was I surprised! I took a closer look and sure enough, my hero, Roy Rogers, his wife, Dale Evans, as well as that beautiful palomino horse named Trigger and Bullet, the dog, were all shown on the big, full-color poster. Wow! I couldn't believe that they were actually all right there in our neighborhood—in that theater. I hadn't yet understood the meaning of cinematography and simply believed this show was to be a live production.

Oh, if I only had a dime, I could see their show right now! Pacing back and forth in front of the theater, I just couldn't let this once-in-a-lifetime opportunity slip away. There was no chance Roy Rogers and his entourage would ever come to that neighborhood again. But I had to buy a ticket to gain entry and couldn't ask the Gordas for the money because ten cents was a lot, and being older folks, they'd probably never heard of Roy Rogers and wouldn't understand why it was so important to me. Continuing to pace anxiously in front of the theater, admiring the poster from every angle, then, lowering my head and staring at the sidewalk in deep thought, figuring out some way I could see that show. A piece of crumpled-up dark green paper lay there at the curbside next to the street. I bent down to pick it up.

"Wow! I can't believe it!" I said to myself.

It was a dollar bill—a bit dirty, but oh, so beautiful! I raced home to inform Mrs. Gorda where I would be for the afternoon. The minute I stepped in to purchase my ticket, I was greeted by that familiar popcorn aroma that I first tasted back in Germany at the Port of Bremen prior to boarding the ship. I could certainly spend another nickel now and enjoy the most thrilling afternoon imaginable with a bag of buttered hot popcorn on my lap. After the show, everyone was leaving and new people were coming in. I asked the cashier if I could just stay and see the show a second time. With a nod, she allowed me to go back in. I bought another bag of popcorn, enjoyed the second show and afterward skipped all the way home as happy as any boy could possibly be. I had such a wonderful time! That pleasure would last me for years to come.

I adjusted very quickly to my new home and surroundings, and in order to prove my worthiness, I washed Mr. Gorda's car every week and even waxed it occasionally. Since it sat out all the time, with pigeons regularly flying about, the car didn't stay clean too long. When the next-door neighbor remarked how clean and shiny our car was, I also washed his, for which he paid me a whole dollar.

A MEMORABLE FISHING TRIP

In order to show his appreciation for my eagerness to pitch in with the house chores, the car washing, and the enthusiastic energy I added to the household, Mr. Gorda invited me to join him on a fishing trip to a very big lake about an hour drive from home. Prior to arriving there, he made a quick stop at a takeout diner to bring along our food for the evening. Placing the paper bag full of food between us on the front seat, he drove just a few minutes farther—right to the edge of the lakeshore. Meanwhile, the tantalizing, mouthwatering aroma emitting from that paper bag had filled the interior of our car. Within a few minutes, we were sitting on a blanket at the end of a rickety old wooden dock overlooking the most picturesque sight imaginable. The magnetic lure of that irresistible aroma from the paper bag circling around the dock made it impossible to wait another second longer.

I was treated to my very first taste of Fish-n-Fries take-out meal, including a bottle of Coca Cola. Mr. Gorda took that opportunity to teach me how to sprinkle a bit of vinegar on the fish and some ketchup on the crispy fries. The vinegar against the hot fish prompted me to deeply and repeatedly fill my lungs with that tantalizing aroma before each bite of that most wonderful-tasting treat.

I was awestruck with the beauty surrounding us, just watching the golden sun slowly sinking into the far end of the tranquil deep blue-colored lake encircled by the lush green pine, poplar, and birch trees and the weeping willows draping over the edge of the shore softly kissing the water below. This most peaceful and ever so aesthetic natural setting imaginable was accompanied by the frolicsome entertainment of a chorus of singing birds all around us. I spotted a curious-looking squirrel eying us before scurrying up one of the pine trees.

While expressing my gratitude to Mr. Gorda for arranging this special fishing excursion and bringing me to this wonderful spot, I also thought of my friend Ted's description of his dream-filled future life in the Canadian Rockies and the beautiful color brochure he had displayed during our Atlantic crossing. Somewhat similar to Ted's description, here was I, enjoying the experience of fishing in the Canadian natural wonderland.

As I continued sipping my Coca Cola and eating the last few crumbs of my meal, Mr. Gorda opened a bottle of beer he had brought for himself from home and began setting up his fishing gear off the dock. He explained that just like people, all of God's living creatures, by inbred natural instinct, search for food at dusk and again at dawn, and the fish in the lake would also now be searching for food in the lake.

Like magic, in no time at all, he had assembled a fishing net with bait inside a 6 by 6-foot tubular square, suspended from a collapsible pole, and simply lowered it off the end of the dock and into the deep water. We settled in for a relaxing long night, just chatting and checking the fishing net from time to time.

After opening another bottle of beer, he began explaining his arrival to Canada from Ukraine as a young teenager.

"During the early years of the twentieth century," he said, "so many people from my village in Ukraine came here to escape the brutality of the Communist-Russian oppression. All we wanted was freedom. The opportunities in this vast new country were boundless. I chose to live here in Hamilton, close to many of my Ukrainian friends, and pursued my trade as a plumber."

I asked him about his son, Bill. Before answering, Mr. Gorda took a deep breath, checked the fishing net which was still empty, sat down, took another sip of beer, and told me all about him.

"Bill grew up as a very smart, determined, opinionated, and tough kid, but also very stubborn and disobedient. He dropped out of high school, got into a few street-fights, and many a time would come home with a bloody nose or a black eye. Against our wishes, he trained to become a professional boxer, which he soon abandoned. He kept reading and collecting all those silly comic books and baseball cards—

still stacked up in our attic, cautioning us not to touch any of them as they would be worth a lot of money in time. What good are they? I don't know why he just doesn't take all that junk to his place instead of keeping it at my house. He's in his thirties now and owns an auto-body shop somewhere in the city."

"We also have a daughter," said Mr. Gorda. While he never mentioned her name, he said that her husband is a professional cartoon artist, creating pictures of Mickey Mouse and other silly-looking animals. Mr. Gorda continued by saying, "I don't understand how anyone can make a living drawing those ugly pictures. They're living in a small apartment downtown and raising two young children."

During our conversation, he kept an eye on his fishing net by repeatedly raising it a bit, then immediately submerging it until we finally had a few decent-sized fish to take home—but the biggest one, unfortunately, got away just as we were about to put it into a net. I thoroughly appreciated this special time alone with Mr. Gorda and hoped we could do it again soon.

Driving back home in the middle of the night, he turned briefly to face me and said, "You know Alex, my son Bill never once wanted to go fishing with me. He was always too busy. You're a good boy, Alex. Thanks for coming along and keeping me company. We'll plan on another fishing trip here soon."

"Oh, I'd sure love to come here again. Maybe we'll catch that big one that got away," I replied. "And we can again stop and have those yummy Fish-N-Fries and Coca Cola."

In order not to ignore Mrs. Gorda, who had so faithfully continued to prepare our meals and kept the house so clean, I pitched in to wash and dry the dishes, the windows, and mop the vinyl floors. Later she complained to her husband that she was no longer able to keep up with certain daily chores. So, the next time I noticed her dusting and polishing the dark wood furniture in the dining room and living room, I immediately took the polish and rag from her hands and took over the cleaning. I did it all and assured her that I would be doing it from now on. During my polishing and cleaning routine, I discovered a small secret door upstairs leading to the attic.

Once inside the dark, low-ceiling attic, I located the switch to turn the lights on and found the comic books and baseball cards that Mr. Gorda had told me about. There were several stacks of new-looking comic books neatly stacked on the floor against the wall. Each one had a different name printed in large letters against a colorful, full-action cover page: Superman, Batman, Flash Gordon, Roy Rogers, Lash Larue, Gene Autrey, Hopalong Cassidy, Tex Ritter, Lone Ranger and Tonto and many others.

I could have spent many days looking through them all. Next to the comic books was a cardboard box filled with new-looking baseball cards showing images of players I never heard of. They meant nothing to me at the time. I assumed they were children's playing cards. Mrs. Gorda explained that her son, Bill, had been collecting those books and cards since he was very young, believing that they would become very valuable someday and telling her not to let anyone touch them. I gave her my word that I wouldn't go to that attic again.

Weeks at the Gordas turned into months and I began to wonder why their son or daughter and grandkids never came by to visit, since they all lived in the city of Hamilton. There were no birthday or holiday celebrations at our place or theirs, but then I recalled Mr. Gordas's unflattering description of his family during our fishing trip, so I decided not to inquire any further.

MEETING BILL GORDA

On a Sunday afternoon, as I was bouncing a soccer ball on the front lawn, an odd-looking shiny green car stopped at the curb in front of our house. Mr. Gorda came out from inside the house and stood on the landing by the front door just staring at that car and with sarcasm remarked to his wife, "What kind of stupid-looking car is that? You can't tell the front from the back."

As the dark-haired, handsome, muscular-looking driver slowly climbed out and very gingerly closed the car-door behind him, Mr. Gorda called out, "Is that your car, Bill?"

"Yes!" responded Bill. "It's a new 1948 Studebaker two-door hard-top. In time, it'll be a collector's item because not too many were in production."

Mr. Gorda told Bill that he had never heard of a Studebaker before. Then he said "Well, no wonder they're only going to make a few of these. If you ask me, it really does look kind of stupid. You can't tell the front from the back."

With that comment, Bill's pride of ownership surely became somewhat deflated—setting the tone of the conversation to follow. After they both entered the house, I continued looking at this strange new Studebaker from every angle, slowly circled it several times, peered through the windows to admire the interior but was very careful not to get too close or touch the gleaming bright green paint. Repeatedly, however, my eyes were drawn to that rear window which really did resemble the front windshield. Through the screen door of the house, I was able to overhear the conversation from within.

"Who is that skinny kid out front, looking at my car so much?" asked Bill. "He'd better not touch it. Do you know him? Is he one of the neighbor's kids?"

"Oh, that's Alex," his father replied. "He's an orphan from Ukraine, and we decided to let him live with us. He's been with us about six months now, going to school and sleeping in your empty room upstairs."

"He's really a pleasure to have in our home and very helpful to both your father and me," said Mrs. Gorda. "Your father and Alex went fishing a couple of weeks ago, and they both really enjoyed it."

"Where did you find him?" asked Bill.

"From the orphanage at Mount Mary Immaculate Convent," replied his father.

Bill's next statement was hurtful for me to overhear, as he, in frustration, raised his voice and cold-heartedly began berating and lecturing his parents.

"Are you both nuts? I can't believe this," he said. "Why, at your age, would you do such a dumb thing? Let someone else step in and take on such a responsibility. Take him back immediately where you got him."

Charging out of the house and into his car, Bill gave me a quick glance and drove away. Thinking about it a bit later, I knew that Bill was right, but he sure had no respect toward his parents. Nevertheless, some wonderful and memorable events occurred during my time there under the name of "Alex Gorda." I thoroughly enjoyed the home atmosphere with that kind-hearted older couple, learned English, earned a diploma to sixth grade, got an award from the Hamilton School District for my artwork, saw the Roy Rogers show, learned how to fish with a net, and was treated to the tastiest Fish-n-Fries take-out dinner in the most picturesque Canadian lakeside setting imaginable. In total, it was a blessing to be able to experience such joy and tenderness.

BACK TO THE ORPHANAGE

When Bill drove his new Studebaker car away, he took with him Mr. Gorda's jovial, grandpa-like "Teddy Bear" image, which I had come to adore. The drive back to the orphanage was not something either one of us had foreseen, but the more we discussed it, the more we both agreed that in the long run, my education and opportunities would be somewhat compromised if I remained there. Having raised two of his own children, he remembered and understood the sacrifices, guidance, and discipline that would be asked of him and his wife, which, at their age, they would find challenging.

After a few moments in Mother Superior's office, Mr. Gorda, clutching a white handkerchief in the palm of his hand and visibly saddened, gave me a huge bear hug, wished me well and said, "You're a good and very bright boy, Alex. I really enjoyed our time together and will miss you. You exemplified the kind of son I wish I had when I was younger. However, as we discussed earlier, I truly believe that a brighter, more rewarding future lies ahead for you."

I thanked him for opening his home to me and allowing me to experience a joyful life as a city dweller in Hamilton and for that special, unforgettable fishing trip. As he slowly drove away, I could see him dabbing his eyes with his white handkerchief. His departure, however, didn't cause my throat to tighten up as it had during my prior permanent separations.

It wasn't such a shock to me anymore. I had no tears or deep sorrow associated with the finality of it all. Perhaps, after so many goodbyes and separations, my emotions had become accustomed and calloused. My eyes followed Mr. Gorda's car until it passed through the iron gates, turned left onto the highway, and drove out of sight.

As I stood there in deep thought, reviewing my feelings of emptiness that followed the end of every relationship to date, I simply recalled my mom's assurance that God, through His angels, would continue to care for me, protect me, and guide me to a safe, joyful, and godly place. All the people that were chosen by God to be my angels, who had cared for me to date, including the Gordas, had something very special in common: They were all kind, loving, caring, and faithful. Although neither Mr. Gorda nor Herr Ludwig Ott in Germany openly displayed their faith, I believe that their steadfast acts of kindness and compassion caused them to be tapped as one of God's angels in bringing me closer toward my destined permanent home a little farther away.

Although I had only been away about a year, my return to the convent and orphanage felt so much different than when I first landed here from Germany. The experience gained from attending an English-speaking school, adapting to the Canadian customs of city life, and the unforgettable wonders and tranquility of the vast natural beauty during my overnight fishing excursion made me ever-so-appreciative just to be living in this wonderful country. I was filled with renewed hope and trust that the best was yet to come, and that another angel was preparing to take over from here.

Mother Superior assigned me to more responsibilities as well as my former altar boy duties and general helper at the chapel. Among my observations, the visiting priests conducting the worship and homily were usually older priests with tired and monotonous voices.

On rare occasions, a younger, more energetic priest would fill in for the older ones causing everyone in attendance to be much more alert. I began to think that if I remained at Mt. Mary Immaculate Convent a long time—beyond the possibility of being adopted—I could, perhaps, become a priest, not only at this chapel but at any regular church in Canada.

CHAPTER 17
WINNIPEG GREEK CATHOLIC CATHEDRAL

I n his Easter sermon in 1948, the bishop of Western Canada, addressing the parishioners at the Ukrainian Greek Catholic Cathedral in Winnipeg, Manitoba, reiterated his appeal to welcome the Ukrainian war orphans temporarily sheltered at Mount Mary Immaculate Convent in Hamilton, Ontario and to consider offering those fatherless and motherless Ukrainian children the precious gift of adoption. Mrs. Melnyk, a devout member of the congregation, who had recently been widowed, volunteered to personally take the bishop's message to some of the smaller more remote churches in the farming communities of Western Manitoba.

Very early, on a chilly Sunday morning, she tied her traditional colorful babushka over her head, put on a warm, full-length wool coat, and headed to the Winnipeg Bus Station to board the first Greyhound bus heading west on Trans-Canada Highway 1 and on to Highway 126 to speak at several Ukrainian Greek Catholic Churches, including a new church recently built in the town of Oakburn.

Prior to the 11:00 a.m. service in Oakburn, after a brief meeting with Father Fornalchuk, Mrs. Melnyk took a seat in the very front pew of the sanctuary, which was so well attended that people stood in the aisles, filled every space in the balcony, and even crowded around the doorway of the entrance. Near the end of the service, after being introduced by Father Fornalchuk, Mrs. Melnyk stood up to face the congregation, fully aware that many of the older folks she was about to address, had sacrificed so much, escaped from their homes in Ukraine because of the ongoing Soviet oppression, and worked tirelessly to create a new home for themselves and their families in those prairie provinces.

Ever-so-eloquently, she presented her impassioned mission to find homes for as many Ukrainian orphans as possible, appealing to the congregation to open their hearts and consider adopting a little boy or girl. She summed up her message with a quote from the Bible:

> *"Then He took a little child and set him in the midst of them. And when He had taken him in His arms, He said to them, "Whoever receives one of these little children in My name receives Me; and whoever receives Me, receives not Me but Him who sent Me"*
> *(Mark 9: 36–37).*

As was customary in most all the Ukrainian Greek Catholic churches at the time, women would generally sit on the left side of the church facing the altar and men on the right. Scanning the worshippers, who remained very silent, except for the occasional cough or unrest of a baby, Mrs. Melnyk, with high hopes of a response or question from someone, noticed an elderly lady among the many head-coverings of colorful babushkas, scarves, and hats, slowly rising to her feet, holding her hand high above her head and proudly declaring, "I'd like to adopt a girl."

The entire congregation, including the priest, was stunned in disbelief. Instantly, the stillness in the church turned into loud chatter, arm-waving, head-shaking, even laughter, as among them stood the bravest of them all—Mrs. Mary Sytnyk, who was tapped by God to be His angel and fulfill an assignment for Him. Most shocked, however, was the lady's husband, who sat in the men's section. Also, her six grown children ranging in age from twenty-two to thirty-seven, who had already blessed Mrs. Sytnyk and her husband with a dozen grandchildren, looked at each other dumbfounded, perplexed, and simply embarrassed to be witnessing their mother making a fool of herself in front of everyone.

The most remarkable characteristic about this special lady was her profound unshakeable faith. She was an ambassador of God, always with a small cross hanging from her neck, a rosary wrapped around her left hand, and she was constantly in prayer. She was not shy about reading scriptures from her old Ukrainian Bible to anyone that came to her home. She also had a high-pitched soprano singing voice and would invariably take advantage of a quiet moment just prior to commencement of each service to honor the Lord by rising to her feet and singing a hymn all alone without any musical accompaniment or assistance from the choir or musical director in the balcony above her.

Although Mary and her husband George (Hnat) Sytnyk (both in their mid-sixties), had already raised six children, their seventh—a baby girl named Lena—had died in the midst of a long harsh winter when she was only two years old. Mary would reveal that painful, never-ending loss before God in deep prayer every morning and evening through the rest of her life. Could this opportunity for adoption be a sign from God—an answered prayer to raise a Ukrainian orphan girl, even at this stage in her life? With submission to God's will, she would honor Him by raising the orphan girl as a nun.

At the end of the church service, Father Fornalchuk asked Mrs. Melnyk, Mrs. Mary Sytnyk and her husband, George, to step into his office and briefly discuss Mary's important decision and then he led them in prayer for guidance, courage, and God's blessing.

With only one potential adoption for a Ukrainian orphan girl, it was enough for Mrs. Melnyk to get the ball rolling, knowing that more success was sure to follow. She took a 1,400-mile train ride to Hamilton, Ontario to become more familiar with the adoption program at Mount Mary Immaculate Convent, which she would rely on to continue with her dedicated mission. She was also hoping to select and return with a young girl for Mary Sytnyk in Oakburn, Manitoba.

Mother Superior greeted her and explained that there had been a lot of activity at the convent to place orphans within the province of Ontario ever since the war ended but that western Canada had been more reluctant in its response. Mrs. Melnyk said that her job was to change that, and she was there to bring back a Ukrainian girl for a farm family in Manitoba.

"Oh, I'm so sorry," said Mother Superior. "You see, girls are usually adopted very quickly and as of now, we have only one older girl still here. However, she has chosen to remain here, at the convent, to be trained as a nun." Exactly the kind of girl Mrs. Sytnyk had requested and prayed for. "In fact, at this moment, even the remaining boys have also all been spoken for, and we're getting them ready to meet their new parents."

"Oh, but wait a minute," she added. "I just remembered that we do have a nine-year-old boy who was just returned to us by an elderly couple in Hamilton. He's a very bright boy, speaks four languages, and recently graduated to sixth grade from Hamilton city school. He's currently serving as Altar Boy in our chapel and helps us with some of the chores around the convent. Perhaps you would consider him?"

Not wanting to return empty-handed or waste the church's money for the train ticket, Mrs. Melnyk was in a quandary. The two ladies spent several minutes wondering how to resolve the dilemma, and decided to talk to me directly. After a series of questions and answers, they proceeded to the chapel, knelt before the altar, and together prayed for God's guidance. Upon returning with Mother Superior to the office where I was waiting and hoping, Mrs. Melnyk, in a leap of faith, took my hand and said, "No, you're certainly not a girl, Alex, but let's go for a long, long train ride, all the way to the countryside of Western Manitoba. It may just work out for everyone, God willing."

With a smile on my face, I sat next to Mrs. Melnyk in the luxurious Canadian National Railway (CNR) passenger cab, closed my eyes, and in thanksgiving, retraced the most wonderful and exciting life that continued to unfold before me. I was, again, on the wings of angels toward my predestined home somewhere far away, and in my mind, Mrs. Melnyk was God's angel chosen to get me there. As the train picked up its speed, leaving the busy city of Hamilton, Mrs. Melnyk filled me in regarding her mission in arranging this potential adoption for me. She asked me to give her as much information as possible about my life as a Ukrainian orphan so that she would be able to represent me in the best possible manner to my potential new parents.

At the end of the long train ride, Mrs. Melnyk and I spent a day at her home in the sprawling city of Winnipeg, Manitoba. She took me shopping to the Hudson's Bay Company department store and, using her personal funds, bought me a new white shirt, a dark blue suit, a tie, and black shoes, making me feel very special.

"Wow! Come and look at yourself here, in the three-way mirror, Alex," she said. "You look quite handsome and all grown-up."

I smiled, thanked her, and glanced at myself from different angles in the mirror, hardly recognizing the new person looking back at me. The next day, we hopped on a bus, heading 180 miles westbound on Trans-Canada Highway 1, arriving at the Children's Aid Society in the city of Brandon, where the anxious Mrs. Mary Sytnyk and her thirty-two-year-old son, Tom, were waiting in the counselor's office to meet the anticipated orphan girl.

Despite being apprehensive about the entire idea of adoption, George Sytnyk, the patriarch of the family, agreed to support his wife's and Tom's decision whatever it may be. Throughout his adult life, George had always avoided travel—preferring to remain close to his farm and home.

Mrs. Melnyk had to do some fast explaining when she presented me instead of a girl. The shocked and disappointed look on Mrs. Sytnyk's face told me that the interview would not turn out too well. There were no smiles, hugs, or even a hint of encouragement. I began to think that this long journey may well end in futility and that I may be sent back to the convent in Hamilton to give it another try. But then, I quickly snapped out of my negativity by trusting that since God's angels brought me this far, I needed to continue to hope, pray, and believe in the power of faith and my mother's assurance that the best was yet to come.

Tom, dressed in a grey suit and matching tie, was bilingual—English and Ukrainian—but his sweet mother, with her floral babushka loosely draped over her head, a small cross hanging from her neck, and a rosary in the clasp of her left hand, only communicated in her native Ukrainian language. As the interview proceeded, I continued to smile, stand at attention and answer all their questions in perfect Ukrainian dialect.

Since no one asked about my miraculous escape and survival from World War II's pit of hell, I knew that it was up to me to sell myself and to explain that through my mom's prayers and deep faith, I was assured that God would protect me and guide me to freedom and safety. Addressing Tom, his mother, the counselor, and Mrs. Melnyk, I summarized my background, ending with one last statement:

"My mom, just before being put to death, told me to run away. God saved me and placed me on the wings of angels, to carry me thousands of miles, across two continents and an ocean, all the way here, to you."

I had to convey to everyone in that room that I wasn't merely another DP or refugee—that I spoke four languages, including English, lived in four European countries, was baptized in Poland and Germany, and served as an altar boy in those countries as well as in the chapel at Mount Mary Immaculate Convent.

When Mrs. Sytnyk heard me say that I had lived in Poland, was baptized, and served as an altar boy, she sat up, smiled, and raised her head in interest because she had been raised in Poland by her Polish father and Ukrainian mother.

Tom, a confirmed bachelor, explained that he would continue to live with his parents who were now semi-retired, and he was now managing the large farm comprising several sections of land as well as a herd of cattle, horses, poultry, and hogs.

With some excitement in my voice, I asked, "Did you say you have horses on your farm?"

"Yes," replied Tom. "We have six or seven horses. Dad tends to them and relies on them throughout the year, especially during spring and harvest times, while I work the fields with tractors and a variety of farm machinery."

"Not long ago," he continued, "I bought a white horse—a very spirited filly. Maybe you can learn to ride her."

This last statement from Tom was most encouraging so far, and my heart began to race with excitement. I was asked to step out of the office and wait in the lobby for a few minutes so they could come to an agreement regarding my potential adoption. Looking out the window of the lobby, I whispered a prayer to thank God for arranging all these miraculous events starting from that far away, most dangerous part of the world all the way here, 7,000 miles west, to this wide open Canadian prairie province of Manitoba—right in the center of North America.

"Dear Lord," I prayed. "Until now, I had no idea where your angels were instructed to take me, but now I realize that each lay-over, each diversion, and each episode brought me closer and better prepared for this place. Thank you for your steadfast guidance and your countless blessings. My heart tells me that this may be the spot that you set aside in answer to my mother's and also Lady Elizabeth's faithful prayers. Help me, Father, to be obedient and respectful—that I may bring an uplifting joy and happiness to this kind and godly household. I pray that you would bless me into becoming a worthy, helpful, and loving addition to this family and to grow up as a strong, faithful, and God-fearing man."

With me continuing to wait in the lobby, everyone in the office was free to express their feelings. Mrs. Sytnyk, not yet willing to overlook the substitution of a boy for the girl that she had requested, again expressed her apprehension about taking on the responsibility of raising a nine-year-old boy at this stage of her life. "Having mourned the loss of my baby girl for over thirty years," lamented Mrs. Sytnyk, "I was looking forward to bringing home a young girl with hopes of raising her into becoming a nun. This boy, cute and smart as he is, cannot replace the girl I had prayed for. I've already raised four sons and two daughters and know from experience that boys, by nature, can be rather difficult."

Tom, on the other hand, acknowledging that he had no plans toward marriage, saw an opportunity to train an eager young boy like myself in many of the farm-related chores, believing that, as he grew older, bigger, and stronger, he may become a reliable assistant with the endless work on the farm. Facing his mother, he promised her that he would absorb most of the behavioral, disciplinary, and scholastic responsibilities.

Though still somewhat reluctant, Tom's mother relented and decided to leave it in God's hands but also sent a silent "Hail Mary" prayer that this young boy may just possibly grow up and become a priest.

In order to relieve Mrs. Sytnyk's concerns, Mrs. Melnyk and the counselor agreed to provide a one-year trial period before finalizing the adoption process by simply bringing me back if it didn't work out and, in that event, the entire process would be voided. It was a win-win situation for everyone, especially for me. Needless to say, Mrs. Melnyk must have felt like a heavy burden was lifted from her shoulders and that her prayers were answered.

CHAPTER 18
SONS OF A PIONEER

I n spring of 1948, happily riding in the back seat of Tom's 1946 tan-colored Ford four-door sedan as a nine-year-old new member of this God-given family, I had ample time to study my new mother and older brother seated in front. With thanksgiving and elation, it felt like I was again on wings of angels in the final segment to that far away happy and safe place of which my dear mom had assured me. I experienced a similar kind of joy when I was four, when Lady Elizabeth, who had come to select a girl, chose and rescued me from a Polish orphanage. Thankfully, this time there would be no fear of being uprooted and pursued by the evil Russians.

As soon as we turned onto the main highway, my new mom rustled through her food basket and offered Tom and me some fresh raspberries, crab-apples picked from her garden, and some of her home-baked bread buns. Immediately, I thought of the bread roll and honey given me by Lady Elizabeth. Now, here I was, being chauffeured in a private Ford sedan, nibbling on hand-picked fresh fruit! Tom explained that his mom's habit was to always bring along some food, regardless of the length of the trip, in the event of bad weather, bad roads, or car-trouble.

Born in Chorzów, Poland, in 1886, Mary Hatchkowsky (her maiden name), arrived in Canada at the age of eight with her parents and five siblings, settling near Oakburn. Her father arranged for her marriage to Hnat (a.k.a. George) Sytnyk, who, at a very young age, had already developed his homestead into a well-managed farm. Such arranged marriages were commonplace in the old country from where they all came. The final touch for a growing and thriving homestead would be the addition of a virtuous wife and Mary certainly was that—working by his side in the field, enduring the many hardships and setbacks, building their new home, and providing for all the needs in the raising of their six children.

In a short while, I would meet my new father and the rest of the large family. How rich are God's blessings that He would continue to lift me up, time-after-time, and make each new step more glorious than the last! I could barely contain the excitement and anticipation of my new home. Starting with my new name, Alex Sytnyk, I was so happy and proud to share their name and, like magic, become a new member of this wonderful family. The paved highway, leaving Brandon northbound, eventually turned into a much narrower, gravel-covered country road, which created a cloud of dust behind us. Like a giant painted canvas, the gentle rolling hills moving by us on both sides of the road displayed vast stretches of soft shades of green fields broken up by an array of bright, vivid colors of yellow, gold, charcoal, and blue.

The blue fields looked like lakes of fresh water. I was in awe, just absorbing the colorful kaleidoscopic beauty surrounding us. From the rearview mirror near the top of the car's windshield, Tom observed me gazing intently at the different colors and deeply inhaling the perfumed aroma emitted from all those flowery fields, so he started naming what each color represented.

"The green fields," he explained, "are young grain crops, such as wheat, barley, and oats. The gold fields are ripened grain crops, the sky-blue fields are blooming flax, and the charcoal-black fields are called summer-fallow, which are purposely left barren for one year to allow the land to rest and regain its fertility for next year's planting."

"How about those bright yellow-colored fields?" I asked.

Before answering, he cleared his throat and with a sly grin, said, "The yellow field—that's called rapeseed, from which cooking oil is produced but we just call it 'rape'." Then, with a broader grin, he continued, "There's a joke going around that we used to get twenty dollars a bushel for rape, now we get twenty years to life."

(The name has more recently been changed to "canola." Canada is its largest producer.)

Our car trip from Brandon to Oakburn, which would now be my home town, lasted about two hours. There was a Catholic cemetery on the right side of the road and an Orthodox cemetery on the left, followed by a large new red brick Catholic church, a school, and a community hall. We turned right at the one and only stop sign and continued much more slowly for the final four miles on a narrow dirt road etched with dried-out weaving ridges created by cars trying to manipulate the slick muddy surface after recent rainstorms.

"Look, there's our house," said Tom, pointing to his right at about a twenty-degree angle. Situated on a slightly higher elevation, about 200 yards from the road, stood a rather large, impressive two-story house facing the bright warm sun, but otherwise protected by a grove of towering, mature pine trees that were planted by Tom's parents years ago when their children were still very young.

MEETING MY NEW PIONEER FATHER

Tom parked his car close to a walkway outlined by a four-foot-high caragana hedge. As we all stepped out of the car, we were greeted by a happy, tail-wagging collie dog named Sandy, who led us to the front door. Just as we were about to step inside, Mr. Sytnyk, my designated new father, joined us. He seemed somewhat puzzled that before him stood a happy-looking boy instead of the little girl he had expected. He shook my hand very gently—I had never touched the palm of a man's hand as rough and calloused as his. It felt like the bark of a tree, obviously caused by his lifelong, daily hard labor.

As time passed, he often handed me a large sewing needle, asking me to remove wooden splinters that repeatedly became lodged in the palm of his hands. With each attempt, I was stunned by the difficulty I had just getting the sharp needle point into that hard, leathery skin, causing the needle to bend. His dark, weather-beaten complexion, caused by being out in the field every day till sundown throughout his life, was softened by his calm and humble demeanor. He sported a thick dark moustache and after removing his faded old cap from his head, surprised me by revealing, in spite of his age, a full head of dark hair without any gray. He whacked the weathered cap a couple of times against his knee to shake off the dust from it. Having raised four boys whom he had taught to acquire and operate their own farms, he seemed to relish the opportunity of teaching another youngster all about farming and the value of hard work. I sensed that he fully approved of his wife's and Tom's decision to add me to the family. We bonded instantly. Without hesitation, Mr. Sytnyk began calling me his son and I would refer to my new family as Dad, Mom, and brother, Tom.

Born in 1885, Hnat (a.k.a. George) Sytnyk had come with his parents to western Canada as a thirteen-year-old boy from the small village of Soroka, in western Ukraine. Although he left Ukraine with a sixth-grade education, he did not have the means of attending school in Canada and neither did his wife nor most of the Ukrainian farmers in the area. However, he had a keen interest in current events and acquired first-hand experience in efficient farming methods as well as sufficient grasp of the English language by working as a hired hand for English-speaking farmers in another village. He was very thankful for this opportunity and would walk 40 miles to work for them during peak spring and harvest seasons while also working hard to clear and develop his own homestead.

THE FORESIGHT OF DOCTOR JOSEF OLESKIW

The mass migration from Ukraine to the untamed rural areas of the western Canadian prairie provinces of Manitoba, Saskatchewan, and Alberta were made possible through the efforts of Doctor Josef Oleskiw, a Ukrainian Greek-Catholic Professor of Agriculture at a Teachers' Seminary in Lemburg,

Austria. In an effort to help free the Ukrainian farmers and their families from the endless oppression under Austrian rule and endless threats from the Turks and Russians, he embarked on a win-win plan for Western Canada and for the oppressed Ukrainian farmers.[1]

In 1895 Dr. Oleskiw sent a letter to the Department of the Interior in the capital city of Ottawa, Canada, requesting approval for possible mass migration of Ukrainian farmers to the prairie provinces of western Canada. The letter was acknowledged by the Superintendent of Immigration, L. M. Fortier, and followed up by Sir Clifford Sifton, Canada's Minister of the Interior.[2] *Inspired by the humanitarian spirit of the Canadian government, Dr. Oleskiw toured the untamed area of Manitoba (also described by many as Freedom of the Frontier), wrote a very positive book about his observation, and distributed pamphlets in western Ukraine, encouraging the people to bring their families here and claim their new homestead. A year later, the mass migration began to unfold. It proved to be an instant success.*

The period from 1896 to 1913 came to be known as the boom of the Canadian economy. Canada continues to be one of the largest agricultural producers in the world.

Since most everyone in this area had migrated from Ukraine, the Ukrainian language was predominantly spoken at home as well as in villages. The Ukrainian church sermons and hymns continued to be conducted in Ukrainian language. In spite of the many challenges, the Ukrainian immigrants were very resourceful and contributed immensely to the growth and development of western Canada.[3]

One of the most popular and highly respected Ukrainian politicians, Stephen Juba, served as mayor of Manitoba's capital city of Winnipeg

---

1. Wikipedia, "Joseph Oleskiw," Wikipedia, accessed August 2025, https://en.wikipedia.org/wiki/Joseph_Oleskiw#:~:text=External%20links-,Joseph%20Oleskiw,-2%20languages.
2. Wikipedia, "Clifford Sifton," Wikipedia, accessed August 2025, https://en.wikipedia.org/wiki/Clifford_Sifton#:~:text=External%20links-,Clifford%20Sifton,-5%20languages.
3. Wikipedia, "Ukrainian Diaspora," Wikipedia, accessed August 2025, https://en.wikipedia.org/wiki/Ukrainian_diaspora#:~:text=External%20links-,Ukrainian%20diaspora,-18%20languages.

from 1956 until his retirement in 1977.[4] He was credited with the city's infrastructure planning and development, lowering of taxes, and also introducing the three-digit phone number into North America.

George Sytnyk was among this mass migration, arriving in Manitoba in 1898. Mary Hatchkowsky (his future wife) and her family had arrived in the same area from Poland a few years earlier. Following a sudden outbreak of scarlet fever shortly after settling near the village of Oakburn, a total of forty-two children and several adults died of this plague within a two-week period. One family, Michael and Anne Holowicky, lost all three of their young children. Young George volunteered to help carry the bodies of the deceased to a gravesite five miles north of Oakburn. A concrete monument now stands as a tearful memorial of that terrible epidemic. In 1924, American pathologists, Gladys and George Dick developed an antitoxin and vaccine to halt this pandemic. It was later replaced by penicillin.[5]

Relentlessly and diligently pursuing his dream of developing his homestead, George became a very successful and admired pioneer farmer in the area and set an excellent example for his growing family of six, all of whom would follow their mom and dad's work ethics and in time, acquire their own farms within a distance of less than twenty miles from home. There were years when devastating hailstorms, dry seasons, early frost, or exceptionally wet seasons would destroy the crops in the field, but the following spring, with hope, prayer, and grit, they would start anew.

In 1935, a rust disease destroyed most of the "Marquis" wheat crops throughout the region. George sprang into action and learned about a new rust-resistant "Thatcher" wheat and purchased a supply from the state of Minnesota, U.S.A. He shared it with other farmers for planting. He loved to reminisce about his pioneering days and enjoyed looking out across his fertile land that once was full of wild brush, trees, rocks, and large boulders. It's hard to imagine that one man was able to turn such a large untamed area into a

---

4. Wikipedia, "Stephen Juba," Wikipedia, accessed August 2025, https://en.wikipedia.org/wiki/Stephen_Juba#:~:text=External%20links-,Stephen%20Juba,-1%20language.
5. Wikipedia, "George Frederick Dick," Wikipedia, accessed August 2025, https://en.wikipedia.org/wiki/George_Frederick_Dick#:~:text=References-,George%20Frederick%20Dick,-2%20languages.

self-sustaining, beautiful farmland, relying on his back-breaking labor, his bare hands, an axe, a saw and his devoted horses. The hand-hewn trees supplied firewood for home-heating as well as a source of bartering for necessary supplies as cords of wood (measuring 4 x 4 x 8 ft.) were hauled into town to be exchanged for flour, salt, sugar and farm-tools. With time and saved-up resources, George acquired more land and more advanced farm equipment.

He was the "Salt of the Earth." The entire community of Oakburn, young and old, respected and admired him. I learned that he was so caring and compassionate about the well-being of his neighbors that he would even plough someone's field with his own horses and equipment if they were ill or if they were falling behind with their field work.

When Ford Motor Co. developed its popular Model-T car, George was one of the first in the area to purchase one and many-a-time would, out of his kindness, drive an ailing neighbor or their child to the doctor in Shoal Lake, some fifteen miles away along a dirt road without accepting any payment in return. That humble, God-fearing, hard-working pioneer, one of the first to settle in that area, would now be my new and permanent father. I was indeed blessed and so thankful and happy to be the fifth and youngest son of a pioneer and spend my adolescent years by his side as he patiently taught me the value of hard physical work involved in the development and operation of a successful farm. Above all, he stressed the importance of honesty, resourcefulness, and honoring God.

With the aid of his reliable team of horses, I learned the basic annual and year-round requirements of farming as well as the never-ending daily chores. On very rare occasions, whenever he felt under the weather, rather than resting in bed or relying on any kind of medication or even an aspirin, he would fill two one-gallon jugs of water from his well, work in the field till sundown, and sweat it out—always returning fully recovered.

Being multilingual and also having escaped the evil communist Russian oppression, as did his parents and most of the people around

Oakburn and hundreds of similar communities, I fit very easily into the fiber of the Canadian-Ukrainian farm life. All of us had one thing in common: We were thankful for our peace, freedom, opportunities, and being permanently far-removed from the ugly Russian barbarism.

MY NEW HOME

Tom was proud to show me the interior layout of the large house, which was finished with stained hardwood floors and ceilings. The wooden staircase leading to the second floor creaked a bit with each step we took. Situated in each corner was a bedroom with a closet. Every bedroom had a metal-framed bed with coil springs, a thin mattress, and a very fluffy homemade feather comforter and pillow. A balcony stretched across the sunny side of Tom's and Dad's rooms giving them a bird's-eye-view of the farm yard and out toward the hundreds of acres beyond. My assigned room was next to Mother's, overlooking the lush garden below and sheltered by the towering fresh-scented whispering pine trees and colorful poplar trees.

Such a cozy and quiet setting was ideal for a good night's rest, especially my room, which was located directly above the seldom used formal dining room. Most homes at that time, including this one, were erected above a full basement where the heating furnace and food storage was located since it was the coldest part of the house. I felt like a prince in this mansion—somewhat similar to my short-lived home back in Poland.

Since we had no indoor plumbing, the water had to be carried in from the outdoor pump. I volunteered to make that among my list of chores. Electricity had only recently been provided to our farm with one light hanging from the ceiling of each room. As was common in every farmhouse, the kitchen was the hub of family activities. It was the largest and warmest, where each day started and ended, where plans were laid out, decisions were made, and visitors were received—with the kitchen table serving as a place for family discussions, eating meals, doing homework, playing cards, and praying.

I was all smiles when Tom and Sandy, the dog, led me into the fenced-off main yard. Like a zoo, there was every farm animal imaginable just freely and lazily roaming about: dozens of chickens, turkeys, ducks, cats, mother hens with yellow-colored tiny chicks following close behind, pigs in their smelly pig-pen enclosures, milking cows, young calves, as well as horses. A multi-colored proud rooster strutted about as if to indicate that he was the official warden—the boss—while Sandy, accompanying our every step, kept a watchful eye on every moving creature. All of them had easy access to the water trough.

Making her appearance from the far corner of the yard, a beautiful, sleek white horse pranced in front of us with its head held high as if to show off that she was special, not like the usual farm animals.

"There she is," said Tom, pointing toward her. "We call her Baby, but she's by no means a baby. She's fast and you won't be able to ride her until she gets to know you because she'll throw you right off and then, she'll just stand there looking at you."

Dad was always first to rise, followed by Mom, Tom, and me to go about our daily chores. Sundays were always of special importance to Mom and also Dad. Everyone had to be up, get the chores done, clean up, dress in their best attire, and never be late to church. Tom, however, required a bit more time in order to shake off his usual Saturday night binge with his lifelong buddies at the local tavern in Oakburn. After repeatedly calling his name without a response, Mom would poke the wooden ceiling under his bedroom with the end of the broom handle. Determined to get just one extra minute of shut-eye, Tom, in response, would pick up his shoes by his bed and toss them across his bedroom floor, hoping that Mom would assume he was up.

Having endured this ritual for many years, Mom would wisely enact her final, fool-proof method by taking her broom to his bedroom and begin cleaning the floor, purposely banging the broom against his bed till, in frustration and grumbling, he'd finally get up. Since Tom was the only driver in our family, Mom made certain she got him behind the wheel with time to spare.

CHAPTER 19
INTRODUCTION TO FAMILY AND COMMUNITY

M y very first church service in Oakburn promised to be very, very special, and Mom was more excited than usual. The bright morning sun was warm and pleasant as the gentle breeze filled our yard with the perfumed scent from the surrounding blooming fields. Mom stepped into the back seat next to me, wearing an ankle-length flower-patterned dress and a beautiful matching babushka loosely draped over her head just above her happy face. I hardly recognized Dad in his striped grey suit, blue tie, and felt hat. With his neatly-trimmed moustache and slicked hair, he looked quite handsome, seated in the passenger side. Tom, the usually good-looking debonair man-about-town, had a crisp starched white shirt under his relatively new suit and matching tie. Wearing the blue suit that Mrs. Melnik had bought for me in Winnipeg, I jumped into the back seat next to Mom and off we drove to church.

That Sunday had been planned to be the official dedication of the new church. The village was abuzz as folks for miles gathered to attend Mass in that beautiful Greek Catholic Church with its onion-shaped dome, topped with a large glistening cross and adjoining bell tower. It was the largest, newest, and most visible brick structure, except for the towering high grain elevator on the other side of town.

We arrived in plenty of time to meet all the members of my new family: Sister Eva, age twenty-two (the youngest sibling), with her broad smile, gave me a big bear hug, as did her twenty-five-year-old sister, Phyllis. Eva's husband, Matt Hrysak (an army vet), and Phyllis's husband, Tony Tutkaluk (tall and good-looking), greeted me warmly with welcoming, firm handshakes. Tom's twin brother Joe and his wife Sophie (a former school teacher), drove there from their home in Shoal Lake. Mike, age thirty-five, with very curly hair and wearing glasses, along with his wife Margaret, greeted me with a smile and invited me to drop by their place any time because their place was only a mile away from ours. Peter, thirty-eight (the oldest sibling), more closely resembled Dad, and lived with his wife, Nellie, in the tiny village of Menzie, only six miles from home. All of them were farmers. In total, they had twelve grandchildren—I would now be their nine-year-old uncle.

As the sound of the large bell struck 11:00 a.m., everyone began making their way up the wide cement stairs through the double-door entry and filed into the wooden pews. Dad, along with all the men, carried their hats and sat on the right side of the sanctuary, women on the left. Tom, who had a rich baritone voice, always went up to the balcony to sing with the choir. I was delighted when he invited me to join him.

Mom made her way to the front, just left of the altar, to light several small candles arranged on a large heart-shaped brass fixture below the statue of the Virgin Mary (I later learned that she had purchased the heart-shaped fixture and donated it to the church).

Mom, as she often did, began singing a Ukrainian hymn without any accompaniment. Before Father Fornalchuk began the service, he addressed the congregation and proceeded to thank Mom and Dad for their steadfast faith and commitment in pursuing the adoption of a war-orphan from Ukraine.

"A week ago, a young boy from Ukraine was one of the many orphans with high hopes of finding a new home in a free land, hoping to find a new mom and dad to replace those that he lost in the war. A home is much more than a house or a place of residence. It's a place of belonging where we are welcomed and loved—a place of peace, joy, and laughter—a place of hope, compassion, healing, encouragement, understanding, moral guidance, also a place for discipline and prayer. The kindness and courage of Mrs. Mary Sytnyk and her husband, Hnat Sytnyk, to add an additional young son to their six adult children," he continued, "reminds us and brings to light that Jesus has a special place in his heart for orphans and widows. Today, that Ukrainian boy is no longer an orphan. He has a new mother and father, a new home, a new name, and a big family right here in Oakburn."

Then, pointing up to the choir in the balcony where I stood next to Tom, he said, "Welcome to Oakburn and to our new church, Alex Sytnyk. We can always use an extra altar boy whenever you're available. I'm happy to see that your brother, Tom, is already teaching you to sing in our choir."

As everyone turned to look up with applause to welcome me, I smiled and waved my hand like a royal prince in appreciation of this awesome welcome to the community.

At the end of the service, everyone was asked to assemble on the wide steps leading out the double doors where a professional photographer captured the entire congregation with the new church as a backdrop. I stood in the front row among the youngest members of the church.

That evening, when I placed my head on the soft feathery down pillow in bed and covered myself with Mom's homemade puffy quilt, I recalled a similar blissful sensation back in Poland when I was rescued from an orphanage. With eyes closed, I could almost hear Lady Elizabeth whispering goodnight to me after tucking me into bed with a very similar cloud-like puffy quilt. Deep in my heart, however, I would always remember my mom back in Ukraine telling me to run away and that God would care for me and lead me to a new home far away.

"You were right, Mom!" I whispered to myself. "God and His angels have indeed brought me all the way here, just as you promised. But, oh what an adventurous and unforgettable voyage it's been! Something in my heart tells me that He's going to continue watching over me a bit longer."

A week later, my new mom arranged for me to be baptized. Though I tried to explain that I had already been baptized four times, she and the priest both said that only this one would be meaningful.

Surrounded by miles and miles of farmland, Oakburn represented similar towns and villages scattered throughout the prairie provinces of Manitoba, Saskatchewan, and Alberta. Adjacent to the elevator was a lone set of railway tracks that weaved its way between those farming communities designed for the purpose of collecting and transporting the harvested grain to market. The church played a big part in the growth of those early settlements. Despite its small size (approximate population under 1,000), there were three churches in Oakburn: the new Ukrainian Greek-Catholic church, a smaller Greek-Orthodox church, and a smaller Roman-Catholic church. Oakburn also had a small hotel with a beer pub (frequented only by men), four small general stores, two coffee/sandwich shops, two auto repair/tire shops, two pool halls, two dance halls, an unmanned fire station with a small fire engine, a post office with limited hours, a school (up to 12th grade), a lumber yard, a barber shop, a blacksmith, and a law office.

From the time I was adopted until I left for college (a span of eight years), my new parents, by example, reinforced basic moral and ethical values as well as the rewards of hard work and daily prayers. As a new member of that kind-hearted Christian family, I quickly became accustomed to the habit of rising very early each morning and tending to the daily chores, most often before breakfast (that habit would stay with me the rest of my life). Without fail, the rooster on the farm served as the master wake-up caller who wouldn't stop until everyone, including all the animals were up and about.

As if on cue, like an orchestra being conducted, cows began mooing, horses snorting, pigs squealing, hens cackling, ducks quacking, calves bawling, turkeys gobbling, all impatiently expressing their joy in greeting their reliable provider and best friend—the old farmer and his team of helpers. Hanging around the barn, however, were the wisest of them all—the cats. Patiently waiting, they knew they'd be the first to get their share of fresh milk the minute someone sat on the milking stool and began milking the cows. I was amazed how cats and cows created a bond between themselves. In return for their daily provision of fresh milk, a cat would invariably hop on a cow's back not only to stay warm and sleep in perfect comfort, but also to scratch and massage the cow's back and, in the process, locate and eliminate any bugs or worms burrowed under the cow's hide.

Throughout the year the cats enjoyed an open season of keeping the mouse population in check, which pleased the old farmer, while the dog provided round-the-clock safety and security of the whole place. Some farmers allowed cats and dogs to sleep and be fed indoors, but Dad strictly forbade such practice, explaining that every living thing on the farm had a purpose in contributing to the harmonious balance and success of farm life, but keeping them indoors made them fat, lazy, and useless.

The first order of business was to assist in the daily chore of milking cows every morning and evening, and everyone was taught how to do it at a young age (I remembered Lady Elizabeth milking a cow during our escape from the Russians back in Poland and also milking the goats at her estate in Poland). Sitting on a short three-legged milk stool or on an upside-down old pail as close as possible in front of the cow's hind leg, with an empty pail wedged between your knees, you were ready to proceed using both hands, one squirt at a time, until there wasn't a drop left. Most of the time, the milking routine continued without incident. With the cats waiting for their share, I would aim a squirt or two directly into their smiling faces and laugh as they would quickly lick every drop from their cheeks with the aid of their front paws.

On rare occasions, a cow inadvertently lifted its filthy hind leg, and in a split-second, placed it directly into the pail partially-filled with milk. Thinking that I'd have to empty the pail and start all over again, I glanced over at Dad who told me to just lift the cow's leg out immediately and continue milking, explaining that the few germs in the milk would build up antibodies and ward off many infections—

even the common cold. I must admit that as unsanitary as that seemed to me, none of us became ill and only on very rare occasions did any of us catch cold. I learned the hard way that a cow may also decide to swiftly kick you during the milking process and send you and your milk-pail flying, perhaps under another cow, splashing milk all over yourself. Dad showed me how to prevent that from happening—by bracing my left arm very firmly against the cow's hind leg.

The men in the family, including the teenage sons, performed most of the heavy lifting and field work. Throughout my time on the farm, aside from school, until I went to college, I was happy to learn and absorb everything I could about farming and worked alongside Dad, Mom and Tom, as well as brothers Peter and Mike—especially during harvest time.

The women, in my opinion, didn't get the recognition of their tremendous value to the overall function of the farm. While the men lubed and checked their tractors and implements for the long and dusty day out in the field, the busy ladies did all the routine chores, prepared all the meals including children's school lunches, did the laundry, tended to the garden, and, at the end of the day, made time to help with the children's homework, listen to how their days went, and hear about their husbands' progress in the field. Yet, no one thought about asking the busy women about their multi-tasked day as they cleaned the kitchen and prepared everyone for bed. After having agreed to adopt me in lieu of the girl she had prayed for, Mom gladly embraced the challenges of raising yet another boy as one of her own. I could well appreciate how much more helpful an orphan girl may have been for her.

MOM'S OUTDOOR BREAD OVEN

Mom took pride in her home baking and knew exactly what she wanted: A big outdoor bread oven made of clay, just like her family had back in the old country. So, she laid out her plan in her mind and approached me one morning with her idea.

"Alex," she said. "Come with me. You and I will build a beautiful outdoor bread oven out of clay in which I will make the best-tasting fresh bread you've ever tasted. The men are much too busy, but you can help me."

I didn't have a clue how Mom was going to carry out her plan, but I was happy to assist her and appreciated the hands-on learning experience it would provide me.

First, using scrap pieces of lumber, we erected a three by four-foot platform about three feet off the ground and overlaid it with used bricks. After locating about two dozen bendable willow branches, we built a dome-like structure above the platform and closed off the end with shorter branches. We then mixed some clay and straw with a bit of water using our bare hands to make a clay compound. Patiently, we covered the willow structure from above, underneath, and end-to-end until the entire structure, including the brick platform, was covered with clay. Next we needed to create a chimney. At the far end of the structure, we inserted a six-inch coffee can through the soft clay after cutting both top and bottom lids off. Once the clay began to harden, we applied a thin layer of soft clay on all surfaces for a smooth finished touch, again using our bare hands. It looked like a miniature Eskimo igloo.

After a couple of days, with the clay dry and white-looking, Mom placed several pieces of dry wood inside the new oven, lit them on fire, and closed off the front by propping an old metal plate against it. Once hot enough, Mom instructed me to carefully remove the ashes from the oven as she proudly placed four kneaded bread dough loaves inside and closed off the front with the metal plate. She moved the metal plate slightly aside every few minutes to check the baking progress. The clay oven retained the heat at a perfect temperature till the end.

I was amazed how Mom was able to follow through with her plans for this unique creation. It didn't take long before the entire big farmyard was engulfed with the most wonderful aroma imaginable. It was so tantalizingly powerful that everyone dropped whatever they were doing and hurried over like bees to honey. Ever-so-proudly, with a smile beaming across her loving face, she gingerly removed those heavenly golden, puffy loaves and led everyone into the kitchen for a generous slice of the best home-baked bread in the world.

Prior to cutting the first slice, she scratched a sign of the cross on the back of the loaf with her knife as a symbol of thanksgiving to God, then offered the first slice to me in appreciation for assisting her.

The taste and aroma were indescribably most memorable! That new clay oven could also have served as a pizza oven.

Without a telephone or toys, playmates or friends, and being isolated five miles from town made for some lonely evenings, mostly during extended rain or snowstorms. There was, however, an old dusty organ in the house that really needed service because the air leaked out from the bellows faster than you could replenish it with the foot pedals. As Mom gleefully sang her favorite church songs, I began to accompany her while Dad took a respite from his daily toil by hitting the sack early since music was of no value to him.

Tom, the confirmed bachelor, enjoyed his time off work at the pub or at a friend's house, playing poker and partaking in someone's home-brewed whiskey into the wee hours of the morning—at times, even getting involved in some fisticuffs but always somehow managing to get home. There were times when the snow or mud on the road home would force him to abandon his car and trudge the rest of the way home. In the morning, while Tom was still in bed sleeping off the effects of the previous night, Dad would lead just one of his horses out to the abandoned, inoperative car and pull it free. He would always sarcastically remark to me that Tom boasts of his car having over a hundred horsepower, but he relies on just one of my horses to pull his car free.

MAKING HOME-BREWED WHISKEY

The long and cold Arctic wind blowing down from the icy Hudson Bay of northern Manitoba, from the town of Churchill, down Moose Lake, Lake Manitoba and Lake Winnipeg, made the province of

Manitoba the coldest of all ten provinces. Most farmers in our area kept their homes warm with wood cut from their own land and remained busy cleaning their barns and feeding their livestock all winter long.

About a half dozen local farmers (close friends of Tom's), took pride during such cold spells in distilling their own whiskey. They clearly understood such illegal endeavors may well have landed them all in jail if caught by the RCMP, but they felt relatively safe under the cover of the cold winter and heavy snow. Despite the risks, they created a very sophisticated-looking apparatus with a large boiling pot above a wood-burning mini-stove. The contraption also had a coiled copper tube condensing dish suspended above the boiling pot. It appeared ready to be launched into space! This odd-looking machine was circulated clandestinely among these friends on an annual basis, usually during the coldest month of January. These illicit partners-in-crime took an oath of sole responsibility to never to reveal one another's name if ever apprehended.

That valuable secret machine was now in the hands of Tom, but no one, not even Dad, who surely would not have allowed its presence or operation on his land, knew where he had stashed it.

One crispy-cold Saturday early morning in January, Tom came to my bedroom, woke me up, and said, "Get up, Alex. Today, you and I are going to make whiskey."

Peeking out from under my warm, cozy, puffy down cover, I was aware that it was Saturday, with no school, and Dad hadn't yet started up the furnace to warm up the house.

"Why so early?" I asked. "It's the middle of the night and it's still dark outside."

"Precisely!" answered Tom, "I'll explain later, but now, dress very warmly and bring out all those old jars of fermented fruit, a pail-full of potatoes, and load it onto the sled outside."

I had always wondered why we kept so many quart-sized jars of spoiled fruit preserves (rhubarb, crab-apple, raspberries, strawberries, and Saskatoon) in our basement year after year. Well, today the answer would be revealed loud and clear. It was show and "don't tell" time. After a quick breakfast of hot porridge, we packed a pail-full of potatoes, a couple of pork-n-beans cans and several empty gallon-sized jugs, and with a light flurry of snow whisking at our faces, we trudged through the deep snow, pulling the sled behind us into the far corner of the field inside the middle of a thick grove of poplar and pine trees with their heavy snow-laden branches hanging low to the ground.

"But Tom," I inquired, "why do we have to come here when it's still dark and snowing outside? No one would be able to find us out here even during the day."

"There have been reports that the RCMP has sent out small planes to take pictures of such remote places as these, especially with smoke coming out from the bushes," answered Tom with a cautious look on his face. "Then, they'd drive out to search the area and take us in for questioning. Dad would disown me and kick me out if that should ever happen here."

Without admitting it, however, Dad and Mom, and for that matter, everyone in town, was aware that this was an illegal activity, but they all discretely condoned it anyway. Notwithstanding the risks, a few young men took their chances and became experts in this most secretive venture.

Finally, we came to a stop and I wondered why Tom would decide to stop here. I could have walked right by this spot a million times, never thinking that there was anything out of the ordinary here. After pushing aside a few branches and removing the accumulated snow and dead leaves, he carefully peeled away a dirty, old, dark brown, weather-beaten, and heavy tarp, revealing that secret whiskey-making machine.

"Wow!" I remarked, "what a superb camouflaging job!"

"Well, here she is," said Tom proudly with some excitement in his voice, as he began checking all the components. "Pull the sled a bit closer and gather some dry wood branches so we can get started."

Obviously, he had performed this ritual before because there was no hesitation in the necessary protocol. We got the fire going, emptied all the fruit jars into the big round boiler, added some potatoes, and filled the condenser with snow. Stirring the sour-smelling mash with a clean branch, Tom instructed me to keep the fire burning and the condenser full of snow.

The white-colored steam from the boiler rising against the cold condensing pan created tiny droplets of liquid dripping into a small catch-basin with a copper tube extending to an empty jug below.

With a broad smile of satisfaction, Tom said, "See what's dripping into the jug? That's real strong whiskey—probably one hundred-proof."

Using a tablespoon, he snagged a few droplets, lit a match, and set the sample on fire to test its potency. Then, he collected another spoonful to taste it.

"Aaah, that's very good stuff. Here, Alex, taste it yourself."

It was the worst thing I had ever tasted in my life. I thought my tongue, mouth, and throat were on fire. I couldn't even breathe and immediately spit it out and filled my mouth with snow so I could resume breathing and stay alive.

Tom began laughing hysterically, "Good, isn't it?"

"No," I replied. "This is poison. How could anyone drink such an awful thing?"

"Oh, you'll get used to it in time," he replied. "It'll make a man out of you."

While the whiskey continued dripping into the gallon-jugs, Tom placed two potatoes and two unopened cans of pork-n-beans into the hot embers, and I kept adding dry wood to the fire and snow into the condenser. Using his Swiss army knife, he opened the cans and cut the potatoes in half. The joy of eating by the fire reminded me of a campfire scene in the Roy Rogers movie. After our snack, Tom opened a small round container of Copenhagen Smokeless Tobacco, pinched a small wad between his fingers, and stuffed it into his mouth between his teeth, cheeks and lower lip. Again, he coaxed me into trying some, making me instantly dizzy, so I spit it out and ate some snow. A bit later, he produced a small pack of tobacco, rolled a cigarette, lit it, and began smoking. As before, he handed me the cigarette to take a puff or two, which I did.

"No, no," he said. "You've got to inhale it deep into your lungs, like this."

Foolishly, I followed his instruction and immediately began coughing profusely, thinking to myself that he was really trying to kill me with all those poisonous things.

However, through the course of my life, thanks to Tom's valuable demonstrations and personal exposure to these vices, ever so common not only around Oakburn but throughout the country, I've refrained from tobacco and alcohol, except for a glass of wine or one beer at social gatherings. I could never understand why people would willingly put those poisonous substances into their bodies.

Tom was the only member of the family that was a regular consumer of those vices, as were his friends. They would usually hide a small bottle of their whiskey in their car or truck and share it among themselves at most social gatherings, also, occasionally, ever-so-discreetly, after church service.

THE QUAINT OLD VILLAGE OF ROGERS

All rural school-age children were assigned to complete their primary education (grades one through nine) in a small country school nearest to their township, which in my case was Rogers School in the little old village of Rogers. It was the same school where all six of Mom and Dad's children had attended years earlier. My fifth-grade diploma from Hamilton, Ontario qualified me to enroll as a sixth grader, and later transferred to Oakburn from tenth through twelfth grade.

Four miles from home, along a dusty country road, stood a small, old, weather-beaten convenience store where a hand-painted sign in the window read: "ROGERS GENERAL STORE AND POST OFFICE." A couple of old redwood benches by the entrance served as a resting spot and meeting place for the dozen-or-so local elderly folks who had been living close by ever since arriving from Ukraine. It was quite common to see several elderly men relaxing on those benches, catching up on the latest news and gossip, sipping a beer, or secretly comparing the taste of some of their home-brewed whiskey. A couple of the tiny old houses close to the store had been abandoned, overtaken by tall weeds and leaning to one side from having endured many storms over the years. Mom and Dad both had a few older relatives still residing in this tiny village where they continued to eke out a living on their small farms (probably similar to their small former Ukrainian farms).

Tom and I stepped out of our car to enter the store. A stack of about two dozen *WEEKLY FREE PRESS* newspapers held open the main door to the store. We opened the old creaky screen door, walked past a cooler filled with bottled sodas to the counter, where we were greeted by the owner who had known Tom and his family his entire life. After introducing me as his adopted young brother from Ukraine, Tom explained that I would be attending school here just as he and his siblings had done. Following a quick glance past the counter, Tom ordered a small circular tin of Copenhagen Chewing Tobacco (about half the size of a hockey puck), opened it, and placed a pinch of it under his tongue.

Upon exiting the store, we were met by a small boy (about four) pulling his little wagon behind him.

"Hey, Bobby, what have you got in your wagon?" asked Tom.

"I found a gallon of whiskey behind daddy's barn," replied Bobby. "Would you like to have some? I can get more."

With a stern look, Tom pointed his index finger against Bobby's face, commanding him, "Bobby, you'd better take this back where you found it right away or both you and your daddy will be in big trouble."

The young lad obeyed, turned his wagon with the whiskey around, and went back to his home down the lane from the store.

With a grin, Tom looked at me, shook his head, and remarked, "That's my cousin, Mike Dietz's kid, Bobby. He's always getting into trouble. I'll have to stop by on the way home and remind Mike to stash his homemade whiskey in a better location."

Directly across the dirt road, on a fenced-off one-acre grass lot stood "ROGERS SCHOOL," a typical one-room country school—one of countless like it throughout the prairie provinces at that time.

"Seems like only yesterday when my brothers, sisters, and I attended this old school," said Tom. "Let's go across the road and check it out."

We walked past the seemingly small wooden schoolhouse with a few cement steps leading to the front door, which was locked. At the far corner of the schoolyard was a small stable—just large enough to secure about four horses.

"Yep, we used to come to school with a wagon in summer and a sleigh in winter and tie up our horse in this little barn just like several other kids did," said Tom. "Now, it'll be your turn, Alex, to carry on the tradition by riding your horse to school and tying it up here like we did. I'll drop off some hay so you can feed your horse during school recess and lunch-break."

In September 1949, I rode my white horse, Baby, to Rogers School with my lunch tied securely to my belt and was ready to enter sixth grade. The barn door was open with three horses already inside. After securing my horse, I entered the school to meet my new teacher and fourteen fellow students ranging from grades one to nine. What an exhilarating experience! Everyone was cheerfully greeting one another and anxiously awaiting the start of a new school year. With a broad smile, Sam, the tallest of all, greeted me warmly, explaining that he had heard about me and was hoping that we'd be in the same grade. When I told him that I rode my horse to school, he jumped with joy and gave me a big hug.

"I did too," he said. "You must have seen my black horse in the barn. We can ride together because you'd be riding past my place on your way home. I'll show you a shortcut that will save us time."

"Sam, with your black horse and me with my white one," I said, "we can pretend to be like *Tonto and The Lone Ranger.*"

The Lone Ranger was a Fictional TV series that ran on ABC Television from 1949–1957. The Lone Ranger rode a white American Saddlebred horse named Silver and Tonto rode a pinto or painted horse named Scout.[1]

The other two horses and the wagon next to the barn belonged to the Kowal family. All four of their kids (first to fifth grade) were part of that year's class with their oldest brother Matt in charge of the horses.

Other students walked to school, rode their bikes, or were dropped off by their father or older siblings. Everyone, including the teacher, was bilingual but we only spoke English in school.

Our teacher, Mrs. Evanuk, a very friendly and personable middle-aged lady, assigned all fifteen students their seats according to their grades. With Sam and me both in sixth grade, we were able to sit next to each other in old wooden desks near the front of the class. Each desk had a small round hole on the top-right side for an ink bottle and also a side bracket for books. A five-foot high slate blackboard stretched across the far end of the classroom behind the teacher's desk facing the students. Displayed above the blackboard was the alphabet—A-Z in small and capitalized script letters—and a black and white framed photo of King George VI. At 9:00 a.m., everyone stood at attention, singing, "O Canada." At 4:00 p.m., we were again required to stand at attention and sing, "God Save the King." Though my lips sang the words, my mind drifted back to Poland and Austria where I had to stand at attention with my right arm extended toward Adolph Hitler's portrait, shouting, "Heil Hitler."

With our first day's school session ended, Sam and I raced to the barn where our horses seemed anxious to get back home. Riding side by side, our daily commute gave both of us an opportunity to open up and share about our past lives and our future wishes and dreams.

---

1. Wikipedia, "The Lone Ranger (TV Series)" Wikipedia, accessed August 2025, https://en.wikipedia.org/wiki/The_Lone_Ranger_(TV_series)#:~:text=The%20Lone%20Ranger%20(TV%20series).

Having attended Rogers School since first grade, Sam explained that Mrs. Evanuk has been his only teacher from the beginning. He went on to tell me some interesting facts about her private life that are not openly discussed. According to Sam, and at a later time verified by Tom, Mrs. Evanuk, was a single lady when she began teaching here and subsequently married one of her students. They settled on a farm not far from the school and raised a son who had since left to attend college in Winnipeg. Mrs. Evanuk had chosen to keep her private life to herself and everyone honored her privacy.

Neither Sam nor I had a saddle, but riding bareback had its advantages by keeping a rider warm in winter and avoiding the rare occurrence of being thrown from the horse with one's foot caught in the stirrup. Sam and I came up with a unique way of riding through blinding snow storms or severe freezing cold winds. We would ride our horses at a slow-walk, sitting backward, resting our hands and face on their cushiony warm back, knowing that regardless of the storm's severity, a horse would generally take the shortest trail straight home—right into the barn without any steering or prompting by its rider.

However, each of us was also prepared to be thrown off our horse without warning, head-first, into the deep snow whenever something would startle our horse, like the crack of a broken tree branch which would sound similar to a rifle shot or the disturbance of a hidden partridge nest in the snow along the trail. In that event, our spooked horses would instantly race home at full gallop without us, giving us no alternative but to trudge through the snow on foot the rest of the way.

TRAMPLED UNDER A WILD HORSE STAMPEDE

One wintry morning, while riding my horse at a slow walk to school along the usual cross-country trail, a light snowfall began blowing against my face, prompting me to pull the hood of my parka over my head. I was about halfway between home and school, in the middle of Dad's half section of land, when about a dozen or more horses suddenly appeared, charging directly toward me and my horse at full gallop, like a stampede. They looked awfully mean and frightening with their ears folded back, similar to a vicious pack of wolves. Not knowing what was to come of this, I knew that I couldn't outrun them, so I squeezed my knees and legs tightly around my horse's belly and pulled the reins tight, hoping that they would just keep running past us.

In no time at all, we were surrounded, getting bitten and kicked from all sides and from every angle. These wild horses, with fire in their eyes, were out for blood, loudly screeching in high pitch with white foam oozing from their wide-open mouths, revealing their big, yellowish teeth, aiming to take a bite out of me and my horse. Some were rearing up with their front legs high in the air attempting to strike my head with their hoofs, while others kicked their hind legs toward us. With my horse frantically jostling about, getting kicked and screaming with pain from getting bitten repeatedly and me trying to defend myself by frantically kicking their mouths with both my feet to avoid getting bitten myself, I knew that I wouldn't be able to stay on my horse much longer.

As much as we tried to break loose from being hemmed in and make a run to safety, they just kept up their vicious attack. I kicked one of them straight in the mouth with my left foot in the nick of time, just barely avoiding getting bit by its protruding bloody teeth. I saw another horse rear up with its head and front hoofs in the air coming within an inch of striking me. Next to me was another horse pushing forcefully against us in an effort to throw my horse off-balance, then raising both its hind hoofs and very swiftly, with full force it kicked me squarely against my left shin below the knee.

With my horse temporarily losing its balance and almost falling, I was thrown off and was beginning to be stomped to death. But my horse sprang up to free itself, and, like a flash of lightning, raced away. In hot pursuit, like a posse in western movies, the whole pack galloped after her at high speed, leaving me disabled in the blood-stained trampled snow. That swift kick to my shin felt like a high-voltage electrical shock through my body.

Lying there helplessly, I was thankful and happy to still be alive. After a few minutes of trying to compose myself, I felt very fortunate that those horses didn't injure me more seriously. The coast now seemed safe enough for me to get up and start walking back home. But, when I tried standing up, my left leg just buckled under me like it had fallen asleep. Very slowly, I tried getting up again and again, then realized that my leg was fractured. Lying there, surrounded by hundreds of acres of snow-covered terrain, totally immobile and no-one within miles, there was no use even attempting to shout for help. I tried crawling an inch at a time on my belly while dragging my broken leg, but the acute throbbing pain made it impossible to continue.

I had heard stories of people being found in a fetal position, frozen to death, and that it would be painless—similar to just falling asleep. Every thought of survival raced through my mind, even wondering how Eskimos in the Arctic managed to stay alive. However, I wasn't wearing a heavy seal-skin parka like them. I began thinking of my very first night alone when I escaped and covered myself with leaves for the night. But there were no leaves here, only mounds of snow and my body was starting to get colder with each passing moment. I just had to keep moving somehow to keep my body temperature up. My leg began throbbing with pain and swelling.

As I looked up to Heaven, an unusually big, fluffy snowflake was slowly parachuting its way toward me and landed on my right sleeve. It was unusually beautiful and perfectly-shaped. While admiring it, my heart led me back to the moment my dear mom tearfully kissed me and transferred me from that fearful Ukrainian warehouse into God's care.

"Mom, is this beautiful big snowflake a message from you? That God would not abandon me?"

WOULD GOD AGAIN SEND AN ANGEL?

With each passing minute, the snowfall was quietly getting heavier. I knew full-well that in order to stay alive, I just had to keep moving to stay warm. On my belly, with one elbow ahead of the other, dragging my broken leg behind me and gritting my teeth from pain through every advancing inch, I looked up to Heaven in desperation and pleaded for God to send an angel to my rescue as time was running out. I thought about my mom back in Ukraine and her profound faith when time was running out for both of us. Her parting words of assurance that God would always protect me and guide me, renewed my hope that He would not let me die here.

"My heavenly Father," I prayed. "I'm so thankful for the countless ways in which you've continued to guide me and protect me all these years. Forgive me for having taken it all for granted without consciously taking the time to kneel in daily prayer and just talk to you like a child would to his father. You have faithfully answered my mom's prayers, brought me safely all the way here, and bonded me with a God-fearing family in a free land. I thought that I could handle it on my own henceforth, but now, I realize that my life is nothing without your constant presence. Have mercy on me, dear Lord—don't let me die out here before I'm able to reveal to other people about the wonders of your endless love in my life. I want to tell the world about the power of faith in the face of gloom and evil."

In spite of my painful effort to stay alive, crawling an inch at a time, I hadn't gained any significant headway, when I thought I heard a faint voice in the far-off distance calling my name. Surely, I must be hallucinating! No one could possibly know that I was out there, in the middle of a 320-acre snow-covered field. I held my breath, listening intently, hoping that it may be real. A minute later, "Yes!" I heard a man's voice, calling my name again.

As loud as possible, while waving my right hand high in the air, I shouted back,

"HERE I AM; HERE I AM; OVER HERE; OVER HERE."

Because of the light snow steadily falling, my vision was obscured, so, I just kept waving and continued shouting as the man's voice was getting a bit nearer with every passing moment. Oh, what a miracle! "Thank you, Lord, for sending an angel to rescue me once again."

Fixated on the hazy image steadily advancing toward me, I kept wondering how God could find an angel way out here in the nick of time. Was I surprised when the man reached me and bent down to help me! It was my new adopted father.

When my horribly bruised horse had galloped home at full speed, frightful and wet with perspiration, foam dripping from its mouth and the reins loosely dangling from its bridle, he knew that something terrible must have occurred. So he immediately set out on foot to find me, hoping and praying to find me alive.

Although the falling snow had covered my horse's tracks, he knew every inch of the vast field which he had personally cleared and developed over the years and also understood which route my horse would have taken to reach home.

Like a sack of potatoes, dad hoisted me onto his back, wrapped my arms around his neck and with a firm hold of my hands, and carried me all the way home without stopping even once—allowing my broken leg to hang down, barely clearing the surface of the snow. His timely appearance in rescuing me and the warmth of his body while carrying me to safety made me feel like I was again on wings of angels. This feeling was somewhat similar to when that German officer rescued me by hoisting me onto the back of his motorcycle in Ukraine during the war before dropping me off at the orphanage in Poland.

Tom drove me over the snow-covered road to Shoal Lake Hospital (about fifteen miles from home). By now, the painful throbbing leg had swollen inside my boot. Dr. Bardell sliced the boot open, took an X-ray of my leg, reset it into place, and applied a full cast from hip to toe. The white plaster cast soon hardened like concrete, and I was able to move about and attend school with the aid of wooden crutches. During my four-month healing and rehab period, with Tom driving me to school, my grades improved significantly since I temporarily had to suspend many of my outdoor activities and devote more time to studying and reading.

Within a few days, my cast was covered with signatures and brief notes of speedy recovery wishes from all my friends, family, schoolmates, and also my teacher. I was so relieved when Dr. Bardell finally removed the plaster cast from my leg and freed me to resume my joyful farm life and my horse riding.

CHAPTER 20
END OF MY PROBATION PERIOD

How quickly a year flew by! I was ten years old and my probation period was about to expire, at which time this wonderful life may have very well come to an abrupt end as it had on several occasions before. A quick self-review of my not-so-proud behavior the past year made me realize that I hadn't been the perfect kid that I had set out to be. Some examples:

- Breaking a small window at the highest point of the attic just to see how far and how good my aim was in throwing small stones or shooting a BB gun.
- Enjoying the staggering and funny behavior of a cow as well as a pig after giving them some of Tom's beer to drink (they actually liked the taste).
- Tying my sled to a steer's tail and getting the thrill of my life with the wild joy ride through the snow.
- Switching eggs from under a sitting mother hen with turkey or duck eggs in order to confuse them once the eggs hatched. While the mother hen was trying to teach the baby hatchlings how to scratch in the dirt for food, the young ducklings just wanted to go swimming in the water.

- Skipping school along with my pal, Sam, and pretending we were The Lone Ranger and Tonto looking for outlaws while leisurely riding our white and black horses.

In truth, I was guilty of more unruliness—certainly more than needed to determine my awaiting fate. Perhaps no one was aware of my shenanigans, but I wasn't going to chance it. I had to conceive a plan that couldn't fail so that Mom and Dad would definitely want to formalize my adoption. It had to be a one-of-a-kind surprise to impress everyone, including Tom. Luck was on my side since Mother's Day was coming up. Yes, I could simply have taken the easiest route by asking Tom for a little money to buy Mom a present from town or picking a bouquet of beautiful flowers from the garden —but those flowers would've been from Mom's own garden which would not have impressed her too much. After some deep thinking, I came up with the best idea imaginable—one that no one would expect.

On Saturday night, prior to Mothers' Day, before going to bed, I located an old alarm clock, wound it up, and set it to wake me up at four o'clock, Sunday morning—plenty of time before anyone would normally rise. Placing it carefully under my pillow to muffle the sound, I lay awake rehearsing every detail of my plan over and over and hardly got any sleep as I kept checking the alarm clock every few minutes. Finally, even before the clock was set to ring, I shut it off, dressed warmly, and quietly tip-toed my way downstairs, remembering to bypass some of the old creaky steps. Then, in slow motion, I exited the house.

With Sandy close behind, surely wondering what could be happening on that dark early morning, I hurried to the barn where the cows were still peacefully asleep. As they lazily began to open their big heavy eyes, wondering what I was up to, I gently nudged each one at a time to rise and began milking them until all six were done. A couple of cats on top of the cows were also rousted from their deep sleep but I rewarded them with a bit of warm milk for their early breakfast. The next task was to separate the cream from the milk with a hand-cranked separator and feed the calves with the skimmed milk and placing the cream can into the ice shed.

I hurried back to my bedroom just as Dad was heard yawning and getting ready to rise. As soon as I heard Mom in the room next to mine moving about, I tip-toed over and greeted her with a big smile, proclaiming, "Happy Mother's Day! Today is your special day, Mom. You can stay in bed as long as you wish because I got up earlier, milked the cows, separated the cream, and fed the calves."

She was totally surprised and speechless, then gave me a hug and thanked me for being so thoughtful. Upon leaving her room, I glanced back as she sat at the edge of her bed with a smile on her face. Then, I quietly closed the door behind me and returned to my bed. That smile on Mom's face made my heart jump with joy—assuring me of a better chance of a permanent bond as her youngest son. Similarly, Dad and Tom were also blown away with my Mother's Day idea.

A couple of weeks later, when a black sedan pulled into our yard, Tom went out to greet the visitors. As expected, they were from the adoption center. I wasn't about to take any chances about this all-important final decision. Rather than relying on God's guiding hand that got me that far, I chickened out and decided to hide atop a high wood-pile until I was assured of a positive outcome. Tom came out to the yard calling for me repeatedly. He must have understood my concern and apprehensiveness in responding. Finally, much more audibly, Tom called out, "Come here, Alex, we've got the adoption papers signed and approved. Come and say good-bye to the counselor."

Oh, what a glorious day! I ran over, happy as ever to receive the news. The counselor was amazed how joyful, healthy, and strong I looked and asked about my school. I didn't say a word about my broken leg and neither did Tom or Dad, since it healed up so well.

When the Children's Aid Society car departed, I looked up in thanksgiving to God for all the angels that participated in my long journey—especially for my dear faithful Ukrainian biological mother and Lady Elizabeth.

They both brought the meaning of faith and hope to reality by their personal sacrifices, continuous prayers, and their firm belief and conviction that what they hoped for was going to happen.

TO CHURCH ON A TRACTOR

On one particularly bright Sunday morning, Mom had wanted to attend a special church service but Tom, the only licensed driver in the family, was away for the weekend. She expressed her disappointment of not being able to attend church and was unable to arrange for other transportation. Although I was only about eleven years old, I knew how to operate our old Massey Harris 44 tractor and offered to take her to church riding on the tractor with me. She was elated but Dad just looked at us like we were both nuts and walked away shaking his head.

It was an old, red, four-cylinder, forty-five horsepower tractor with a top speed of ten mph and only one metal seat right behind the steering wheel. Mom, with her babushka tied under her chin, climbed aboard, braced herself against the narrow rear fender, and with a smile said, "Let's go to church." The open-air five-mile ride was loud and bumpy, but she never complained. Once we neared the church, I parked the tractor out of sight a block away. Holding my hand, she climbed down, appearing radiant and joyful, re-arranged her colorful babushka and thanked me for getting her here. I'm sure it also put a smile on God's face.

During my final year of school at Rogers, in 1952, the black and white portrait of King George VI was replaced by a new portrait of his twenty-five-year-old daughter, Princess Elizabeth, who would now be Queen Elizabeth II. Having been a heavy smoker, her father, King George, had died of lung cancer on February 6, 1952 at age fifty-six. We began singing, "God Save the Queen" henceforth.

As fourteen year old boys, Sam and I graduated from eighth grade in our final year at Rogers School. We continued working diligently with our parents on the farm all summer long and into the fall before enrolling into Oakburn High School.

The location of Oakburn High School wasn't as remote as the smaller school in the quaint old village of Rogers. Our commute by horseback was brought to an abrupt end since the town of Oakburn had no barn to stable our horses. So, Sam and I commuted the five-mile distance to the much larger school on our bicycles. Over the next four years our interests and plans would follow a very similar path. While devoting most of our time to school and helping with the farm-work at home, we both began thinking about and discussing our plans after high school.

Meanwhile, Mom, now in her seventies, who had had enough of farming, wanted to change her lifestyle and move into town as many of her friends had done and be able to attend church on a daily basis. Dad, on the other hand, wouldn't hear of it—vowing to spend the rest of his days on his beloved farm. So, without any hesitation, Mom located a small old house with a nice little garden for herself in Oakburn and on occasion would visit the farm, where Tom, Dad, and I continued to live. That worked out perfectly fine for me because during the harsh winter months I was able to stay with her in town to attend school.

Luckily for Sam, he also was able to live in town during the winter with his aunt, Mrs. Antonyshen, who had moved into town several years earlier following the passing of her husband. While there were a variety of after-school programs and sports activities during our high school years, such as baseball, hockey, touch football, and curling, Sam and I generally rushed home to help with the endless farm-work. I must admit that I didn't particularly enjoy attending high school. I viewed it only as a requirement in preparation toward a productive career other than farming.

In our final year of high school, Sam and I met privately with our school principal, Mr. Martin, at his home, to discuss our options and potential careers available to us after high school. He explained to us that there were countless little country schools, just like the one at Rogers, throughout the prairie provinces and that there was a dire need to find enough teachers for them.

"Speaking from personal experience," he said, "a teaching career can be a very rewarding lifelong career. Most of the current little country schools will soon disappear and school buses will bring students to bigger, more structured schools where you'd be able to select the grade level and specific subject you want to teach."

With his winning smile, Mr. Martin gave each of us a warm hug, assuring us that we'd both make excellent teachers and that he'd be very proud if we chose to follow in his footsteps.

DAD'S GENEROUS OFFER

Prior to high school graduation, Dad sat me down to help me come to terms concerning my future plans. Tom, on the other hand, assumed that I would continue living on the farm and work with him.

"At seventeen, you're now a strong and smart young man with many opportunities awaiting you as you venture out on your own," Dad said. "Since joining our family eight years ago, you've learned a lot about farming and you've also excelled scholastically beyond all my grown children and certainly beyond me. Those opportunities were not open to us, but we made the most with what God provided, thankful for our freedom from communist oppression. All my time from a young age was spent right here—developing my homestead, as did our neighboring pioneers. As much as I wanted my four boys to continue their education, I needed their help and took them out of school. Eventually, they all acquired their own farmland within twenty miles from here and have become more successful than I could have envisioned. My two girls married at a young age and also live on their farms close-by."

I explained to Dad that my friend, Sam, and I had spoken to Mr. Martin, our school principal, who indicated that there was a dire need for teachers in many of Canada's country schools and that both of us would do very well in that career.

"That sounds like a good opportunity and we would all be very proud to have a teacher in our family," said Dad. "However, if you really enjoy farming and wish to follow my sons' and daughters' examples, we would be equally proud of you and assist you in any way we can."

He reiterated the many challenges, endless hard work, and disappointments from time to time due to bad weather, crop failures, frost, hail, drought, and crop-disease. As encouragement, however, he explained that if I were to pursue a lifelong career in farming, he would consider following through with a helpful plan to get me started.

Apparently, Dad and one our neighbors, John, who owned a farm close to us, had discussed me and had tentatively agreed that if I chose a farm life, they would each contribute a quarter section of land (totaling 320 acres), a number of cows, and some farm machinery if I married one of his two daughters. John, a widower, also offered to include his home in the dowry providing he could live out the rest of his life in the guest house.

"That's mighty generous of you both," I said, in total surprise (I wondered why I had never met his daughters in town or at any school functions or community dances for weddings).

"Tell me a little about them," I asked Dad.

Dad explained that John, due to his failing health, had completely relied upon his daughters to run his farm.

"I've watched them. They're just as experienced as any man, and either one of them would make a perfect wife and lifelong partner for you. Maybe they'll be in church next Sunday and you can meet them."

From the church balcony, standing next to me, Tom pointed out John and his two daughters making their way to an open pew near the front of the church. A quick glimpse was all I needed not to pursue Dad's matchmaking idea. Such arrangements were common-place in the old country and even in Dad's own marriage to Mom.

I promised Dad that I would work hard all summer-long with Tom and him while seriously considering a teaching career and thanked him for his desire to help me in any way he could.

Similar to my commitment, Sam also worked at his parents' farm that summer. Because he had full use of his family's car, he'd generally swing by to pick me up on our way to a Saturday night dance in one of the nearby towns. Like most of us farm boys, simply scanning the vast number of pretty girls seemed more interesting than the actual act of dancing. Besides, neither Sam nor I had yet learned how to dance. The most popular dancing venue in the area, by far, was at the scenic lake shore of "Silver Beach."

Since it was unlawful in Canada to dance on Sundays, the widely-popular "Midnight Frolic," as it was called, held weekly through the summer months, didn't start until Sunday at midnight, ending around 2:00 or 3:00 a.m. Monday morning. No sooner did I get home—only to see Dad getting ready for the busy day ahead. I had just enough time to change my clothes, eat some oatmeal, and venture into the field to work all day, just as I had promised. Without a word, Dad would only glance at me with a smile on his face, surely recalling the growing years of his other sons.

In 1949, when I first became a member of the Sytnyk farm family, all the field work on the farm was done through long hours of manual labor. Horses and small tractors, like Tom's 4-cylinder Massey Harris, were in regular use. Dad kept his horses busy year-round.

I often witnessed very interesting discussions between my older brothers, Tom, Joe, and my brother-in-law, Tony, concerning the ever-changing ways of farming. Much larger and more expensive machinery would soon be replacing the labor intensive and back-breaking long hours they experienced while growing up. Until then, Dad continued working with his horses as Tom and I spent countless long days and into the night combing hundreds of acres with our old Massey Harris 45-hp tractor pulling a ten-foot cultivator. At the end of each day, having been exposed to the hot sun and dust, I would glance in the mirror before washing my face. All I could see were the whites of my eyes—the rest of me was totally black with dust.

At harvest time, our family shared one large old stationary threshing machine which required a threshing gang of six to eight men (mostly all family members, including me) to keep it fully operational. Upon completing the harvesting of one family member, the threshing gang with the old machine in tow was quickly relocated to the next farm until everyone's fields were completely done. The end result in each family's yard, revealed a huge straw-stack like a rounded pyramid and several storage bins filled with prized golden grains of wheat, barley, oats, or the slippery black flax seeds.

As summer turned into late fall, and now at the age of eighteen, Sam and I followed through with our school principal's suggestion and enrolled into Manitoba Teachers College in Winnipeg. It was like a vacation compared to the hard life and endless labor on the farm. Sam was a lady's man and often took a date by bus to the city for a movie on Saturday nights. There certainly were countless attractive girls at college, and I wanted to arrange a date for myself. However, since I was neither given an allowance nor would I ask Tom or Dad for one, I set off to get a job. One Saturday, I hopped on the same bus to a job I landed at a bowling alley.

My job was to set pins at the far end between two bowling lanes. Now I was "arranging pins" so that I could start "arranging dates."

With the wooden pins flying at me simultaneously from the left lane and from the right, like bullets, it reminded me of my time in the trench during the war. There were only five pins in each lane and the black balls were about the size of cantaloupes. If it was a strike (with all the pins down), I had to quickly set them back up for the next set. Many times, only some of the pins got knocked down which I had to remove right away for the game to continue.

At the end of my shift, riding the bus back to college, there was Sam— sitting near the back, arm-in-arm with his date. Though Sam obviously had a more enjoyable evening, my temporary job commitment strengthened my resolve to remain self-reliant and productive, knowing that there would be plenty of time for dates once I graduated and began teaching.

A SAD ENDING OF A BY-GONE ERA

Coming home to the farm several times during college opened my eyes to the steady, irreversible transformation of the farm life I had fully embraced. With each passing year, much larger, more efficient and technically advanced machinery slowly began to creep in, replacing the older ones. Years later, the last time I checked, that reliable old 45-hp tractor that I had worked with was demoted to a motorized gardening and yard maintenance piece of equipment. Towering over it was a huge half-million dollar 500-600-hp John Deere monster of a machine resembling a commercial earth-mover. Similarly, the old eight-foot cultivator I had first worked with grew to ten, twelve, then fourteen feet, and kept on expanding until it became a giant tarantula-looking spider with arms spanning fifty to sixty feet wide.

The high-tech harvester/combine put all the threshing gangs out of work and those threshing machines that used to be moved from farm to farm became useless rusty relics behind the barn, surrounded by tall weeds among poplar trees. One farmer was now able to do it all much more efficiently and cover thousands of acres from his air-conditioned cab—but at a cost of about a million dollars. The upward mobility of such technological progress caused the younger, more aggressive farmers to purchase and rent more and more land.

In addition to the heavy debt to pay for all this, plus the tremendous cost of fertilizer, many young farmers got themselves in financial trouble. Had I chosen to remain on the farm, I may well have been caught up in this web.

In many ways, it was sad for me to witness this transformation. During one of my subsequent visitations to the farm, I spotted Dad in his yard casually leaning against the handle of a three-pronged pitchfork which he had temporarily anchored into the ground. As I came by his side, he continued to focus on the distant field where Tom, inside the comfort of his air-conditioned cab of his big new tractor, was about to finish cultivating a vast section of land. Dad looked at me with his sad eyes, lamenting the only life he had ever known, and

understood it was now fading away into the past like a puff of dust—
that a new generation with new ideas and modern machinery was
taking over.

"Before you were adopted and became a member of our family," he
said, "most of the work on the farm relied on back-breaking long hours
of manual labor. There weren't any available men looking for work—
we had to do it all ourselves. When the war ended, we were happy
when the Canadian government provided German war prisoners as
day-laborers to help us farmers at harvest time. An Army bus would
drop them off early each day and pick them up in the evenings. We
enjoyed having them and you would've been able to converse with
them fluently. They were all strong, young workers with a good
attitude."

Alas, Dad and his faithful horses could only watch those big machines
zipping around the field, engulfed in a cloud of dust. Neither he nor
his horses would be needed anymore. However, he also understood
and had always believed that nothing on this side of Heaven was
permanent.

Pointing to his horses, he said, "As a teenager, right here on this land,
after clearing this untamed homestead, I trudged for days on end
behind that old rusty plow you see over there behind the barn, being
pulled by horses just like these. I guided them in a straight line by
wrapping the reins around my waist or my neck while balancing the
plow with my hands firmly grasping the extended handles. I was very
happy when wheels and metal seats were later introduced. But, I'm
also very grateful, as little by little, with God's blessings, I was able to
reap the fruits of my labor, raise my family, and watch my sons'
advanced opportunities beyond my imagination."

Out of a lifelong habit, Dad continued to rise at the crack of dawn just
in time for the rooster to crow and Sandy to lead his way to the horse
barn. Each morning, after opening the old creaky wooden door—
slightly tilting off-center and suspended by big rusty hinges—his mere
comforting presence prompted his horses to greet him with a
welcoming snort and swishing of their tails.

That familiar, nostalgic scent of the dry hay and sweet clover in and around the barn and the sight of the aging, well-worn horses' bridles, breast collars, traces, reins, and metal bits hanging from rusty hooks and nails against the old distressed and weather-beaten wooden wall behind the horses would linger in his heart the rest of his life.

Each time I viited my home on the farm, I would also, as a reminder of those bygone times which I was blessed to have witnessed and experienced, walk into that horse-barn where Baby, my white horse (no longer there), used to greet me. I'd close my eyes to delight my senses and savor those joyful, most memorable growing years with that humble pioneer father. A tear in my eye always reminded me of my dear Ukrainian mother's profound faith which had assured me that God's angels would safely carry me to that special place.

CHAPTER 21
MY FIRST JOB – A TEACHER

O ur high school principal was right! There was a great demand to fill teaching positions throughout western Canada's vast rural country, Yukon Territory, and Native Indian Reservations. The starting pay was $2,000–$2,200 per year (depending on the remoteness of the school's location), payable in ten monthly installments during the school year. That seemed like a lot of money to me at the time.

Upon graduating from Winnipeg Teachers College, Sam and I made our selections, signed our contracts, and prepared to head out as new teachers. Sam went up north to Thompson, Manitoba and I chose a small country school in the village of Regent, just south of the city of Brandon, Manitoba. Tom drove me there, dropped me off at the Regent General Store and Postal Service and drove back home without getting out of his car. At first glance, this tiny village seemed very similar to Rogers, where I had attended primary school.

As I walked into the store with my suitcase, I was warmly greeted by an elderly gentleman. With a broad smile, extending his hand to greet me, he said, "You must be our new teacher. Everyone in our little community is anxious to meet you. Welcome to Regent! My name is Terry Foster, the proprietor. You'll love it here in Regent and you'll feel right at home. Everyone will be your friend."

"In addition to this store and postal service," he continued, "we have the school, of course, a small church, a curling rink, a baseball field, a grain elevator and just a few small houses. The school is next to the baseball field over there (pointing out the window). Mrs. Johnson's house sits just around the corner behind this store and she's already prepared to offer you a room to stay in. She's also a great cook, I must say."

"I'm very pleased to meet you, Mr. Foster. My name is Alex Sytnyk. You've been very helpful in answering all my concerns. This is my very first teaching position," I said. "And I'm eager to meet all my new students and their parents. I'll walk right over to meet Mrs. Johnson. Thank you for all the information."

Mrs. Johnson, a humble and friendly elderly widow, opened the door even before I knocked and greeted me with a warm smile, inviting me into her pristine home. The room she had prepared for me was perfect. Glancing at a Spinet piano in the living room, I asked if she enjoyed playing it.

"Yes, I love playing and singing hymns," she said. "The ones we sing in our church."

"That's fantastic," I said. "I also love music. Perhaps you can teach me a few songs?"

"It would be my pleasure, especially during those long cold winters," she said.

This being my very first job, I was most enthusiastic to begin day one of my teaching career.

Arriving very early, I made sure the school was clean with desks neatly arranged to face the large blackboard behind my desk. Standing by the doorway with a broad smile, I greeted every parent with a warm handshake and thanked them for leaving their child in my care. Addressing my students for the first time, I told them a little bit about myself, and at exactly 9:00 a.m., we all stood at attention to sing "O Canada" just as we would do every morning thereafter. This one room, first through ninth-grade country school with fifteen students was very similar to Rogers School I had attended only five years ago.

I made it a point to befriend every one of my students' parents, attend church with them, sang in the church choir, participate in ball games and ice-curling events, and, at their invitation, dine with them at their homes—usually on Sundays after church. I was amazed at the sincere acceptance, respect, dignity, and embrace of a teacher's position within the community. At the end of the month, when I received my first pay in cash, I was so elated! Since it was my first ever earned pay, I had never seen that much money before—a whopping $200! I laid it all out on my bedspread, wondering what I could buy that would bring me the most joy.

Having observed different bands playing at dances and weddings over the years, I had always been fascinated by the accordion because of its unique sound, world-wide popularity, as well as its being portable. Whether it's a polka, a waltz, a fox-trot, a country-western, a love song, or a sing-along, the accordion, in my opinion, added so much more depth and quality to any music. So, I arranged for a ride into Brandon, bought my first accordion for $75, and began practicing by following Mrs. Johnson's lead on the piano, learning all the hymns she played, and then I began practicing some of the many popular tunes of the time, especially the standard country songs. Several self-taught musicians in the community soon asked me to join their small band to play at house parties, local dances, and weddings. My new life as a teacher in this little community was very rewarding. In fact, it turned out to be my best, most rewarding teaching experience along with some lifelong friendships.

After two wonderful years, I was informed that the school would soon be closed for good. Alas, those small, cute country schools throughout western Canada simply vanished as yellow-colored school buses began transporting students to larger schools in more-populated towns. I continued to teach in the relatively small city of Brandon for a couple of years, then transferred to Manitoba's capital city of Winnipeg to an even bigger school.

With each move, the schools and class sizes became bigger and bigger. The personal one-on-one parent-teacher-student bond would now be replaced by bigger class sizes (three dozen or more) with bullies and unruly students, together with some unconcerned or overly-critical parents, who were just too preoccupied with their personal activities to make time for parent-teacher meetings.

After five years, my joy of teaching slowly began to wane as student behavioral and disciplinary measures took away from quality teaching time. My heart began tugging at me that a lifelong teaching career in this cold prairie province of Manitoba may not be my calling in the long run.

During one of my visits to the farm, I stopped at the village of Regent, where I left my fondest teaching memories. Mr. Foster's store and postal service was shut, Mrs. Johnson's house was vacant, and the old school was now used for grain storage by one of the farmers.

As I searched my heart for where my life would take me, a series of events began developing rather rapidly:

1). I really liked country music and, after purchasing a much better electronic accordion, I joined a five-piece country music band. We often traveled up to one hundred miles to perform at various gigs. Between rehearsals and the various performances, my weekends became fully booked and most enjoyable.

2). On the afternoon of November 22, 1963, the principal of the school where I was teaching made a shocking announcement over the P.A. speakers, that American President John F. Kennedy had been shot in Dallas, Texas. Everyone in my class and in the entire school seemed paralyzed with disbelief. He was only forty-six years old and, ever-so-popular throughout the world!

3) During an extended car trip to visit Niagara Falls, Toronto, Ottawa, and Montreal, I was driving through the city of Hamilton and remembered Bill Gorda's name. I couldn't resist. So, I stopped to check the city phone book and located the name, "Gorda's Auto Body Shop."

Recalling his visit to his parents' house with his shiny new Studebaker car and how he berated his parents for giving me a home to live in, this was my opportunity to confront him.

I drove my shiny white 1960 Cadillac convertible as close as possible to the wide-open doors of Bill's shop. With the top down to display its rich red leather interior, I stepped gingerly out of my car just as he had done a dozen years earlier with his Studebaker. Upon entering his shop, I immediately recognized him busily repairing the fender of a client's car. He appeared much older, heavier around his waist, and tired from working alone in his shop.

"What can I do for you?" asked Bill, while carefully eying my car, perhaps assuming that I needed some repair work.

"Oh, I was in the area," I said, "and thought I'd drop by and just say, hi.

Looking somewhat puzzled, Bill asked, "Do I know you?"

"Yes," I answered. "You may remember me. My name is Alex, that skinny little kid who lived with your parents for a short time many years ago when you drove up in your new Studebaker."

With his mouth agape, ogling my Cadillac, he remarked, "Well, I'll be!"

After a brief exchange of information, I learned that his parents had both passed away, that their house had been sold, and that he was still single, devoted to his work. After I drove away, I felt a bit guilty but also relieved by the sense of closure to his past disrespect of his parents and me.

4). In June, 1964, at the start of spring break, I drove up to spend a few days at the farm at home. Sam happened to be visiting his folks at the same time. We got together to review our teaching experience thus far as well as our future plans. Recalling our happy times when we rode our horses to Rogers school, we decided to drive over and see if it was still there. The old Rogers store and post office was gone but the school looked good as new with a fresh coat of paint. It was fenced off and dedicated as a historic place.

"Alex, do you remember Zane from high school?" asked Sam. "He graduated from Teachers College two years before us and has been teaching school in Portage La Prairie, Manitoba."

"Yes," I replied." I remember him very well but haven't seen him in a long while. Why do you ask?"

"Well, he contacted me recently about accepting an English-language teaching position in Germany and I'm seriously considering joining him," replied Sam.

"We thought of you, Alex, and would love for you to come with us. Considering your background, having attended school in Germany, and being multilingual, you'd be a natural fit and of great help to Zane and me," he added.

It seemed like a great idea and the timing for me joining them was perfect, since I was already contemplating my own next move. For a moment, the thought of revisiting Germany and maybe reconnecting with Lady Elizabeth, Nikolai, and Irma stirred my heart. However, considering the absence of regular communication with them, the heart-aches, painful memories, and the post-war European turmoil I had left behind, my response to Sam was swift and decisive.

"Thanks for asking me to join you, Sam," I said. "But seventeen years ago, when I was eight, I landed by ship in Halifax, Nova Scotia from Germany and stepped on this, the most wonderful part of the world. I left my memories of the war and its after-effects behind me and joyfully embraced all that God has provided for me here in the land of freedom, where hopes and dreams are boundless. This is where God has faithfully brought me and this is where I'm staying. I'm here for good, Sam."

He totally understood as I went on to explain to him the possibility of a career change, away from Winnipeg—the coldest place on earth— perhaps relocating to California. With a brotherly bear hug, we wished each other well and promised to stay in touch. As it turned out, however, I would never hear from him again. A short time after having arrived in Germany, Sam and Zane were involved in a car accident. Zane, who was the driver, survived, but Sam, who was in the passenger seat, didn't make it. He was able to make one phone call to his parents from the German hospital before expiring. His sudden departure took many of my happy, innocent, adolescent years with him—leaving me feeling so sad and empty. Such a young, handsome, tall, and wonderful friend, just gone.

MY DECISION-MAKING TRIP TO CALIFORNIA

During the long summer break (June to September, 1964), I prepped my red 1957 Ford Fairlane Convertible for a long trip (perhaps a life-changing one), all the way to southern California. With the car-top down and the warm summer wind blowing through my hair and gently caressing my cheeks, I felt free as a bird, without a care in the world, drifting along the endless open road in a west–south-westerly direction, deeply absorbing the natural beauty of the ever-changing landscape and inhaling the perfumed scent of blooming wildflowers. What a wonderful feeling—just watching the colorful farms, vast ranches, forests densely filled with a variety of tall trees, the lakes, streams, and the majestic mountain ranges moving by me on both sides of the car! It brought back memories of our horse and wagon voyage across Europe.

By avoiding the fastest, most direct highways, I chose the less-traveled, most scenic route through South Dakota, Wyoming, Nevada, and down the long California coastline. At times, I would park my car close to a slow-moving river among the whispering pines, roll out my sleeping bag, and allow the rippling sound of the trout stream and the hooting of the owls to lull me into the most peaceful sleep imaginable. With a smile, I thought of my first night alone in Ukraine when I covered myself with leaves in my quest to freedom and a new home. Here I was, at twenty-five, still in search of a new home, wondering if I was destined to remain a wanderer like a gypsy.

Awakened at early dawn by a chorus of singing birds, I was reminded that it was time to get back on the road again. I would've loved to spend much more time in South Dakota's historic Black Hills, known for its landmark Gold Rush Era, the Old West lawless town of Deadwood, and the wonder of Mount Rushmore, but my mission reminded me that I had a lot more country to see. Driving through Wyoming's rangelands and Rocky Mountains, continuing through Utah, Nevada, and scenic Lake Tahoe, I was in Northern California, but the lure of southern California's coastline prepared me to expect that the best was yet to come.

As I continued my westward journey, I stopped for a hearty breakfast at a Denny's restaurant and overheard several folks saying that President Lyndon B. Johnson would be visiting Sacramento, California's capital city, that day. I happened to be very close to the capitol building, so I parked my car and walked over—just in time to watch the motorcade slowly pass by with the president just inches from me, smiling and waving his hand.

From the Wine Country of Napa Valley, where I sipped the finest samples at several wineries, I drove over the Golden Gate Bridge to Fisherman's Wharf at the shore of San Francisco Bay—where I sat at a bench watching fishing boats unloading their catch with seagulls swarming around them. Tourists from every corner of the world filled the walkways and crowded every shop and restaurant. As soon as I sat down to enjoy my prize-winning clam chowder soup, a couple of seagulls joined me, hoping I'd share some of my crackers with them.

After a short ride on the famous cable car, I resumed my south-bound trip along the most picturesque coastline imaginable—down old Highway 1. At every turn and every mile, the most beautiful coastline beckoned me to stop and absorb such an unbelievable natural wonder.

There was no end to it! For hundreds of miles, hour after hour, through Monterey, Big Sur, Carmel, Morro Bay, Santa Barbara, Ventura, all with their quaint seaside inns, restaurants, shops, and homes above the rocky shoreline being sprayed by the breaking surf. There was no shortage of sandy beaches, seals, and sea lions basking lazily in warm sandy coves. From time to time, I'd pull over to stretch my legs and rest my eyes while gazing into the tantalizing blue Pacific, at times being entertained by schools of porpoises, the occasional pair of whales, or groups of pelicans gliding effortlessly in formation only a foot or two above the water.

I'd never been too fond of big cities. So, when I reached Los Angeles and Long Beach and looked out at the busy port with waiting cargo ships and countless truck traffic, I didn't even bother getting out of the car. However, continuing southbound past Huntington Beach along the Pacific Coast Highway, the seaside cities of Newport Beach, Laguna Beach, Dana Point, and Oceanside, all the way to San Diego with its sandy beaches prompted me to make several stops and wade into the salty water and experience its therapeutic and invigorating effect. This most southern part of California's coastline, with its vast numbers of pleasure boats, was much less touristy, and well planned out with spacious residential communities along, near, or within view of the shore. I dared to dream that someday, perhaps, I may be lucky enough to actually own a home with a peek-a-boo view of that magical Pacific Ocean.

Having spent over a month absorbing the unforgettable life-changing prodigious sights and sounds of California's 800-mile scenic coastal drive and being a mere stone's throw from the Mexican border, I decided to make a quick stop into Tijuana, just for curiosity's sake, before heading back to Canada (a distance of about 2,000 miles) to resume my teaching position in Winnipeg.

Traveling north-north-east through Las Vegas was exciting to see. Then, cutting through the north-western corner of Arizona and south-eastern Utah, across the majestic Colorado Rockies, straight north through Nebraska, South Dakota, and North Dakota, I finally made it back to Winnipeg, Manitoba. During this exhausting long return trip, in which I picked up three speeding tickets, I had ample time to think through all that I saw and lay out a plan of action toward my future. I also began to feel somewhat selfish for having enjoyed this extended spell-bound voyage all alone. Sure, it would've been nice if I could've shared and discussed all the wonders I'd seen with someone!

I decided to teach one final year (September, 1964 to June, 1965) in Winnipeg, during which time I would work on acquiring my U.S Visa and Green Card for permanent residency in California.

CHAPTER 22
A SPECIAL, MOST BEAUTIFUL ANGEL

Ron Wilding, a sixteen-year-old junior high student, required more help and discipline than the rest of the students in my class. His prior year's report card also indicated Ron's lack of ambition and disregard of school protocol. So, I arranged a parent-teacher conference at his parents' home in a cooperative effort to help their son take school more seriously by completing his homework assignments and being more attentive and responsible. His parents, James and Erma Wilding, appreciated my concern and explained that they'd been aware of their youngest son's lack of ambition and interest in school and that he just wanted to get this year over with so he could get a job as a delivery driver like his older brother, Jimmy.

"Our two older girls were excellent students," said Mr. Wilding, "but the two boys turned out to be completely opposite."

"I'll try to devote some extra time to Ron," I said. "Hopefully, I can encourage him to stay with me an extra half hour after school a couple of times a week so that he gets to understand the priority in completing homework assignments. As parents, perhaps you could think of some small incentive to offer him as he begins to show some positive signs of progress, such as a night at the ball game or hockey game? Let's give it a try."

I could never have anticipated that my visit to Ron's parents would end up turning my own life around in a most profound way for good. As we sat there, in the living room discussing their son, the front door slowly and quietly began to open. We all stopped talking. Mr. and Mrs. Wilding looked at each other, wondering who may be coming to visit them. But when I glanced up toward the door, I stopped breathing, as the most beautiful, stylish, and stately young lady I had ever laid eyes on came into the living room to join us. I felt immediate heart palpitations.

"Patricia, we'd like you to meet Mr. Sytnyk, your brother, Ron's teacher," said Mrs. Wilding. "Mr. Sytnyk, this is our daughter, Patricia."

This most charming, polite, soft-spoken, angelic young lady greeted me with the warmest smile and loveliest hazel-blue eyes. As I held her delicate soft hand ever-so-gently, I was in awe with the sheer perfection to her finest detail—her attire, her softest silky skin, her hair, her lips, her polished poise, and her manners. As if struck by lightning, all my dreams and plans came to a grinding halt.

When Patricia was just four years old, her biological mother, Aileen, passed away at age forty-two from ovarian cancer, leaving Patricia, her older sister, Audrey (six), and Jimmy (ten) in the care of their widowed father. Aileen's younger sister, Patricia's Aunt Erma, who was thirty-three, single, and an excellent cook and housekeeper, volunteered to tend to the children's needs. Realizing how much he and his children depended on and adored her, Mr. Wilding decided to make it a permanent arrangement. They were soon married, and to everyone's delight, Aunt Erma became the children's official new mom. Five years later, they were blessed with a baby boy named Ron.

I had just a little bit of a similar reaction when I was four, back at the Polish orphanage when another charming lady, Lady Elizabeth, swept me off my feet and not only changed my life but literally saved it.

Had it not been for the kind words Patricia's parents impressed upon her on my behalf, I may not have been able to see her again, as she had scores of lady friends and most likely, a special gentleman friend. My work was cut out for me and I'd better go about it very thoughtfully and gentlemanly. If only I could see her one more time to realize that she was real and not an illusion! A month later, when I came by to follow up on Ron's progress, Patricia was on her way out to meet some friends. We spent a few moments in idle conversation after which I mustered up enough courage and asked her to join me for dinner the following week. At that dinner, I relayed my desire to relocate to Southern California.

During our courtship, Patricia's stunning beauty, delicate femininity, sincerity, honesty, moral Christian standards, work ethics, sense of humor, and adherence to the etiquette of her English-Irish heritage made me realize that she was indeed someone very different and special—a rare gift.

Over the next few months of dating, during which time I would patiently describe the wonders of the California coastline and the possibility of us moving there, we were at an impasse. She was totally disinterested whenever I brought up the subject of California and would simply wish me well. I began to think that I could temporarily postpone my California plans so as not to lose the woman I loved. As much as Patricia also loved me, the mere thought of leaving the only home she had ever known and the isolation from all her lifelong friends and family (totally different from my roller-coaster background) remained non-negotiable.

Each time I came to pick up Patricia on a date, I had time to chat with her parents as Patricia usually needed a bit more time to get ready.

"Might as well get used to it, Alex," said her father. "Women always need extra time. Let's play a round of cards while you wait." I was wise enough to allow him to win most hands.

Mrs. Wilding, discreet and hospitable, always brought out a tray with a fresh pot of tea and delicate English-style cups and saucers. Her husband, with a twinkle in his eye, generally followed with one of his favorite jokes, ending the punch-line with his own laughter.

He often repeated the same joke, knowing full-well that I had heard it a number of times before but enjoying the laughter it provided.

The turning point in our dating occurred one evening when I came to pick Patricia up to join me for dinner at an exclusive restaurant called The Old Watermill (it reminded me of the one near Ludwigs Ott's farm in Germany). As she came down the stairs to greet me, she looked stunningly gorgeous—like a movie star. I gently reached out, held her hand in mine and complimented her lovely appearance. Her parents could tell how much we loved each other and understood the dilemma between us regarding my dreams for California. As we began walking out toward the door, her dad, realizing how I was smitten by his daughter's beauty, decided that this was as good a time as ever to intervene and help us confront the subject of California.

Addressing his daughter, Mr. Wilding said, "Alex and I were just talking about America, honey. Did he tell you that he's planning to move to California?"

"Yes, we discussed it several times," responded Patricia, "and I wished him well."

"Please sit down here for a minute, Patricia," said her father. "Honey, I've never told you this before, but during the depression in the 1930s, before I married your mom, there were no jobs in this city or, for that matter, anywhere in Canada. I loved your mom very much and planned to marry her and provide her the best life I could. As a trained plumbing inspector, I felt I had a good chance of finding work in America. I had saved a little money and made a bus trip to Detroit, Michigan in search of a job but came back empty-handed and eked out a living as a plumber. We got married, settled down in this very house, raised our family, and until recently, I rode my bike to various job sites. Eventually, I gained my position as plumbing inspector at the University of Manitoba."

"My three older brothers, your uncles, had a head-start," he continued. "They all moved to America before the depression and have all done well. One got a job at Chrysler Auto manufacturing, another moved to Florida, and your Uncle Seth started his own heating and air-conditioning business in Ventura, California."

Then, he turned his attention to me and said, "Alex, if I were a young man like you, I'd be going to California too."

For a minute I wondered if he was suggesting for me to go to California alone as his daughter had implied, or if he was hoping that Patricia would seriously consider going with me. As Patricia and I proceeded to walk out the door, I shook Mr. Wilding's hand. His return smile and a wink in his eye assured me that I could count on his blessing. In a short time, thanks to her dad's encouragement and positive comments about America, Patricia and I were able to seriously address her concerns. We decided to make plans to become Americans and settle in southern California.

Her dad's brief talk reminded me of Spencer Tracy's final speech in the 1967 Academy Award-winning romantic comedy-drama film, *Guess Who's Coming to Dinner*, starring Spencer Tracy (who died only seventeen days after filming was completed), Katherine Hepburn (best actress award), Sidney Poitier, and Katherine Houghton.

In the film, their daughter was engaged to Sydney Poitier, a highly respected black professor whom her parents had not previously met or heard of. He arrived for dinner, totally shocking the hosts. My situation was the opposite—the parents had to convince their daughter.

In many ways, Mr. Wilding also reminded me of Archie Bunker, portrayed by actor Carrol O'Connor in the popular sitcom, *All in the Family*, in which Archie would sarcastically and negatively comment on any subject, especially on politicians and ethnic groups of people. Since he was of English descent, he often remarked with sarcasm about the Canadian Native Indians, the French-Canadians, the Italians, the Poles, and the Ukrainians, saying that they should all keep to themselves north of the tracks (a less-desirable part of the city) where, according to him, people steal the clothes from their neighbors' clotheslines and make a second trip for the clothes-pegs. Realizing that I was a Ukrainian, he would try to back-walk his comment by saying, "Well, we're not talking about you, of course. You and your family don't come from that area and our very popular Ukrainian Mayor Juba —he's the best we've ever had."

Several weeks later, Patricia and I drove out to the farm to meet my family. Everyone immediately loved her. However, Dad took me aside to express his opinion.

"Alex, she's too frail and skinny and would never have made a good wife on the farm," he said. "In fact, her mere presence and scent of perfume spooked the cattle the minute she arrived. I think you'll do well in California and I wish you both all the best."

When we stopped at my mom's house in town, Patricia was cheerfully and warmly greeted and embraced by Mom, who immediately started bringing out some of her home-baked goodies and then began reading several verses from her old Ukrainian Bible. It was her way of bestowing God's blessing upon us. Patricia gracefully and politely gave Mom her full attention and thanked her, even though she didn't understand one word from the reading.

A couple of weeks later, with blessings of both our parents, Patricia and I became engaged, committed our lives and love to one another, and applied for permanent residency in America. On Tuesday, June 29, 1965, right after my teaching contract ended, we exchanged our vows at the United Church of Canada in the presence of close friends and Patricia's family, then, headed out to the farm where my family hosted a reception for us at sister Phyllis's and Tony's house. Afterward, we left for California—our permanent one-way honeymoon—in our new 1965 Pontiac Parisienne convertible.

Holding my bride's delicate, soft hand, I was as happy as a song-bird, never ceasing to be amazed with her beauty and charm right from the first moment I saw her.

When I heard the beautiful love song, "The First Time I Ever Saw Your Face" by Roberta Flack, I wished that I could have expressed my feelings to Patricia in the same heart-warming way.

CHAPTER 23
OUR NEW LIFE AS AMERICANS

I n our mid-twenties, now joined as husband and wife and filled with dreams to begin our new life as Americans, we placed our future into God's hands, trusting that He would guide us and bless us each day going forward.

Thinking back to when I was eight, prior to boarding the ship out of Europe, America's magnetic appeal had never left me. People from around the world, even the people of America's enemy nations, continue to risk their lives to come there by any means possible because it represents a bastion of freedom, security, boundless opportunity, growth, and adventure.

Recalling my spellbound voyage down the California coastline a year earlier, how selfish I felt in not having someone to share it with—well, not anymore. This trip would be immensely more enjoyable with my beautiful wife by my side. However, I quickly learned my first lesson in being the husband of a stylish lady: The canvas top and the windows of our convertible had to remain up when traveling on open roads and highways.

I enjoyed listening to Patricia's wondrous comments on the endless magnificent coastal scenery. Remembering my stop in Newport Beach a year earlier and my dream of someday possibly living there overlooking the Pacific, I had no doubt that Patricia would feel likewise. We stopped for a hamburger on Balboa Boulevard, took off our shoes, and walked hand-in-hand along the sandy beach. The next morning, after driving through several residential neighborhoods, I asked her opinion about living in this lovely Newport Beach area.

Her answer, however, came as a complete surprise to me. "No, I don't like it at all," she said. "Look at the people around here! They're in torn shorts, sandals, and not-so-clean T-shirts. I would not be happy living among them. It's not at all what I had envisioned and hoped for."

HOLLYWOOD

I was wise enough not to pursue that subject any further, drove up the freeway into the heart of glitzy Hollywood, and began to see a sparkle in her eyes. The short walk from our one-bedroom Hollywood apartment brought us to the main intersection of Hollywood Boulevard and Vine Street where the iconic Capitol Records tower stood. All the sidewalks in that historic part of the city were inlaid with large black granite star-shapes honoring many of the award-winning names in the motion picture and music industry.

Patricia walked into the Capitol Records tower to drop off her resume and I crossed the street to United California Bank to open our checking account. While processing my new account and discussing my immediate plans, the bank manager, Mr. Cohen, explained that this particular branch of United California Bank was one of the busiest in the city and that he needed to hire more people in the Operations Department.

"As you can see," said Mr. Cohen, "in addition to my Branch Management duties, I'm covering the New Accounts Department as well as the Human Resource and Training Department until we find someone suitable to bring aboard. Considering your teaching background," he said, "and since you're new to the city, looking to get established and live close-by, would you consider a position here at our bank?"

"Yes," I answered, "I'd like to give it a try. Thanks for the opportunity."

"Good," said Mr. Cohen. "Please fill out this Employment Application, come in next Monday morning at 8:00 a.m., and you can be my assistant in the Operations Department."

We shook hands and as I turned to leave, Patricia had just come in with a beaming smile on her face.

"Oh honey," she said, "What a lucky break! I was hired to start working next Monday morning at Capitol Records in the Data Processing Department. I'm so happy!"

With a hug, I said, "Wow, honey, that's fantastic. I'm so proud of you! What a coincidence! The bank manager hired me to start next Monday morning also. This calls for a celebration. Let's walk up a few blocks to the world-famous Brown Derby restaurant for lunch."

Little did we know that The Brown Derby was known as the place to see and be seen for heavy-hitters in the motion picture industry and the wide array of popular stars and social climbers that would regularly gather there. A steady stream of tourists—on foot, in slow-moving cars, and in tour buses trying to get a glimpse of the patrons within, prompted us to come at another time. We were told that the Cobb salad, named after its owner, Robert Cobb, became the signature dish. "Meet me at the Derby" was a common invitation among the elites from 1926 until its closing in 1985 because of a lease dispute. On our way back to our apartment, we stopped at a café near the popular Grauman's Chinese Theater, which is known for the cement handprints, footprints, and signatures of famous movie stars.

Occasionally, on her way up or down the elevator to her fifth-floor office at Capitol Records, Patricia would be accompanied by famous singers, such as Nat King Cole, Frank Sinatra, Dean Martin, Sammy Davis, Jr., The Beach Boys, Glen Campbell, Duane Eddy, and countless others.

As Assistant Operations Manager, at United California Bank, I regularly provided special assistance to recording stars and executives with their banking needs. When Herb Alpert of the Tijuana Brass or Neil Diamond would come in to open another of their many multi-million-dollar accounts, I would take a double look. Observing my look of surprise, Mr. Cohen tapped me on the shoulder and said that I'd soon get used to this very unusual activity.

The apartment unit next to ours was occupied by retired L.A. Police Detective David Russell and his wife, Delores. Our friendship with them quickly blossomed and proved to be immensely helpful to us as naïve newcomers in the vast area of Los Angeles county and its many cities. David had one son, from his previous marriage, who owned an air-conditioning business outside the city limits but they very rarely spent time visiting each other. Delores didn't have any children.

On August 11, 1965, less than thirty days after we settled into our apartment, a deadly riot in the black L.A. section of Watts broke out, sparked near a traffic stop by an L.A. police officer and nineteen-year-old-black man and the ensuing struggle of the attempted arrest for suspicion of DUI. The riot lasted six days causing thirty-four deaths, over a thousand injuries, and hundreds of buildings set on fire. David cautioned us which areas to avoid.

SAN FERNANDO VALLEY

About two years later, Dave and Delores notified us that they were buying a house in the Valley, just a short distance from Hollywood, and that we may also want to consider doing so. Patricia and I agreed that it was a good time for us to move from apartment dwellers to homeowners. So, we also acquired our cute little house with a pool in a quiet neighborhood of North Hollywood in the San Fernando Valley, about a mile from Dave and Delores and paid $23,000. After a couple of years in our new home, Patricia suggested that we should decorate the smallest bedroom for a baby soon to arrive.

"WOW!" I gleefully shouted. "What great news—a new baby in our new house. What a great house-warming gift for both of us!"

I held Patricia's body close to mine as we joyfully danced across the living room floor in celebration of the announcement. On Friday, February 27, 1970, with her little carry-on bag that she had prepared a week before, I rushed my 29-year-old sweetheart to Hollywood Presbyterian Hospital on Sunset Boulevard, and within an hour of our arrival, our six-and-a-half pound son, Jason Alexander, was born.

That miraculous sweet little bundle of joy, with wee-little fingers and toes no bigger than dew-drops and barely-open soft blue eyes, represented God's precious gift to us—to love and be loved in return, to safeguard, nurture, teach, and encourage him in the pursuit of his natural talents. His arrival automatically reshuffled some of our previous sets of priorities.

That innocent and helpless tiny baby, an extension of us, would look to us for all his needs and guidance during the developing and growing years.

Patricia left her job in order to be a full-time mom for the first three years of our baby's life. When he was about three, I came home early from work and saw Patricia comfortably nestled into the corner of the sectional couch, cuddling little Jason in her lap.

"Good timing, honey," she said. "We're all set to watch a special children's movie on TV, called *The Wizard of Oz*. Jason has his own little picnic table with a glass of milk and some cookies which he'll have at intermission. I saw the movie when I lived in Canada," Patricia said, "and still remember everything about it."

Having never seen the movie, I joined the party as the three of us thoroughly enjoyed the exciting story together. Looking at our three-year-old boy so content and happy with his warm, loving mother's arms cradled around him, I smiled and said a quiet prayer in thanksgiving of being able to watch my baby boy with his mother enjoying the kind of life and bonding that every family should have—of which I was deprived.

The Wizard of Oz debuted in 1939. It was the most loved and watched iconic film in cinema history and became an annual tradition for millions of families around the free world to watch its annual TV presentation. Judy Garland's song, "Over the Rainbow," opened children's dreams of joy and happiness.

(1939 was also a historic year when two evil dictators, Adolf Hitler and Joseph Stalin created fear, destruction and death throughout Europe, igniting World War II. I was born that same year trying to escape, as an orphan, the onslaught of those dictators.)

OUR WORST FEAR

Patricia rightfully wanted to share the joy of our baby boy with her parents and close friends in Canada as well as my family out on the farm. In an effort to ease the void of family closeness, we made many memorable cross-country trips by car from southern California to Winnipeg. Our youngster loved those car trips, enjoying the freedom of the entire back seat to play with his favorite toys and sleep with the comfort of his own pillow and blanket.

During one of those trips, in 1973, when he was three, we stopped for the night at Salisbury House, a motel and restaurant along Trans-Canada Highway 1 in Moose Jaw, Saskatchewan. It looked so picturesque and inviting!

Behind the restaurant was a pond with a few ducks frolicking about, and on the other side of the pond were a dozen-or-so quaint motel rooms. It was the last place on earth we would expect to encounter the worst fear of our lives. After a light dinner and restful night's sleep, we began gathering our belongings in preparation to check out and resume our travel while Jason played with his toys in the grass right by our open door.

"Let's have some breakfast before we begin driving," said Patricia.

"Good idea," I said. "You go ahead, get a table, and I'll join you as soon as I load the suitcases into the car."

I took a quick look to make sure that nothing was left behind, locked the room, and drove up to join my family inside the restaurant. Patricia was sitting alone at a table looking at the breakfast menu.

"Where is Jason?" I asked.

"I left him with you," replied Patricia.

"He wasn't with me, so I assumed that he went with you to the restaurant."

In a flash, I raced out to find him, thinking that I must have missed seeing him at play by our room. I checked the room and its surroundings, then frantically ran around the pond, calling his name repeatedly. Meanwhile, Patricia checked inside the restaurant, including the restrooms and kitchen, then came outside to join me.

By this time, visibly shaken with fear, we asked the manager to please help us find our little boy. He summoned his workers to check everywhere, then made an emergency call to the RCMP Using his master key, he checked every room and spoke with every person on the property. We also checked the pond over and over again. Each passing minute seemed like a torturous eternity.

As I held my trembling wife close to me, I could barely withhold my own emotional reaction. Totally broken and helpless, we knelt down next to the highway—praying, holding on to each other with faith and hope. In my mind, this had all the signs of a kidnapping, especially with the busy highway next to us. All we could do was to look up to Heaven and in desperation continue to plead for God's intervention to bring our baby boy back to us. With tear-filled eyes, we focused intently into the window of every car and truck that drove by from either direction, hoping that someone may have some news for us. Each time a car or truck stopped at the café, we sprang to our feet and rushed over with anticipation of some positive information for us but with each attempt, our hearts sank lower and lower in desperation.

About a mile or two down the road, we saw a motorcycle heading our way and assumed it must be the RCMP responding to our call. However, there was no accompanying flashing red light or siren.

As the sound of its motor decelerated and began turning toward us, a young bearded biker stopped right in front of my wife and me, then glanced behind him and said the sweetest, most heavenly words we could ever have hoped for:

"Are these your parents?" he asked.

Behind the biker was a tiny passenger, holding on very tightly. It was our dear little boy, delivered to us safely by a young bearded angel—not with wings, but with a motorcycle. With tears of uncontrollable joy, thankfulness, and jubilation, after wrapping ourselves around our most precious gift which God returned to us, we also embraced the biker and showered him with kisses and the longest bear-hug he had ever experienced. He explained that when he saw a little boy running as fast as he could down the highway, waving his arms for a lift, he decided to pitch in and help. This reminded me of the time when Nikolai, riding on his motorcycle, picked me up in Ukraine at the railroad tracks. He then took me to safety across the border into Poland, dropping me off at the Polish orphanage.

"Yes, Mom," said Jason. "I was playing in the grass by the motel and saw dad locking the door and driving away. Thinking that you and Dad had left without me, I began running down the highway as fast as I could to catch up to you."

The biker said that he could see the urgency and sincerity in the little boy's demeanor and decided to hoist him up and race down the highway for several miles to catch up to us but then wisely decided to turn back to the motel. We offered to reward him and also treat him to a meal, but he refused and drove off.

It took a while for Patricia to release her tight embrace of her baby boy. As I watched the biker slowly disappearing into the horizon, my mind drifted back to my own motorcycle ride behind a German officer when I was the same age as our son.

We thanked the motel manager for his and his staff's assistance and asked him to please notify the RCMP with the good news. The three of us were so grateful and ecstatic for this miraculous outcome that we forgot all about breakfast, jumped into our car, and spent the rest of the day trying to quell the stressful ordeal we had all endured. We were so thankful how the Lord turned our greatest fear into the most wonderful and joyful blessing. Instead of putting our son in the back seat as usual, Patricia put him on her lap and held him close to her bosom until the next stop.

That frightful event we experienced in Moose Jaw made us realize that the tender love of a parent—especially that of a mother—for a child may be the purest and most sacrificial kind. There is no greater pain than losing a child. Nothing can compare to it, no matter the child's age. We had just experienced a brief jolt of that kind of pain, but to carry such an unbearable deep wound of losing one's child—a wound that would never heal through the rest of that parent's life—would be like walking around with a knife permanently wedged in one's heart.

My current mother lost two of her children: her two-year-old baby girl, Tina, and her adult son, Michael, who had been suffering from Multiple Sclerosis (MS) and passed away at age sixty-three.

Yet, such tragedy failed to undermine her continued deep faith, her daily devotional prayers, or her decision to step up and be a mother to a war orphan.

CHAPTER 24
ESCAPING THE SMOG

L ike everyone around us in the Los Angeles basin, we reluctantly had come to accept the Los Angeles, Hollywood, and Valley smoggy air quality which, many-a-time, caused our eyes to itch and burn. Thinking about those pure tiny lungs of our young baby as well as our own health concerns of breathing that on a daily basis, I felt that I had to step up and make some hard choices. David and Delores, both having spent their lives there, kept telling us that we'd get used to it, also explaining that the adjoining Riverside and San Bernardino counties, east of L.A., were much smoggier.

Having given up her job at Capitol Records in order to devote all her attention to our baby's needs, Patricia spent much of her time with Delores, who adored her and our baby like her own family. David, like an uncle, likewise opened his heart to us. He owned a tiny, very basic oceanfront cabin in Ensenada, Mexico and invited me along to enjoy deep-sea fishing in the Mexican Pacific Ocean.

I was impressed how fluently he communicated with the locals on the fishing boat and in the village. Toward evening and into the night, as the two of us strolled along the narrow old cobblestone streets, the festivity of Ensenada began to reverberate its historic celebratory past

—reminiscent of many scenes from old Western movies. Happy older women, dressed in traditional colorful dresses, kneaded small portions of dough on their portable taco stands. The irresistible, tantalizing aroma of baked tacos, in addition to the misty whiff of tequila and the romantic sounds of Ranchera music floated through the air from all directions.

Among the many cantinas, the most popular one was Hussong's. Dave and I walked in to join a crowded group of locals (mostly wearing dirty old cowboy hats) and Gringos (a derogatory term for Americans who were not Hispanic). After ordering a couple of bottles of Dos Equis Cerveza and freshly baked tacos, a strolling Mariachi band, consisting of a violin, a concertina, a trumpet, and a bass guitar, approached our table. Dave tipped the band, requested a traditional song called "Jalisco," and sang it along with many of the patrons.

When I asked how he acquired his fluency in Spanish language, he reminded me that as an LAPD officer and detective, one learned the language very quickly because the city had among the largest Spanish-speaking population in America. That memorable experience reminded me of my fishing trip with Mr. Gorda in Canada. We spent most every holiday with David and Delores, and when it came to Thanksgiving and Christmas, Delores went all out to decorate her house and prepare the finest array of food and gifts. They were just the warmest and dearest friends to us.

On Easter Sunday, 1973, David's sister, Sue, and brother-in-law, Bill, invited us to join them along with their adult children and grandchildren for Easter dinner at their beachfront home in Sunset Beach (just north of Huntington Beach). We thoroughly enjoyed this special celebration at the beach, including the traditional egg-hunt for the kids, the delicious variety of food accompanied by the constant sound of the breaking waves, and the clean smog-free, salt-scented ocean breeze. David asked his sister and her husband why they never wanted to come up and visit him and Delores in the Valley. Bill's answer was quick and to the point, "We don't want to spend any time in that heat and smog." That comment was my cue not to put off any longer those very same concerns that I'd been wrestling with.

Soon after our Easter visit to Sunset Beach, as the usual heat and smog was again beginning to overtake the valley and the L.A. basin, I explained to Patricia that I would be looking into a healthier, smog-free place for us to live. She responded with a very similar answer to the one about moving to California when we were dating.

"You go right ahead and look, but I'm happy right here. We've got a cute little house, all our friends are here, David and Delores are like family to us, I've got a pre-school picked out for Jason, and our doctor, dentist, and hospital are all near us."

Over the next few weekends, I began my search for an affordable home near the coast, away from the heat and smog, and perhaps even with a bit of an ocean view. I started out in Santa Monica and worked my way down through Long Beach, Sunset Beach, and Huntington Beach until I eventually came to the intersection of Coast Highway and Balboa Boulevard in Newport Beach—the same intersection where I had originally brought Patricia during our honeymoon in 1965. Instead of driving down the popular, congested Balboa Peninsula, I turned left on Superior Avenue, proceeded up a slight incline, and saw a Grand Opening sign of a newly-completed housing development called Newport Crest, within walking distance to the beach.

The salesman, Mr. Miller, showed me an artist's rendition of the master plan, then invited me to ride with him in his golf cart, pointing out the luxurious pool and tennis court in the center of the development, its fine amenities, as well as its proximity to the beach, the new Hoag Hospital, and the rest of the city.

"This is a new condominium development with two units sharing a common wall," he explained, "The purchase price per unit is $50,000 and those with a view are $5,000 more."

Back at the office, he went on to explain to me that during the month-long Grand Opening celebration, only a 5 percent ($2,500) down payment was needed to purchase one of the many available homes.

He opened and showed me four or five of the best-located units. I was stunned by how good the view was in each of them.

When I stepped out to the balcony, I could hear the waves crashing against the shore at the bottom of the hill where rows of old waterfront homes were crammed close to each other.

"Let's do it," I said. "I just hope I can qualify for the financing."

A few minutes after my application was approved, Mr. Miller said, "Alex, your credit score is so good, you could buy a second unit if you wished and rent one of them out. Since Hoag Hospital is only two blocks from here, you'd never have to worry about a vacancy. If you decide to buy two units, we'll waive the additional $5,000 charge for the view."

"It's a deal," I said. "Here's my deposit check for $5,000 for two side-by-side ocean view units."

"Congratulations, Alex," said Mr. Miller, as we shook hands. I guarantee you that those ocean view homes will be gone very quickly. You'll be glad you acted now."

On my one-hour drive home, remembering Patricia's response from nine years earlier about living near the beach, I had to be careful not to upset her with my acquisition. Patricia was starting to prepare dinner when I came home, and Jason was playing with his toys on the family room floor. I embraced her and swept her off her feet in jubilation.

"Honey, you won't believe it but I found a great business investment for us," I said. "Two side-by-side new condominium rental homes in Newport Beach with a view of the ocean and only two blocks from one of Orange County's biggest new hospitals, which will aid in providing tenants with its countless medical staff. Why don't we drive out there next weekend and check it out?" Patricia was happy about the condo purchase, and I was wise not to discuss my hopeful intent to make Newport Beach our future home.

The following weekend, as usual, was hot and smoggy in L.A. and the Valley—a perfect time to take a drive to Newport Beach. After walking through the decorated model home next to the sales office, our salesman, with his golf cart, took us to our two newly-purchased units and pointed out the up-to-date amenities in the kitchen and the rest of the home. When we stepped out to the balcony overlooking the blue ocean, with the sound of the surf and the scent of the fresh breeze, I withheld my comments—just enjoying Patricia's awe-inspired reaction.

"Look out there," said Mr. Miller excitedly, pointing straight out toward the ocean. "Can you see those two whales, out there? They're heading north for the summer."

That was the clincher! Nothing else needed to be said by me or Mr. Miller. Patricia looked at me and asked, "So, you're planning to rent out these two places?"

"Yes," I responded. "I don't think it'll be a problem, considering the view, location, and proximity to Hoag Hospital."

"Well, honey," said Patricia, "I love all the new kitchen appliances and carpeting. I agree that the closeness to the ocean, the fresh sea air and the view would make it easy to rent out. Perhaps we should think about moving into one of these homes ourselves?"

In response, I said, "I was thinking the same thing. We could probably sell our house in the Valley for almost the same amount as one of these units. Why don't you decide which one of these you'd prefer to move into?"

When Mr. Miller handed us the keys, he also presented us with a complimentary membership to the famous Balboa Bay Club as a gift in welcoming us to Newport Beach.

"The Bay Club, located on Coast Highway, is in the heart of Newport Beach, only a mile down Pacific Coast Highway," he explained. "It is recognized throughout America as a place patronized by movie stars, like John Wayne, Buddy Ebsen, Joey Bishop, and others who also own homes and boats here. The club offers a fine restaurant, a tennis court, a sauna for men and one for women, as well as a place for children to play in the sand. You will all enjoy it for years to come—I promise you."

I had recently joined a retail chain as H.R. (Human Resource) manager, Patricia was an instructor at Valley Business College close to our home in the Valley and Jason had started pre-school.

In the next thirty days, our life would be turned on its end. Because of the fast-moving events during my childhood, I had become accustomed to such sudden changes with inbred trust and subsequent rewarding joy. But my wife's steadfast, normal upbringing hadn't prepared her for this or for the continuing challenges of living with me.

We didn't even have a chance to say goodbye to our dear friends, Dave and Delores. David was in the hospital suffering with a serious aneurysm and Delores had died in her sleep at her home a week earlier. I continued to stay in touch with David during his confinement at Kaiser Hospital. In our final conversation, he informed me that he would be moving in with his son whenever he got discharged from the hospital, as he would no longer be able to function alone in his home.

We sold our Valley house for $49,000, close to the price of our new place in Newport Beach. Patricia ended her job at the Valley Business College and took our son out of pre-school to enroll him into a pre-school located within a short walk from our new home. I continued my work as H.R. manager in the retail chain, commuting between its many stores. As we were moving in, I stopped at the sales office to thank Mr. Miller for all he had done for us with the purchase of our new home.

"Do you have a minute, Alex?" he asked. "I told you that these places would sell out quickly. We have only two ocean view homes left. If you're interested, we'll honor the same arrangement we gave you before, even though the prices have since risen."

"With the proceeds from the sale of our Valley home, I think we can swing it. I'll discuss it with my wife and give you my answer by tomorrow."

We bought them, and a few months later acquired two more new condos in another new development called Jasmine Creek in Corona

Del Mar and rented them out too. Patricia, by nature, had always been more pragmatic, not the risk-taker that I'd grown up to be. She openly expressed her concerns but always supported me and never ridiculed me later for decisions that didn't quite work out as planned, always giving thanks to God for His providence.

CHAPTER 25
AS A REALTOR

Getting hooked on the real estate potential, especially in the exclusive Newport Beach area, I acquired a realtor's license and learned the skills of marketing, negotiating, selling, listing, exchanging, leveraging, financing, leasing, leasing with option to purchase, tax lien certificates, and property management. I also attended the Orange County Property Auctions and bought a couple of houses at less than half their value—renting one out and reselling the other one for a quick profit in less than thirty days.

After having successfully listed and sold a client's expensive home in Newport Beach in record time, the owner, Mr. Allen, asked if I knew of anyone who'd be interested in buying his truck stop in L.A.

"I'll be happy to look it over," I said, "and inquire with my sources or refer you to a commercial broker for that area."

The next day, I met Mr. Allen at his truck stop, and after completing a report on its assets, liabilities, income, expenses, and method of operation, we decided to discuss it further over lunch at a nearby coffee shop.

"You can see that this is a good cash business," he said. "I bought this simple truck stop business for my son, hoping he'd settle down and manage it. Unfortunately, he dropped the ball, got into some bad habits, and even left his wife and kids. I'm getting out of California and moving into my new house in Las Vegas where I own another truck stop. I'm also in the process of acquiring a motel in nearby Henderson. I've decided to put all my time and assets in Las Vegas and need to divest myself of this truck stop—my only remaining responsibility here in California."

"Alex, would you consider managing this truck stop for me until you find a buyer?" he asked. "Looks like you're a fast learner and a man of your word. I'll introduce you to my foreman, and once you see how simple the operation is, you may want to own it yourself and if you do, I'll even carry the financing for you."

Well, I couldn't resist. Managing the truck stop was a no-brainer and the financial rewards were very attractive. A year later, in 1974, Mr. Allen came by the truck stop and seemed quite impressed by how efficiently I managed it.

"Let's go get some lunch," he said. "I'd like to tell you what I've been doing in Las Vegas."

After we ordered lunch, he began explaining how well his motel acquisition in Henderson turned out and how Las Vegas and the surrounding area was booming. On a paper napkin, he drew a rough sketch of all the forthcoming planned developments and the massive ongoing construction projects taking place.

"I recently bought a vacant piece of property off the 15 Freeway in North Las Vegas," he said.

On another paper napkin, he sketched the layout of a new truck stop he had just built—an all-inclusive Truckstop with self-service fuel, a coffee shop with slot machines, and a truck cleaning service.

"I was hoping that my son would manage it, but he left me holding the bag just as he did in L.A. I currently have several irons in the fire," he continued, "and don't have time to oversee the truck stop operation. Now that you understand how simple and lucrative the business is, why don't you drive up to Vegas and see what you could do with it. If you're interested, I'll offer to carry the financing of the entire package for you, including the business and the property."

The following weekend, I drove out to inspect it. We shook hands in agreement. Prior to assuming the business, I had to appear before the Nevada Gaming Commission in Carson City to transfer the slot machines into my name, get a liquor license, and a food and beverage sales permit. Not planning to be a full-time operator of the truck stop, I wasted no time in finding a lessee that agreed to operate it with a Lease/Option agreement.

Naturally, each new acquisition came with added management time, stress, travel, maintenance costs, taxes, employee, tenant problems, and unforeseen surprises. I simply reasoned that over time, the property values and income would simultaneously increase, making it all worthwhile. I also had an exit strategy—selling, leasing, or exchanging each and every location when the time was right. Overlooking the two truck stops and our rentals, driving hundreds of miles each week, coming home later and later while pursuing my seemingly selfish ambitions, I relished the euphoria it provided me, believing that there was no downside to my ventures.

I didn't have much time left to spend with my God-given, beautiful young family, and almost none for my spiritual nourishment. I didn't take time to stop to honor or thank the Almighty God, who, in spite of my lack of experience, limited funds, and naivety, had patiently allowed me the freedom of doing it my way, yet kept a watchful eye that I didn't squander it all, especially the love of my faithful wife, my marriage, and the development of my growing son. My sweet Patricia enrolled our son into a private school near our home and accepted a teaching position at Orange County Business College in Anaheim. She sensed that my exuberance and excessive time spent away from home would ultimately affect our family bond and our son's important father-son connection.

Through quiet and, at times, tearful prayers, she asked for the Lord's help to intervene. In the meantime, she took the initiative to ensure that our son would not be deprived of a spiritual upbringing. She arranged children's Bible-study classes, camping trips, and church-related volunteer work for him, thereby planting enough of a seed in his young heart to later mature into a handsome, upright, moral, and God-loving adult.

CHAPTER 26
A HARSH DIVINE DISCIPLINE

D iscipline, according to Webster's dictionary, is "a form of punishment to correct, mold, train, develop or perfect mental faculties or behavioral and moral character."[1]

God heard and answered Patricia's prayers. In 1976, driving my shiny silver Jaguar XKE sports-car through the city of Pico Rivera, heading to L.A., I stopped at a red light at an intersection. When the traffic light turned green, I began crossing the intersection, but God stopped everything right in the middle of the street. In less than the blink of an eye, I was at death's doorstep.

As paramedics were frantically trying to bring me back to life, the fire department engaged the "jaws of life" machine in an effort to remove me from the heap of twisted metal that only moments earlier was my symbol of success—and now looked more like an oversized metal pretzel. A large crowd gathered to witness the aftermath of a horrible car accident resulting from a large old station-wagon that, according to several eye-witnesses, had run the red light at full speed ramming directly into the driver's door where I was seated.

---

1. Merriam-Webster, "Definition of discipline," *Merriam-Webster Dictionary*, accessed July 14, 2025, https://www.merriam-webster.com/dictionary/discipline.

One of the paramedics quickly sprayed both cars with a fire retardant, the other one hurriedly applied an oxygen mask over my mouth and nose, and with large scissors cut away my coat, shirt, and tie in order to help relieve the pressure from the wooden steering wheel sunk deep into my chest. The noxious smell of gasoline and burnt rubber permeated the entire area. Millions of tiny particles of glass covered my entire body—through my hair and neck, into my ears, under my armpits, even inside my pants and shoes. Unable to breathe, I could feel my broken ribs cutting against my lungs and heart. The excruciating pain throughout my body, mostly my head, left femur, and chest (which absorbed the direct impact), caused me to pass out.

Following the high-pitched blaring ambulance sirens and pain shots, I awoke briefly in the Pico Rivera Community Hospital where wires, tubes, and a beeping heart-monitor were quickly attached to me. It became clear to me that my time was up and that I wouldn't last much longer. With every bit of strength left in me, I turned my attention to the Lord, and I tearfully begged His forgiveness for having walked away from Him, instead following my own choices that led to my selfishness, foolish pride, greed, and disregard to His abundant providence.

"Dear Lord," I prayed. "Considering my mom's profound faith when she placed me as a tiny tot into your care in her final hour, I've turned out to be a big disappointment to her, to all the angels that protected me and cared for me, to my wife, and most of all to you, Lord. I totally deserve this punishment. Father in Heaven, hear my prayer—I humbly ask for your forgiveness.

If this is to be my final hour at the age of thirty-seven, I only ask that you comfort and protect my wife and help her raise my young boy. Please guide him and hold him close to you as you've so faithfully and patiently watched over me all these years."

As they wheeled me into the emergency room for X-rays and tests, one of the doctors asked if there was anyone they could notify on my behalf.

"Yes," I whispered. "Please send for a priest so I could receive my Last Rites."

"What about your immediate family, your wife, or next of kin?" inquired the doctor.

"No, please do not call my wife just yet," I whispered. "It'll just upset her seeing me in this hopeless condition during the final moments of my life and not being able to help me. I deserve this, but spare her the bad news a bit longer and call her when I'm gone. I'm not worthy of her tears and pity. Just get me a priest and please hurry. I don't have much time left."

Very soon, a young priest was at my side, deep in prayer, and I was prepared to meet my Lord Jesus. I felt at peace, warm, and comfortable —ready to meet my Maker. The doctors concentrated on my heart by closely observing the heart monitor, but totally ignored my internal bleeding and broken ribs. While they kept checking all the tubes and wires, my whole life flashed by like a video in fast-forward. I saw an image of myself—as that little orphan boy running to safety and wandering aimlessly through the war zone of Ukraine. Then, that image of me transformed into my own little boy—my Jason, similarly wandering aimlessly through life's rough terrain as an orphan. When the doctor injected more pain-killers, the image of Jason slowly began fading away but not before I heard him cry, "Dad, I barely got to know you. You were always so busy with work. Are you now going to leave me as an orphan just like you were?"

Several hours of unconsciousness must have passed when the soothing touch of a soft hand on my cheek felt like someone in Heaven was reaching out to greet me. As I slowly opened my eyes, the sweetest angel, my dear Patricia, was at my bedside. Tears flooded my eyes from the sheer joy of seeing her one more time, even if only for a brief moment.

Ever-so-thankful and relieved to see me still alive, she experienced an instant surge of power and resolve. Not yet knowing my condition, she became very concerned about all the tubes, suspended liquids dripping into my veins and nose, and the beeping heart monitors. The doctor foolishly assured her that I would soon be as good as new, except for my bruised head, leg, and fractured ribs. My whole body remained in a state of shock and my color was deteriorating before her eyes. She wisely determined that this small Pico Rivera hospital was not adequately equipped to help me. Rather than asking for a second opinion or arguing with the doctor, who seemed to treat my condition much too lightly, she took matters into her own hands.

By then it was getting dark. She contacted our neighbors, Kathy and Dave Lenton, imploring them to help transport me in their Volkswagen van to Hoag Hospital in Newport Beach without delay, and she would be waiting for them to accompany me. Once the nurses laid me into the back of the van, Patricia sat next to me and held me steady during the one-hour drive back. Both Kathy and Patricia were in continuous prayer as I groaned in agony at every turn or bump in the road.

Doctor Orin J. Riddell admitted me into the emergency ward of Hoag Hospital, which was only a couple of blocks from our home. When Patricia, with Kathy by her side, presented the medical report from the Pico Rivera Hospital to Dr. Riddell, he quickly read it and shook his head in disbelief, took a closer look at me, and rushed me right into the operating room.

A few minutes later, Dr. Riddell re-emerged and explained to Patricia, "Your husband has been bleeding extensively internally for some time. His belly is bloated abnormally, and his stomach is pushed to the side because of the bleeding. I can't tell if it's his liver, kidneys, or spleen, but I must open him up immediately."

Poor Patricia was crying and trembling with fear, while her friend Kathy did her best to console her. We had no family in California, and there wasn't any time to call our parents in Canada for support. Realizing the dire urgency of the situation, Kathy telephoned her step-father, who was a retired pastor, to rush over in support and prayer. They all joined hands as he so eloquently led a very spiritual prayer of hope and faith by invoking upon God's mercy and healing power. He also read a few select passages from a small Bible he had brought with him as, together, they continued in prayer throughout the operating procedure.

About two hours later, the door from the operating room finally opened and Dr. Riddell re-emerged. After removing his surgical mask, the smile on his face was like a message from Heaven, that my wife's and her friends' prayers had been answered. Addressing Patricia, Dr. Riddell summarized the entire surgical procedure.

"We opened him up. There was so much blood in him that his stomach and vital organs were pushed to the side. I literally scooped the blood out with my hands so that I could locate the source of the bleeding. Fortunately, none of his vital organs were damaged. His spleen, however, was ruptured from the impact of the accident, causing continuous bleeding. We removed his spleen and he can live a normal life without it. We also replaced some of the blood he lost. However, most of his ribs are broken and can only heal on their own from within. His head and left leg are severely bruised. He'll be in a lot of pain for some time, but because of his overall healthy body, physical strength, and young age, he'll soon recover."

Then, Dr. Riddell held Patricia's trembling hand and said, "Your husband is a very lucky man. Had you not brought him here when you did, he may not have survived till morning."

After the anesthesia began to wear off, I felt a very familiar, ever-so-soft and gentle touch on my face. I opened my eyes to be greeted with the warmest, most wonderful smile imaginable. My lovely angel, my Patricia, through faith, prayer, hope, and the loving support of her friends, followed God's direction and saved my life. Apart from the ten-inch zipper down my belly, which would remain as my constant disciplinary reminder, and the ensuing pain that would hopefully begin to subside, my spirit, focus, and priorities would immediately be reset for the better.

By the grace of God, my wife wasn't going to be a young widow, and our little boy wasn't going to grow up as an orphan. How marvelous—that in addition to saving and renewing, God can turn a loss into a gift that is even more beautiful and precious than before.

In the movie, *City Slickers*,[2] starring Billy Crystal and Jack Palance[3] (one of my favorite actors, whose parents were Ukrainian immigrants), Jack takes the part of a tough trail boss and asks Billy, "Do you know what the secret of life is?"

"No, what is it?" asks Billy.

Without even a word, Jack simply looks at Billy and holds up his index finger.

Billy asks, "What—your finger?"

With his index finger still pointing up, Jack answers, "One thing—just one thing."[4]

"What is that one thing?" asked Billy.

To which Jack replied, "That's what you gotta figure out. When you do, stick to it, cause that's all that really matters."

Anyone who comes close to losing the most precious gift of all will clearly realize what that one thing is. Most certainly it would not be a valuable possession or a supposed power. When a reporter on the street recently asked different folks what the most important thing in their life was, what one thing they simply could not afford to lose, surprisingly, most of them answered, "Oh, my smartphone, of course! I can't live without my smartphone. My whole life depends on it."

Two to three days following my operation, I was fully alert but my inner and outer body was acutely painful. The most basic attempt to inhale a shallow breath—just a hint of air into my lungs or to move an inch in any direction felt like my ribs were being broken anew. With

---

2. Wikipedia, "City Slickers," Wikipedia, accessed August 2025, https://en.wikipedia.org/wiki/City_Slickers#:~:text=table%20of%20contents-,City%20Slickers,-29%20languages.

3. Wikipedia, "Jack Palance," Wikipedia, accessed August 2025, https://en.wikipedia.org/wiki/Jack_Palance#:~:text=table%20of%20contents-,Jack%20Palance,-55%20languages.

4. Gregory Scott, "The meaning of the one thing in *City Slickers*," Gregory Scott Blog, accessed August 2025, https://www.gregoryscottblog.com/the-meaning-of-the-one-thing-in-city-slickers/.

prayer, God's miraculous healing power, and my inbred grit and determination, I was going to get out of that hospital bed one inch at a time in spite of the resulting torturous pain. A week later, I wasn't even able to sit up yet, but very slowly, I was able to lower one foot to the floor. After many more tries, gingerly, I stood upright and made my first, although very, very short, step forward. I was on my way to recovery.

While dragging along an assortment of tubes and liquids suspended on a wheeled portable lightweight stand, I kept increasing the length of my trek around the hospital hallway on the seventh floor, always glancing out through a window at the beckoning blue ocean in the horizon.

On several occasions, I stopped to observe a tiny white triangular-shaped image of a sailboat a couple of miles off shore, lazily gliding along the sparkling blue sea. It made me realize that I had become so preoccupied with myself that I overlooked such simple family pleasures available to us right here in Newport Beach. Imagining the thrill of the three of us sailing to Catalina Island, dropping anchor close to the shore, swimming, snorkeling, barbecuing, and being rocked to sleep with the soothing gentle rippling sound of the water lapping against the side of the boat—Oh, I had some catching up to do after I got home.

After about ten days at the hospital, when Dr. Riddell again came to examine me, he was taken aback with my speedy rate of recovery and said, "You are healing extremely well. It's a bit soon, but would you like to go home, Alex, and be with your wife and son in time for Easter? We'll call your wife to pick you up tomorrow morning and schedule a post-op visit to remove the stitches within the next two weeks. I know you're anxious to get back to normal. You'll be in pain for a few months but you'll be fine. May you and your family enjoy a happy Easter together!"

Approaching our driveway and seeing my jubilant young son running to greet me, excitedly calling, "DADDY, DADDY," filled my eyes with tears of joy. As much as I wanted to toss him up into the air and smother him with a bear-hug on his way down, it would have to wait. Patricia explained to him that I needed time to heal. For a moment, as I slowly walked into the house, I felt like I was a visitor—a stranger in my own house—that I no longer was its rightful owner but was granted a second chance by God. Just the joy of being alive, back with my Patricia and my little boy was all that really mattered. After Easter Sunday church service, we attended the Balboa Bay Club's Annual Easter Egg Hunt and enjoyed watching dozens of youngsters, including Jason, scrambling excitedly about the sandy playground in search of those brightly-colored hidden treasures.

Upon my return for the post-op appointment, I saw Dr. Riddell stepping out of his car. It was a Mercedes Benz sedan. When he saw me, he said, "Alex, had you been in a Mercedes Benz rather than a Jaguar sports car, you may very well have walked away from your accident because of the superior crash-resistant features built into every Mercedes car." I took that statement to heart for my future car purchases.

After removing the stitches from my belly, Dr. Riddell assured me that everything was healing up very nicely. When I questioned him about my chest, which appeared somewhat uneven because of the broken ribs and continued to ache profusely even when lying in bed, he explained that the pain would begin to subside over the next month or two, then handed me a list of therapeutic exercises and stressed the importance of adhering to them on a daily basis.

"When you're able, Alex, try doing some push-ups," he said. "It's a very effective upper body training regimen in boot camps throughout the various armed services and in all police academies. It'll help strengthen and rebuild your chest close to normal."

The therapeutic exercises were very beneficial and each week I felt stronger with a little less pain. However, I couldn't even do one push up without crying out in pain when I first started. I continued pushing myself little-by-little with a rest-day between until I did two in a row. With sheer determination, I kept increasing the number of push-ups bit-by-bit to a point of obsession until I reached 200 at a time.

Eventually, my chest filled out, making me more muscular and athletic-looking than ever before. I even did some push-ups on my knuckles or fingers and a few with my son on my back, pretending I was a horse. I became a devoted believer in the lasting benefits of regular exercise.

Keeping in mind what had brought me to the point of almost ending my life, I began selling my rentals in order to clear my mind, simplify my life, and enjoy it without the endless stress. The quality time it afforded me to spend with my loving family was priceless. Strolling hand-in-hand around Balboa Island, looking at all the boats in the water, I pointed out to Patricia a small sailboat moored about 20 yards off shore. There was a "FOR SALE" sign on it. I jotted down the number and related to Patricia my hope-filled feelings when I saw a tiny triangular white image of a sailboat from the hospital window.

"But, honey," she said, "you don't know anything about sailing. Besides, where would you keep it?"

She was right, but I called the number anyway and arranged a showing. The owner, Mr. Prince, an elderly, soft-spoken gentleman, picked us up at the Bay Club with his boat, and as we leisurely sailed around the harbor, he described every detail of his 27' Catalina sailboat. He asked if I'd like to take the helm. I said that I had never owned or operated a boat.

"Oh, that's no problem," he said. "You can take sailing classes right over there on Coast Highway by the Bay Club to learn the basics, and I can show you the rest. It's generally hard to find a dock or slip in this popular harbor, but I secured my mooring from the Harbor Master years ago and if you buy the boat, the mooring will come with it."

CHAPTER 27
"AHOY THERE"

After completing the "Principles of Safe Sailing" class offered by the Coast Guard Auxiliary, I arranged to meet Mr. Prince at the Bay Club where he kept his eight-foot dinghy. We rowed the dinghy along the shore past John Wayne's house to the mooring about twenty yards from shore where the Catalina sailboat was tied. He pointed out that the mooring was located close to James Cagney's homes in the guarded-gated community of Bayshore. With Mr. Prince's observation, I piloted the boat around the bay, tacking back and forth into the light wind just as I had learned at the sailing class. Returning to the mooring, we locked the boat and rowed back to the Bay Club to finalize our transaction.

Just as I had envisioned, when I looked out at that lone sailboat in the calm Pacific Ocean from the hospital window following my surgery, we would now be spending some memorable weekends sailing to Catalina Island (twenty-six miles west), playing in the sand, swimming, barbecuing, exploring the untamed shoreline, and visiting the quaint island shops and restaurants. Although it seemed like a bit of a hassle to use the eight-foot dinghy as a means of boarding and disembarking, it was but a small price to pay for the joy it brought us. Countless other boat owners in the harbor were just as thankful as we were because there was a waiting list to secure a mooring through the Newport Beach Harbor Master.

One Saturday afternoon in 1978, as Patricia and I tied our boat to the mooring, locked it up, and began disembarking into our dinghy to head back to the Bay Club, a lady who had been watching us for a few weeks walked down the private dock of her waterfront home toward us and shouted, "AHOY, THERE! Why don't you tie your sailboat to our dock right here and come in for a drink?"

That invitation by Betty and her husband, Don, both in their late fifties, was the beginning of a long-lasting friendship. Their lovely home was next-door to James Cagney's house, who according to Betty, wasn't very sociable and hardly ever came out. Betty immediately gave our son a big bear hug and told him to call her "Aunt Betty."

She was the friendliest lady and took to Patricia like a sister. Don, sitting in his La-Z-Boy armchair, balanced his lit cigarette on the edge of his personal ashtray and greeted us cordially, then resumed watching the news on their big screen TV and smoking his cigarette. About five feet to the side of Don, also facing the TV, was Betty's matching La-Z-Boy armchair with a small wooden stand next to it holding her own ashtray that was also filled with short left-over stubs.

They had two adult children—a boy in his mid-twenties living away from home and a twenty-year-old daughter still living with them.

When we prepared to leave, Betty said, "Alex, you may as well keep your sailboat tied to our dock from now on and park your car in front of our house whenever you want to go sailing."

"Wow, that's mighty generous of you," I said. "Thank you very much."

A few days later, when we prepared to sail again, Betty greeted us by the dock and gave Jason a big hug. I asked if she and Don would like to accompany us and sail around the harbor for an hour or so. She jumped at the chance, but Don had to be coaxed into leaving the comfort of his armchair and the TV. After about a half hour of leisurely drifting through the harbor and in idle conversation, with the warm ocean breeze filling the sail and gliding us along, Don said, "When are we going to turn it on and get going?"

Before I could answer, Betty explained to him, "That's the beauty of sailing, dear. Just relax, fill your nicotine-lined lungs with this wonderful, clean ocean air. There's no motor noise or fumes and no phones ringing—just a peaceful appreciation of sailing."

During our idle conversation, occasionally interrupted by the sound of a passing motorboat, Don began to relax, lit a cigarette, and explained that he owned and operated a large furniture manufacturing plant in the city of Santa Ana with over 600 factory workers, a dozen supervisors, about two dozen office personnel, and a team of national sales reps. After inquiring about Patricia's and my backgrounds and current lines of work, he said that he needed a Human Resource manager to administer related functions in his factory with its 100 percent Hispanic employees as well as the office staff.

"Alex, based on your background, you'd be just the right person that I'm looking for. Would you be interested in such a position?"

"I'd like to look into it," I responded.

"Why don't you come and meet me at the factory tomorrow?" asked Don. "Betty and I will show you around and if you're interested, we can discuss it further."

Don explained that when he was growing up, he didn't get along with his father, dropped out of school before finishing high school, and supported himself by working at a variety of jobs. Betty boasted about Don having graduated from the "School of Hard Knocks with a degree in Common Sense." Though his communication skills were limited, he was a man of few words, and relied on his wife and secretary to read to him and prepare written business letters and agreements for his signature. He was street smart, a good listener, a risk-taker, a good negotiator, and ran his company with day-to-day hands-on control to every detail—always with an eye on the bottom line.

Nothing slipped by him without his approval. He didn't believe in annual budgets or annual raises, but relied on his shrewdness and keen eye in running a tight ship. His company was revered as being one of the finest in the furniture industry on the west coast.

By accepting the job (only twenty minutes from home), I not only eliminated the daily commute of my management position at the retail chain but felt that I would learn a lot from watching Don run a big manufacturing plant that deviated from the norm. I certainly wasn't disappointed.

These were but a few examples:

- When the Workers Union reps attempted to unionize the company, Don told them he would simply close the place down and no one would have a job. They left and never tried again.

- When Don saw me working on a Federal E.E.O. report inquiring how many Asians, Hispanics, Blacks, Caucasians, male, and female employees were there, he said, "Don't waste your time—just write across the report in big letters 'WE DON'T DISCRIMINATE' and send it back." We were never contacted again.

- When I brought to Don's attention that some of the employees in the factory hadn't received a raise in over a year, and that the plant manager requested additional workers on the assembly line, Don explained to me that he does not believe in automatic annual raises— only merit and promotional raises. As for additional workers, he said, "Come with me, Alex; let's walk along the assembly line together."

- He selected fifteen employees, without regard to their seniority, to be immediately terminated, making the plant manager furious. But the very next day, even with 10 percent fewer workers, the assembly line became more productive. While the plant manager had concentrated on increasing the number of workers, Don merely weeded out the slow moving, tired-looking ones, and the rest, fearing that they may be next, worked much more efficiently.

Prior to meeting Don, I had been taught and continued to believe that a good manager delegates and oversees rather than insisting on doing it all himself. In order to relieve the mounting stress caused by his iron-fisted, hands-on approach (from 10:00 a.m. till 4:45 p.m.), Don smoked two packs of cigarettes a day and had to be home by 5:00 p.m. to open a fresh bottle of I.W. Harper Bourbon, enjoying the alcohol's calming effect until the last drop signified that it was bedtime. Betty did the same—smoked two packs a day and matched her husband drink-for-drink with her favorite, Chivas Regal Scotch.

That initial short sailboat outing with them thrilled Betty and must've also had some impact on Don, even though it was much too slow-moving for him. About a year after I joined the company, they flew to Florida, bought a 110′ luxury motor yacht, sailed it through Panama Canal, up the Pacific Coastline, and into a prime slip at the Balboa Bay Club facing the popular First Cabin bar and restaurant, which I had arranged for them through my membership.

The big yacht was like a new toy for Don and Betty—a place where they would unwind and go deep-sea fishing down to the Mexican waters, around the Channel Islands, to San Simeon, and up the coast to San Francisco Bay. They counted Patricia, our son, and me to accompany them whenever we wanted.

The yacht required a full-time captain and a crew of six to operate and maintain it. In addition to my regular position as H.R. manager at the factory, I was asked to oversee the crew, keep the galley and bar fully stocked, and plan special excursions (mostly on weekends) hosting business-related guests, charitable events, weddings, birthdays, boat parades, and whale-watching. When our son mentioned that his teacher was planning to take his class to the Newport Pier for the annual whale migration, Betty invited the teacher and the whole class to come aboard their yacht to see the whales up close.

As our friendship grew, the four of us and our young son enjoyed more and more time together on the yacht or at their bay-front home. Rather than relying on their TV-watching habits, they preferred the music I provided with my accordion and joined me in singing many of the old familiar country songs we had all grown up with, especially when we were out at sea or moored at a fishing village.

This lifestyle continued for ten years. However, as much as Patricia and I enjoyed the perks that came with my job and the resulting friendship and trust between us all, I could not stand by and just ignore our friends' continued destruction to their health without interceding. Common sense assured me that filling their lungs to such an extent with nicotine and filtering that amount of alcohol through their liver each and every day would surely end both their lives much too soon. The longer I waited to challenge them, the more pronounced their slurred and off-color speech became.

In the evening during one of our fishing trips, I asked for their undivided attention for just a few minutes before they started drinking to explain my concerns by relating the busy life I led (although to a much, much lesser degree than theirs) prior to my near-death experience and how, through divine intervention, Patricia's prayers, and her swift action, my life was spared.

"Because of God's grace," I said, "I was given a second chance to turn my life around. I came to my senses by realizing and appreciating what the most important thing in my life was. Yes, each one of us is different and our challenges in life vary greatly. I care for you both and want to see you live a long and enjoyable life with the resources and wisdom given to you by the Almighty God. Your common sense and wisdom, Don, must tell you that continuing to smoke and drink as much as you do, will definitely shorten your lifespan and deprive you and your loved ones of the one thing that really matters. I'm here to pray with you and help you get professional help if you'll let me and if you're ready. Don't wait until it's too late. Life is so precious and so short! You may not get a second chance."

They both allowed me to present my concerns, but continued smoking while I spoke. After reiterating their joy and dependence on these vices to help relieve the daily pressure associated with their business (which they reminded me I would never comprehend), they were happy when I quit talking so they could resume their smoking and drinking.

Their son, John (from Betty's former marriage), and daughter, Kim, spent very little time with their parents and showed no interest in their yacht. Since Don and Betty worked long hours together building their company, they relied on a nanny to raise their children. Neither child finished high school or showed any interest in finding a job, but both picked up their parents' bad smoking habits. I observed Don and Betty's happiest moment when their son and his girlfriend, Donna, decided to get married on the yacht. The parents spared no expense decorating it. The entire celebration simulated a Hollywood feature. To her credit, Donna, a kindergarten teacher, transformed her new husband's dependency on his parents into building a new life for themselves. He started working, and together, they saved their own money, bought a house, and began raising a family.

Over the next five to six years, Don started coughing more and more. Betty and I insisted that he see a doctor. The X-ray revealed a malignant spot on his lungs and the blood test alerted him of some inflammation and damage to his liver.

The attending doctor recommended lung surgery without delay. As Don was wheeled into surgery, I held Betty's hand and led her in prayer. It bothered me that her children weren't by her side. She thanked me, and, teary-eyed, admitted that she didn't know how to pray. Thankfully, the surgery was successful and Don would be back at home in a couple of days.

When we brought Don home, the attending nurse informed Betty and me that Don, on numerous occasions from his hospital bed, while awaiting to be wheeled into surgery and during recovery, had offered her fellow nurses and her one hundred dollars for just one cigarette, which they laughingly rejected (the nurses and doctors had been trained in handling such common acts of desperation).

In the evening, a couple of days after his release from the hospital, I went to Don and Betty's home and was distraught to find their living room filled with smoke, as before. There they were, in their usual sofa chairs—drink in one hand, lit cigarette in the other, and their individual ashtrays waiting to be emptied.

Don and Betty, foolishly, in spite of my desperate plea, resumed their smoking and drinking habits with the dumb excuse that the doctor got the cancer out in time, and Don was now cancer-free. I stooped down between them so I could be as close to them as possible in order to confront them with my final appeal.

Unbuttoning my shirt to reveal the aftermath of my own life-saving operation, I looked at both of them and said, "Look, this ten-inch scar on my belly is a reminder that I almost didn't get to enjoy the life that God had provided for me. It represents the second chance I was given to shed the encumbrances that rob and shorten a man's life. Don, don't you see? You've been given a second chance, but you have to stop your smoking as well as your drinking. One deadly habit is as bad as the other, but together, your life will be shortened twice as fast. The rest of your life and yours, Betty, can be so much more rewarding and sweeter than the past. The withdrawal period may be extremely challenging, but it'll be well worth it. The internal and external injuries caused by my accident were also extremely severe. God's healing power was able to bring me back, allowing me to alter my priorities for my own good. Won't you let Him help you? With your permission, I can arrange professional help for both of you."

There was no sign of agreement or willingness from either of them. It took a family tragedy to immediately stop his and Betty's drinking. Early one morning in 1988, Don called to inform me that their daughter, Kim, had died overnight from an overdose of liquor and an unknown substance. She was only twenty-nine years old. They were devastated, in shock, and wanted me to come over to share their grief.

Don soon sold his business and yacht and put all their assets into a family trust. Patricia and I continued visiting Don and Betty each week. Though they no longer drank, neither of them was able to stop their lifelong smoking habits. Sadly, their health and quality of life began to decline rapidly. Dark blue-colored spots started showing up on Don's skin necessitating a series of medical treatments. Their remaining days continued to be spent smoking in their sagging old La-Z-Boy armchairs in front of their big screen TV. In 1999, at age 71, Don passed away, and Betty, who then moved in with her son, died four years later.

Having worked with this self-made wealthy and seemingly successful couple, whom my wife and I embraced as friends for almost ten years, I found it painful to watch the anticipated ending. I gave it my best shot, but in spite of my attempt and plea, I found myself helpless to prevent its sad outcome. It reinforced my focus on the only thing in life that truly matters. Patricia and I felt that with our son going through college and venturing out into the world, he'd surely be exposed to such vices and hopefully resist the temptation by remembering the damaging and deadly effects of tobacco, liquor, and other harmful substances that shortened Don's, Betty's and their daughter, Kim's life.

CHAPTER 28
A LETTER FROM THE PAST

E venings, upon arriving home from work, I usually found Patricia planning our evening dinner and Jason absorbed in his special projects or playing with a friend. One evening, the garage door was open, and in my parking spot, next to Patricia's car, was Jason— busy fine-tuning and polishing his special Hutch racing bicycle. I parked in the driveway, emptied the mailbox, discarded junk mail, and while walking toward the front door, sorting through the letters and bills, I came upon a handwritten letter addressed to me. The unusual and most interesting style of calligraphy on the envelope caused me to stop and study it. The return name and address in the upper left corner read:

Mr. and Mrs. Helmut Kohler

7428 Pacific Heights Drive

San Francisco, California

Patricia and I looked at each other, shrugging our shoulders, indicating that neither of us had any idea who it could be from. However, the minute I opened the envelope and began reading the letter, dated August 15, 1982, I realized that it was from Irma, my little sister I had left behind in Schwabmünchen, Germany in 1947 when I was eight years old—about forty years ago.

As I continued reading, my memory flashed back to the Bremen shipyard with the image of my angel mom standing at the shipping dock, waving her white hankie, which, in my heart, resembled a white dove sending her final goodbye and love to me. Irma's letter went on to explain that after Dad and Mom passed away, she and Helmut (her German husband) moved from Munich, Germany to San Francisco through her job transfer with Lufthansa Airlines, and they were proud parents of twin three-year-old girls, Lisa and Nicole (named after her Irma's parents, Elizabeth and Nikolai).

She had found my old letter from Oakburn, Manitoba, written in 1949, among her mom's possessions and followed through in locating my current address (I recall sending a brief letter to Schwabmünchen about two years after I left Germany to express my joy of being legally adopted by a kind-hearted Ukrainian farm family in Oakburn, Manitoba, Canada and that my new surname was legally changed from Marcel to Sytnyk. I don't remember getting a response but I was too absorbed with my exciting new life to dwell on the past or write again).

I called the number she submitted in the letter to express my jubilation, and told her that my wife, our young son, and I would be driving up to see them the following weekend and catch up on the immeasurable amount of information between us that occurred over the past forty years. I can still picture that cute seven-year-old blond girl on St.-Rochus-Straße in Schwabmünchen. So, when we were greeted by a tall, mature, attractive, blond-haired lady with that familiar smile, demeanor, and blue eyes, there was no doubt that it was the same Irma I had left behind. I embraced her tenderly while she cried on my shoulder. Patricia turned her attention to the twin girls and Helmut, while Irma and I excitedly and endlessly rattled on and on.

"Mom cried a lot about the devastating, destructive effects of the war, not only taking a toll on her and Dad, but also about the loss of their loved ones who didn't survive," she said. "For many years, Germany remained but a remnant of what once was a most vibrant, proud, and powerful nation leaving its survivors heartbroken, poor, hopeless, and in tears, trying to rebuild their lives from among deadly piles of smoldering embers and ashes."

Irma remained at her parents' side to the end, providing them the love, kindness, and compassion they relied on. She worked a part-time job while continuing her education and subsequently accepted a secretarial position with Lufthansa Airlines.

"Dad always was a man of few words, and he subdued his feelings of the war's devastation. When he passed away," said Irma, "I was Mom's sole companion until she died two years later to reunite with Dad in Heaven."

During Irma's and Helmut's visit to spend the following Thanksgiving holiday with us in Newport Beach, Irma expressed her desire to devote her time to raising her darling twin girls and begin planning their upcoming educational needs. Being the protective person she was, Irma also worried about her husband's safety in his profession as a house-painter, which often required tall ladders and makeshift scaffolding.

Helmut explained that with the vast influx of Asian workers in San Francisco who were taking over the house-painting business and underbidding jobs with inferior workmanship, he was unable to be competitive any longer but refused to compromise the quality of his work.

Patricia and Irma drove by the local primary, secondary, and high school, which were all within walking distance from our home, and Patricia pointed out the location of University of California, Irvine (UCI), only ten minutes away by car. Meanwhile, Helmut and I drove to my truck stop in L.A., where I showed him the simplicity of operating the business. The following day, we all got in the car and toured our immediate neighborhood, the layout of the city, the beach, and the many local parks and playgrounds. I could tell from their reactions and comments that it wouldn't take much for them to consider establishing their home in Newport Beach. So, I laid out a win-win-proposal for them to consider.

"Taking into account your desire, Irma, to be a stay-at-home mom," I said, "and your career concerns, Helmut, allow me to share my thoughts with you: Since I'm a licensed realtor, I'd like to show you some of the more desirable family homes nearby, close to the finest schools, and within your budget. As for your career concerns, Helmut, I'd be happy to work out a plan for you to take over my L.A. truck stop, which would provide you with adequate income. You would no longer have to scale the high ladders and scaffolding or be subjected to underbidding."

It all worked out. They made two more trips, located a perfect home in the desirable, family-oriented community of Harbor View, within walking distance to our house and also to one of the finest schools in California. In no time at all, Helmut was able to run the truck stop on his own and took full control of it, thereby allowing me to carry on with my real estate interests.

Irma and Helmut were very happy that they made the move to southern California and loved their new home. Their next-door neighbors were also from Germany. After they got settled, I asked Irma if her mom may have been praying all along for this kind of ending—with both of us living so close to each other in such a wonderful place in the free world.

"As hard as life was for her and Dad," said Irma, "Mom was very thankful for having been able to rescue both of us as orphans from the midst of the ongoing war and live out her life with her loving husband by her side. She missed you a lot, Alex, and kept asking herself if she made the right decision in sending you away but never ceased hoping and praying that you would find a good home and develop your inner strengths and natural musical talent. When she learned that you were adopted by a Ukrainian farmer, she was a little disheartened but happy that you had a permanent home with a loving Christian family."

"Your parents did much more than save my life," I said. "They opened a new world for me by sending me to a land of freedom and opportunity at a young enough age to enjoy a better life. But you, Irma, you were an angel—a priceless blessing by devoting your young life to them. I'm so sorry that I wasn't there with you. As you can see, I'm not a farmer and have pursued even more than music."

During a lighter moment of our conversation, Irma smiled and revealed that Mom had been secretly hoping that the two of us would someday reunite and get married.

"Well, as you can see," I responded, "her wishes came true. We did indeed reunite and get married but each to someone of our own choosing."

We saw a lot of each other, and we watched their daughters grow up into beautiful, tall, blond ladies. They did extremely well in school and in college, graduating with law degrees from UCI. Sadly, however, pancreatic cancer took Irma from us when she was sixty-eight. Helmut sold his business in L.A. and watches his little granddaughter while his daughter works as a legal aide.

CHAPTER 29
HAVE YOU READ THE BIBLE, DAD?

During her fifteen-year teaching career at Orange County Business College in Anaheim (1974-1989), Patricia habitually looked like a model. All her adult students and fellow teachers idolized her. She did more than teach the required material and went the extra mile to find jobs for her graduates. The owner of the college noticed that Patricia's uplifting, positive demeanor, professionalism, pride, and respect for her job caused his entire staff to take note regarding their own work ethics and personal appearance. In appreciation, he assigned the front, most visible classroom to her and painted her name on the parking spot closest to the main entrance.

On her way home from her job, Patricia often made a quick stop at a small fashion boutique near our home to try on some of the latest trends. With her model-like figure, she always looked gorgeous, no matter what she tried on. But she was also thrifty and generally waited a month or more for the price of her favorite item to be reduced. The owner of the boutique enjoyed Patricia's patronage and usually gave her a house discount on all her purchases.

After a few months, when the boutique owner mentioned to Patricia that she and her husband were moving to Florida and would be selling the boutique, we jumped right on it. Thirty days later, Patricia was the boutique's happy new proprietor. She thoroughly loved it, and many of her lady friends became her regular customers. It was a win-win decision—no more freeway commuting. Her boutique was only two miles from our house, giving her more time to enjoy her home and time with her friends. With her newfound popularity in the community and among her peers, she volunteered her time to some modeling and fundraising events, especially during the aggressive construction and development of Segerstrom's South Coast Music Center.

With our son devoting every spare hour to perfecting his illusion skills while attending University of Southern California (USC), he began doing magic shows on most weekends for children and private events. After earning several awards for his close-up and stage performances, he became a regular member of the Magic Castle in Hollywood where he enjoyed meeting many of the top illusionists from around the world and also performed his stage and close-up act several times each year.

Midway through college, he was eager to join a seasoned professional magician on a tour through Australia and New Zealand but decided to follow our advice to first graduate college and earn his B.A. degree. I assured him that not only would it benefit him in his work as a self-employed entrepreneur, but it would also make his mom and me very proud.

During his final year in college, Jason called me one Thursday morning and asked if I could meet with him in L.A. to discuss a serious matter. The tone in his request caused my mind to race through a list of possible serious situations: Was he in trouble at school, did he crash his car or run someone over, did he get into drugs, does he have a health issue, or could he be in legal trouble?

I suggested Denny's restaurant in Long Beach and got there before him. It wasn't the healthy, happy, energetic boy whom we sent off to college but a thin and serious-looking young man who came to my table and sat across from me. I felt a big lump in my throat and braced myself for the worst possible news as the waitress poured us both some coffee and handed us menus.

Clearing my throat, I asked, "Do you want to order some lunch, son? Looks like you really need it."

"No thanks, Dad, you go ahead. I'm not going to eat," he answered. "In fact, I haven't eaten anything for two days."

My heart sank to the floor and I felt it beating like a machine gun. Clenching my coffee mug tightly with unsteady hands, I looked deep into his eyes, but he just sat there calmly searching for the right words with which to begin.

"Talk to me openly and freely, son—what's going on?" I pleaded. "I'm your father, your best friend, who loves you dearly. Whatever it is, we'll work it out."

With the most peaceful and loving look, he began, "Dad, you may be thinking that I'm having the time of my life at USC. I'm watching the amount of liquor and drugs flowing freely throughout the campus and in my dorm and want no part of it. It's much, much different than your time in college, Dad. I'd rather spend my time perfecting my magic. I'm smart enough not to fall into that trap, and as promised, I'll soon graduate."

"Now that I'm a grown man," he continued, "preparing to venture out on my own and developing my magic act, I've also been thinking long and hard about my relationship with God and with you and Mom. I love you both so much and feel that God has called on me to ensure that someday we would all be in Heaven together."

"Although I attended the Catholic church with you and Mom, where I was confirmed and baptized by Bishop Johnson, I never really got to know God until I attended a small Bible study class with some friends in college. I'm sorry to have to say this, Dad, but you, Mom and I have all fallen short of the life that God laid out for us—a life in partnership with Jesus—to learn about Him and become more like Him."

"The reason I haven't been eating the past few days," he explained, "is because I'm fasting in order to clear my mind and body of earthly distractions. On Saturday, a group of us will be baptized at Malibu

Beach, and I'd very much like you and Mom to be there and witness me openly accept Jesus into my life."

Whew! With a sigh of relief and gratefulness, I exhaled my pent-up tenseness as my unfounded concerns turned into admiration.

"But son, we also baptized you in Canada when you were a baby," I said. "Uncle Tom is your godfather and we have continually guided you through a good Christian upbringing."

With patience and understanding, Jason responded, "Dad, of what value is my baptism as a six-month-old baby which I can't even recall or the significance of my godfather who lives on a farm up in Canada if I go through life striving to achieve success through my education and pursuit of my talents, interests, and opportunities if I don't wholeheartedly ask Jesus into my heart and follow His teachings? Did we, as a family, ever open a Bible at home and reinforce God's word into our daily lives as He instructs us to do? You're a good man, Dad— the best any child could wish for, and Mom is the sweetest lady in the world, but no one will enter God's Kingdom based solely on their good deeds."

What a blessed turn of events! Here I was, worried about our son's well-being in college while he's more concerned about our hereafter and knocking at the door of my soul—pointing me to God's teaching. Without missing a beat, Jason opened his Bible, which he brought with him, and read several passages to make his point. He was absolutely right in everything he said. I was speechless but extremely impressed and proud of him. Before heading back to his classes, he gave me a warm bear-hug, again expressing his deep love for me and his mom and how he looked forward to our presence at Malibu Beach for his baptism on Saturday.

As I drove home, I felt a sense of guilt and shame that after all those years, especially considering how God had so faithfully cared for me, guided me, loved me, and provided all our needs for over a half century, that I didn't take the initiative to read the Holy Bible and understand the depth of His grace and unfailing love. My thoughts turned to the time when I lay near death at the Pico Rivera Hospital begging the Lord to spare my life so that I could raise our little boy and help him grow up as a God-fearing and righteous young man.

"Dear God, thank you," I prayed. "Not only did You answer that prayer, Lord, but You have faithfully continued to watch over me in answer to my mom's prayers and extended Your grace by nudging our grown son as a vessel in bringing Patricia and me closer to You."

Having been baptized four times as a youngster and serving as an altar boy didn't make me any more familiar with the Bible because we had always left the reading of the scripture and its interpretation to the officiating priest who read either from a Latin or a Greek Bible. However, I remember my adopted mother, in Oakburn, who owned a very old Ukrainian Bible. She read it regularly and was not shy about reading it to anyone who visited her, regardless of whether they understood the Ukrainian language or not.

When I arrived home and related our son's decision to get baptized, Patricia was caught off-guard like I was. Nevertheless, early Saturday morning, we drove up in support of his spiritual commitment. About two dozen of his college friends all walked into the cold waist-deep water at Malibu Beach where their pastor, with an assistant, waited to submerge each one of them for a second, then hug them as born-again Christians. We watched Jason beaming with joy—a kind of joy we hadn't seen in some time. They all joined hands in a circle around the pastor on the sandy shore and invited us and a few other parents to join them in singing praises to the Lord.

On our drive home, Patricia and I agreed that we would set aside a time each day to read the Bible for ourselves. She mentioned that one of her friends, Mrs. Thompson, an elderly widow, had recently extended an invitation for us both to join a Bible study group at her Spyglass Hill home, which we did. It was a ninety-minute weekly gathering of ten to twelve Christian folks, eager to follow a planned program designed to get through the Bible in one year and discuss its contents applicable to one's everyday life. Being part of this group broadened our Biblical knowledge and created a new, long-lasting circle of friends.

Mrs. Thompson's home was a very cute three bedroom, two bath, single story house on a large double-size lot at the end of a hidden cul-de-sac with a fantastic coastal view extending all the way up to Santa Monica and Palos Verdes. In the summer of 2002, while we were attending Bible study at her home, she informed us that her son, Chuck, who was the District Attorney in Las Vegas, was making arrangements to relocate her to a newly-built senior housing development in Las Vegas and that her home would be going on the market.

"This has been my home for the past thirty years," she said. "All my friends and doctors and my golfing partners are here. But, I'm in my mid-nineties and my son doesn't want me to continue living here alone this far away from him."

Patricia and I said that we'd be very interested in buying it, as did several other people in our group.

"Well, my son, Chuck, is handling the whole thing," said Mrs. Thompson, "and he tells me that he's had a lot of offers already. You'll have to contact him."

Patricia and I prayed about it, hoping to make this desirable place our new home by using the proceeds from the sale of our two-story condominium in Harbor Ridge. I contacted Chuck Thompson in Las Vegas who said that he would be visiting his mom the following weekend to review all the offers and that I could present mine at the same time. After careful consideration of our financial position, the property's location, its view, lot size, privacy, upgrading or rebuilding costs, future resale value, and joy of ownership, Patricia and I continued to pray for God's guidance and wisdom in pursuing our wishes.

Although I've been through a fair number of residential and commercial real estate transactions and represented both buyers and sellers, Mrs. Thompson's charming home had a special, personal appeal for us, but it was also thirty years old, more expensive, and challenging than we were ready to face at that time.

I knew that if I were to submit the standard offer subject to the sale of our home, we could swing it, but Chuck Thompson would just look for the highest cash offer and ignore ours along with the other contingent offers.

So, in a leap of faith, I prepared the simplest, most basic offer which would surely get his attention. Mr. Thompson greeted me at his mother's home where we've been attending Bible Studies and asked me to join him in the living room, without any small-talk or friendly conversation. It was all business with him.

"So, let's see what your offer is," he said.

"Mr. Thompson," I said, "thank you for allowing me to present my offer directly to you. Your mother is a dear friend of ours and we've enjoyed being part of the weekly Bible study being conducted here in her lovely home. We will all miss her when she moves to Las Vegas, and we'll plan on visiting her after she gets settled."

"Mr. Thompson," I continued, "you and I both know the real estate market and what the current comps are in the Spyglass Hill community. I am a licensed realtor, representing myself and my wife. We'd love to make this our new home and after careful consideration and by stretching our resources, we humbly and in a leap of faith, hereby submit our sincere offer for your review. As indicated on this simple, one-page document, we propose to purchase this home in 'AS-IS' condition—no repairs, no city inspection, no termite inspection, no physical or roof inspection, and you won't be paying any commissions to me or anyone. Attached is our 'non-refundable' deposit check in the amount of $50,000. If, for any reason, we're unable to complete the transaction in forty-five days, the $50,000 is yours to keep and you'd be free to pursue one of your other offers."

"Well, I do appreciate your sincerity and straightforward offer devoid of all the usual 'Open House' showings, fees, inspections, and endless number of legal documents," he said. "This is the way we were used to doing business before the government, with all their rules and disclosures and fees got involved. My mother speaks very highly of your wife and also of you. When I informed her that you were coming over to present your offer, she implied that it would please her to sell her home to you and your wife. Congratulations, Alex, you've got yourself a deal. Let's get the ball rolling."

Within a couple of days after listing our Harbor Ridge condo for sale, we had a full-price offer and were in our new home as initially proposed. At the Five Crowns Restaurant, where we and her many friends arranged a farewell dinner, Mrs. Thompson expressed her gratitude for the love and support of everyone and extended a special blessing to Patricia and me.

"I pray that my friend Patricia and her husband Alex will enjoy many happy years living in the place that I've called home for over thirty years. I'm also thankful that they've agreed to continue hosting the weekly Bible study gatherings for the balance of the year in their new home."

Patricia and I enjoyed our newly-acquired home immensely. She continued managing her boutique while I, as a part time realtor, sold a few homes in our community. Both of these business interests required a minimal amount of our personal time, thereby allowing us ample opportunities to spend quality time together in our home.

We didn't get to see much of our son, who, upon graduating from college, relocated to Las Vegas and performed his magic act on cruise ships. Sometimes he would call us from the Princess cruise ship departing Long Beach on its way to Alaska, South America, or the Pacific Islands. We often tried to spot him with our binoculars and watched the ship slowly fade into the distance. On several occasions, over the years, we were able to join him as passengers to far-away places and spend quality family time together.

CHAPTER 30
THE BEST SHAPE OF
MY LIFE

THE LAGUNA BEACH FIRE

Each October, California has historically been under threat of wildfires due to the dry weather, dry vegetation, and extreme high temperatures. Back on October 27, 1993, I remember seeing a threatening wall of flames and black smoke heading our way from Laguna Beach. It was one of fourteen wildfires that simultaneously broke out across southern California. The Laguna Beach fire was among the twentieth largest fire losses in American history that swept through this popular resort area nestled against the picturesque forested hills above the Pacific shoreline. Energized by a ninety-two-mile per hour wind, the intense inferno raced through the hills and into the multi-million-dollar estates of Emerald Bay, consuming everything in its path at the rate of one-hundred acres per minute.

People by the thousands quickly threw their pets and few valuables into their cars and fled to safety down the overcrowded narrow Pacific Coast Highway. Although our home in Corona Del Mar was ten miles north of Laguna Beach, the choking black smoke and towering hot flames were rapidly heading toward us. By 10:00 p.m., fearing that the wood-shake roofs could be set ablaze at any moment, our neighborhood was alerted to prepare for evacuation protocol.

While Patricia nervously gathered a few of her most precious items, I stood still, closed my eyes, and reminiscently thought of my angel mom placing her most important possessions—Irma and me—into her horse-drawn wagon to flee the advancing inferno of Russian brutality. Many of our neighbors in Corona Del Mar began to evacuate. Others started spraying water on their roofs with garden hoses. One of our friends, who lived twenty miles inland, invited us to stay at their home if needed. Miraculously, the wind suddenly shifted, then subsided.

By midnight the spread of the fire was contained. Seventeen thousand acres and 400 homes were consumed with a loss of 530 million dollars (over two billion dollars in today's value). Thankfully and miraculously, there were no human casualties. However, there was a tremendously large amount of wildlife loss while countless deer, coyotes, bobcats, mountain lions, and rabbits were seen trying to outrun the blazing fire.

Throughout history, whether through natural causes or enemy attacks, people have had to leave their homes and all their belongings to try to save their lives. I learned, at a very young age, that the only thing that really mattered was freedom and peace at any cost.

About six months after the Laguna Beach fire, I decided to hike through the charred hills of El Morro above Crystal Cove on the outskirts of Laguna Beach. What was once such a beautiful natural preserve, where families hiked or trained for cross-country races, was now a lifeless, devastated wasteland with mounds of gray ashes as far as I could see. I stopped to examine the flattened remains of a grand old cactus with its arms spread out just lying there resembling a human corpse. It reminded me of the soldier in the trench who had shielded me from enemy fire but ended up lying dead next to me.

Upon closer examination of the big lifeless cactus, I spotted a speck of pink color. With a smile on my face, I bent down to study the tiniest baby cactus sprouting up from the ashes of its deceased mother and happily displaying a very tiny pink bloom from its wee little green stem as if to tell me, "You, Alex, are just like me—spared by God in a world of trial and tribulation, from the ashes of our brave moms—to bloom in full color and to praise our gracious Lord for the full and joyful life which He has given us."

In 1999, at age sixty, after having negotiated a tax-free real estate exchange involving the sale of my Las Vegas truck stop for two homes in the heart of Newport Beach (both of which I rented for a couple of years before selling them), I had more time to devote toward a regular exercise program in order to maximize my overall health and exercise routine. Rather than joining a gym or taking up tennis or golf, I started jogging on a daily basis and aggressively began to extend my mileage. On a Saturday morning in September, at about 7:00 a.m., as I jogged by Corona Del Mar High School, I observed a group of about four dozen adults, dressed like me in jogging shorts and T-shirts, standing next to the oval-shaped race track, intently listening to coach, Bill Sumner, who was also dressed in his jogging attire. I walked over and stood near the back of the group, close enough to hear him.

"I don't care how out of shape you are, how old you are, or whether you've had any experience running long distance, but if you'll show up here every Saturday morning at 7:00 a.m. and follow the training schedule I'm passing out, we will all finish running the San Diego Marathon on January 16, 2000—four months from now."

After distributing the schedule to everyone, including me, he said, "Each week we'll review all the important items, such as stretching, warm-up, hydrating, injury prevention, and proper footwear. Let's get started! Follow me as we all leisurely jog once around the race track to warm up, then, we'll stretch, do a slow two-mile run and meet here again next week."

I looked at some of the men and women in the group and thought to myself, "Do they realize that the distance of a marathon is 26.2 miles?"

Everyone was raring to go, so I joined them and thus began my new commitment. When I told Patricia about it, she couldn't understand why anyone, in their right mind, would want to run that far and asked if I was getting paid for it. After explaining that it had become a very popular sporting event around the world, raised money for many local charity programs, and that we actually contributed one-hundred dollars to participate, she just looked at me and said, "I don't even enjoy driving that far. I prefer my ways of contributing my time and energy to fundraising and charity events."

Without exception, I followed the training schedule to a tee, using Newport Beach's ten-mile natural Back Bay loop and continuing along the jogging trails of Irvine, steadily extending the mileage every week until we all reached the twenty-six mile focus. On race day, my body could sense the energy among the overcrowded start-line as we joined in the singing of the "Star-Spangled Banner," then off we went.

I remember the coach cautioning us to preserve our energy and to not get too excited by forging ahead like many beginners tend to do. Sure enough, by mile eighteen, as many runners began to run out of steam, some even walking the rest of the way, I had enough energy to pass hundreds of them, crossing the finish line with a time of 3:52, which earned me a surprising third place finish in my age category. After two days' rest, I felt twenty years younger, full of energy, and in the best shape of my life. I was hooked and began running four marathons every year, usually placing first, second, or third in my age category.

In order to make it more interesting and include Patricia, I planned some races in far-away places, including Canada, San Francisco, the wine country of Napa Valley, Boston, New York, Disney World, even Dublin, Ireland and Venice, Italy. We combined sight-seeing vacations with each race and, of course, allowed time for Patricia's love of shopping.

On three occasions, at the finish line, a sports reporter asked to do a brief story on me for the local paper by asking what motivated me to run. I was happy to relate that it brought back memories of my very first race, as an orphan, when I was three—running to freedom during the height of World War II.

San Francisco Marathon, July 26, 2009
Alex (70 years old)
Finish Time 05:04:38, Fourth Place Finish in age group
Average Finish Time all runners - 04:31:48
(Source: July 26, 2009 - MarathonGuide.com)

Ukrainian Catholic Church - 1950
Alex (10 years old) Adopted by Mary & George Sytnyk

ACKNOWLEDGMENTS

I am eternally grateful to my wife, Patricia, who for years listened patiently while I recounted memorable moments of my life over and over until she was able to convince me to write this book.

A special note of appreciation to my friend, Joseph Shockey, whose personal interest in my story touched his heart and moved him to devote his time and resources in making this book possible.

BIBLIOGRAPHY

Beevor, Antony. *The Second World War*. New York: Little, Brown, 2012.

Buchanan, Patrick J. "Stalin's terror: the forgotten holocaust," *Santa Ana Orange County Register*. September 30, 1993, 26. Accessed August 2025. orangecountyregister.newspaperarchive.com/santa-ana-orange-county-register/1993-09-20/page-26/.

Kershaw, Ian. "Adolf Hitler: Hitler: 1889–1936" *Encyclopaedia Britannica*. Hubris 1998.

Martin, Hugo Martin. "Sad Reminder of Slaughter Is Unveiled: Holocaust: About 700 people gather in West Hollywood for dedication of a monument to the victims of a Nazi massacre at Babi Yar in the Soviet Union," *Los Angeles Times*. September 30, 1991.

Merriam-Webster. "Definition of discipline," *Merriam-Webster Dictionary*. Accessed July 14, 2025. https://www.merriam-webster.com/dictionary/discipline.

Scott, Gregory. "The meaning of the one thing in *City Slickers*," Gregory Scott Blog. Accessed August 2025. https://www.gregoryscottblog.com/the-meaning-of-the-one-thing-in-city-slickers/.

The White House National Archives. "Remarks by the President Honoring Those Who Died at Babi Yar." The White House Office of the Press Secretary (Kiev, Ukraine). May 12, 1995. https://clintonwhitehouse6.archives.gov/1995/05/1995-05-12-president-remarks-at-babi-yar-kiev-ukraine.html.

United States Holocaust Memorial Museum. Washington D.C.

Wikipedia. "Adolf Hitler," Wikipedia. Accessed August 2025. https://en.wikipedia.org/wiki/Adolf_Hitler?wprov=srpw1_4.

Wikipedia. "Bombing of Dresden," Wikipedia. Accessed August 2025. https://en.wikipedia.org/wiki/Bombing_of_Dresden.

Wikipedia. "City Slickers," Wikipedia. Accessed August 2025. https://en.wikipedia.org/wiki/City_Slickers#:~:text=table%20of%20contents-,City%20Slickers,-29%20languages.

Wikipedia. "Clifford Sifton," Wikipedia. Accessed August 2025. https://en.wikipedia.org/wiki/Clifford_Sifton#:~:text=External%20links-,Clifford%20Sifton,-5%20languages.

Wikipedia. "George Frederick Dick," Wikipedia. Accessed August 2025. https://en.wikipedia.org/wiki/George_Frederick_Dick#:~:text=References-,George%20Frederick%20Dick,-2%20languages.

Wikipedia. "Invasion of Poland," Wikipedia. Accessed August 2025. https://en.wikipedia.org/wiki/InvasionofPoland.

Wikipedia. "Jack Palance," Wikipedia. Accessed August 2025. https://en.wikipedia.org/wiki/Jack_Palance#:~:text=table%20of%20contents-,Jack%20Palance,-55%20languages.

Wikipedia. "Joseph Oleskiw," Wikipedia. Accessed August 2025. https://en.wikipedia.org/wiki/Joseph_Oleskiw#:~:text=External%20links-,Joseph%20Oleskiw,-2%20languages.

BIBLIOGRAPHY

Wikipedia. "Operation Barbarossa," Wikipedia. Accessed August 2025. https://en.wikipedia.org/wiki/Operation_Barbarossa.

Wikipedia. "Stephen Juba," Wikipedia. Accessed August 2025. https://en.wikipedia.org/wiki/Stephen_Juba#:~:text=External%20links-,Stephen%20Juba,-1%20language.

Wikipedia, "The Lone Ranger (TV Series)" Wikipedia. Accessed August 2025.https://en.wikipedia.org/wiki/The_Lone_Ranger_(TV_series)#:~:text.

Wikipedia. "Ukrainian Diaspora," Wikipedia. Accessed August 2025. https://en.wikipedia.org/wiki/Ukrainian_diaspora#:~:text=External%20links-,Ukrainian%20diaspora,-18%20languages.

Wikipedia. "Victims of Nazi Germany," Wikipedia. Accessed August 2025. https://en.wikipedia.org/wiki/Victims_of_Nazi_Germany#:~:text=External%20links-,Victims%20of%20Nazi%20Germany,-13%20languages.

Wikipedia. "World War II," Wikipedia. Accessed August 2025.https://en.wikipedia.org/wiki/World_War_II#:~:text=External%20links-,World%20War%20II,-234%20languages.

Wikipedia. "Word War II Casualties," Wikipedia. Accessed August 2025. https://en.wikipedia.org/wiki/World_War_II_casualties#:~:text=External%20links-,World%20War%20II%20casualties,-37%20languages.

ABOUT THE AUTHOR

Alex Sytnyk is an American citizen currently residing in southern California with his wife, Patricia. This book is an autobiography of his life. Alex was born in Ukraine in 1939 and, at the age of three, began a journey that was unimaginable for anyone, let alone a boy of that age. His struggles throughout his early years and many blessings are recounted here, and now, at the ripe old age of eighty-six, he is sharing his life with you.

With God's direction, protection, and the angels assigned to him, Alex's adventurous journey took him halfway around the world, eventually landing him in the most beautiful spot on Earth.

Joseph G. Shockey is an American Businessman and Entrepreneur who currently resides in southern California with his wife, Teri. During the last forty years, he has built his career establishing de novo businesses and orchestrating the complex issues involved in turnaround situations within the consumer, commercial financial and insurance services business sectors. Most recently, in a new and unique industry, he has joined Alex Sytnyk in completing the writing and publication of Alex's Autobiography.

Alex, Patricia & Jason Circa 1995

www.ingramcontent.com/pod-product-compliance
Lightning Source LLC
Chambersburg PA
CBHW062322120626
46553CB00015B/228